The Science of Consciousness

A User's Manual

by

Paolo Tiberi

Your life is your initiation.

Life Secrets, Principles, and Hacks
to a Meaningful, Purposeful,
and Happy Existence.

Your life is about to change.
Are you ready?

www.paolotiberi.com

Copyright © 2020 by Paolo F. Tiberi All rights reserved

Parts of this book can be reproduced (for non-commercial use) by any mechanical, photographic, electronic process, or in the form of an audio recording if ownership and authorship of the work has been added. It may be stored in any retrieval system, transmitted, and copied for public or private use with consent from the author. Parts of this book can also be use under *"fair use"* as quotations in the embodiment of other books, articles, reviews ad events, if authorship is given.

INTENT
The author has three intents with this book: 1) To offer a book with knowledge, information and case studies to open one's mind and heart so that it may rekindle the inner fire contained within one's soul. 2) To help individuals in their quest for spiritual well-being and developing a more fulfilled life. 3) To awaken and therefore unplug from the Matrix and the delusion of separation.

DISCLAIMER
This publication is intended to provide helpful and informative material. It is not intended to diagnose, treat, cure, or prevent any health problem or condition, nor is intended to replace the advice of a physician. No action should be taken solely on the contents of this book. Always consult your physician or qualified health-care professional on any matters regarding your health and before adopting any suggestions in this book or drawing inferences from it. The author and publisher specifically disclaim all responsibility for any liability, loss or risk, personal or otherwise, which is incurred as a consequence, directly or indirectly, from the use or application of any contents of this book. Any and all product names referenced within this book are the trademarks of their respective owners. None of these owners have sponsored, authorized, endorsed, or approved this book.

CIP catalog record for this book is available from the Australian Library

Author: Tiberi, Paolo F.
Title: The Science of Consciousness
Series: Awakening
Cover by: Paolo F. Tiberi
Published by Effective Life Strategies
ISBN: 978-1-921851-45-2
Audience: 12+
1st Edition, May 2020

CONTENTS

PREFACE ... 1

PART I: A NEW PARADIGM
CHAPTER 1: A New Paradigm of Understanding ... 9
CHAPTER 2: Unifying Science and Spirituality ... 29
CHAPTER 3: The Messenger Is Irrelevant ... 41
CHAPTER 4: Confirmation Bias ... 51

PART II: THE SCIENCE OF CONSCIOUSNESS
CHAPTER 5: Everything Is Consciousness ... 67
CHAPTER 6: Is Physicality an Illusion? ... 79
CHAPTER 7: The Energy Field & Consciousness ... 99
CHAPTER 8: Consciousness and the Physical Body ... 121
CHAPTER 9: Is the Universe, a Particle Self-Aware? ... 135
CHAPTER 10: The Quantum Field and Consciousness ... 155
CHAPTER 11: Light at the base of Consciousness Expression ... 175
CHAPTER 12: The Art of Manifestation ... 195

PART III: THE GENESIS OF CONSCIOUSNESS
CHAPTER 13: We are all Connected: Quantum Entanglement ... 225
CHAPTER 14: The Genesis of Life and Consciousness ... 237
CHAPTER 15: Involution and Evolution ... 257
CHAPTER 16: The Vibrational Scale & Missing Teachings of Jesus ... 271

PART IV: INTERACTING WITH THE MATRIX FIELD
CHAPTER 17: Empty Space Is Not Empty at All ... 285
CHAPTER 18: Can the 'Void' be programmed through Intent? ... 295
CHAPTER 19: From Chaos to Coherence ... 311
CHAPTER 20: The Holographic Universe & Coherence ... 319
CHAPTER 21: The Fractal Nature of the Universe ... 331

PART V: CONCLUSIONS
CHAPTER 22: From Caterpillar to Butterfly ... 351
THE NEXT STEP: Book II: *How to Create Miracles* ... 367
GET INVOLVED ... 381
ABOUT PAOLO F. TIBERI ... 383
SUGGESTED READING ... 389
ACKNOWLEDGMENTS ... 393
GOALS AND IDEALS OF THIS WORK ... 395

PREFACE

This book is about you, and how your thoughts, emotions and intent seed the fabric of reality. Yet there are only a few books that have dedicated their pages to the science of thought and consciousness.

In school, we learned about complex algebra and geometry, how to differentiate between different types of dinosaurs, and even had to dissect poor sacrificial frogs. Yet, most of these skills we will never use in our daily lives. Although we use our mind and awareness at any conscious moment of our lives, not many have explored in detail the science of consciousness itself.

This book is a life and consciousness manual that can truly guide you through many of life's challenges, obstacles, and fallout. This material has changed the lives of thousands of others for the better, and it is my hope that it will improve yours, too.

As you read more, you'll realize, like many before you have, that this is more than a simple book: it's a guide on how to manifest anything you desire, as well as a manifesto of self-sovereignty.

"All truths are easy to understand once they are discovered; the point is to discover them." ~ Galileo Galilei

There will be science and case studies covered in this book, which for some might be superfluous or not as exciting. However, you must realize that the books in this series have two functions: one is to tame your ego (the monkey mind) by showing the true nature of reality, and second is to help you break down the limitations of what you think you and life are.

The first challenge is to convince this monkey mind/intellect to collaborate. Duality and separation can only be partially overcome by using the tools, weapons, and trickery of the ego — logic, reasoning, scientific discoveries and case studies.

This can take us only so far, however. As the monkey mind is like smoke, it is a temporary avatar, transient in nature, a characteristic that more closely resembles a computer program than what you truly are. A being of energy and light. To awaken any individual at the start, you need to make the intellect collaborate. It is only then that the servant (the ego) can stop believing it is the King and act as it was always meant to act: as the servant of the higher self.

This is the path of the initiate, which will be covered in one of the following books.

This is also one of the reasons the personality is dropped as you die and move to higher dimensional realities, and our core self is reborn and fully revealed. Therefore, we will need to cover some scientific facts, some case studies, to unify the personality and your higher self.

How are you otherwise going to unveil and showcase that you are a creator, for example, if you don't fully understand and realize how your thoughts and emotions create a magnetic field attracting and repelling realities, potentialities, people, places, things, times and events in your life?

"Every feeling makes a subconscious impression and, unless it is counteracted by a more powerful feeling of an opposite nature, must be expressed. The dominant of two feelings is the one expressed. I am healthy is a stronger feeling than I will be healthy. To feel I will be is to confess I am not; I am is stronger than I am not. What you feel you are, always dominates what you feel you like to be; therefore, to be realized, the wish must be felt as a state that is, rather than a state that is not. Sensation precedes manifestation and is the foundation upon which all manifestations rest." ~ Neville Goddard

How are you going to understand that you live in a frequency, resonance, energetic universe if you do not understand what frequency is?

How are you going to unveil the fact that physicality is an illusion of sorts, if you do not examine the nature of reality, some elements of quantum physics and the vibrational nature of matter?

Preface

How are you going to conceive the concept of synchronicities if you don't realize that our brains are decoders of frequencies, information?

How can you grasp the fact that you can heal potentially any or all diseases simply by becoming coherent with a new potentiality, if coherence, and resonance are not covered?

How can you recognize that what you experience is a limited interpretation of reality, if you don't cover what cognitive bias is?

How can you explain that even science is discovering, expanding, and truly uncovering the nature of this universe and getting closer and closer to including a divine infinite intelligence, God, if you don't reconcile the Big Bang theory with ancient mysticism and religions?

"The world, and all within it, is man's conditioned consciousness objectified. Consciousness is the cause as well as the substance of the entire world. So it is to consciousness that we must turn if we would discover the secret of creation." ~ Neville Goddard

Every chapter in this book serves a purpose: the exciting ones, the plain ones, the scientific ones, the spiritual ones, and the heart-expanding ones. They are all like keys working on your subconscious mind, on a deeper level while incognito, camouflaged, concealed, and disguised as mere information.

Think of it as a spiritual university curriculum for the evolution and growth of your inner self.

"You must first have the knowledge of your power; second, the courage to dare; third, the faith to do." ~ Charles F. Haanel

By the end of this book, your life will be changed, as the understanding of who you are, what you are here for, and what reality is (to mention a few out of hundreds key concepts and paradigm shifts) will have evolved.

You can't have a different perspective, an expanded understanding, a broader self-identity, and still have the same limited life, it's not possible. Your world is a reflection of yourself, not only perceptually but also on an energetic and on practical level.

So enjoy the ride; as many have attested, it might be one of the most exhilarating journeys of your life as you plunge into the field of self-discovery!

PARTICIPANTS' PAST EXPERIENCES

Below are a few testimonials from participants of the live events on which parts of these books are based.

"I am no novice in participating in workshops. Over the years I have done many courses on self-empowering, business networking, spiritual principals. All valuable in their own way, but none so powerful as this workshop. Paolo's workshop is the glue that brings it all together. It's thought-provoking, challenging, and exciting. It has given me the tools to make the changes in my life that I have only dreamed about.

As soon as I recognized the potent power of my thoughts and their relationship with my perceived outside world, the synchronicities, miracles started happening! Literally within the first few hours of the workshop (Friday), I received a text from someone that offered me an opportunity that I have been dreaming about for the past two years. When I eventually spoke with them, they commented on how I kept popping up in their mind, and how they just couldn't wait till Monday to contact me. That was only the beginning. As the weekend and my week unfolded more life-changing miraculous events began to present themselves, each in perfect synchronicity, and in the most unexpected ways.

Set yourself free, live your life to your fullest potential. I have! You won't believe it until you experience it for yourself, it's pure magic! Thank you, Paolo, for being so dedicated to your life's journey, sharing your knowledge and giving us the tools to change our world. You are a blessing to anyone who has the desire to make a difference." ~ G. Mammone ~ (Seminar Attendee)

Preface

"Like C.S. Lewis' famous children story, The Lion, the Witch, and the Wardrobe, *I feel like I have opened up a doorway into a reality that I had no idea existed. My level of consciousness has been challenged, and the most satisfying outcome for me personally is an understanding of self and the sense of centeredness I now feel.*

Paolo's commitment to the message and the amount of energy and attention he displays in delivering it is phenomenal. I was touched by his generosity of spirit and his devotion to ensuring that everyone in the room got the maximum benefit.

I have left secure in the knowledge that I am the author of my personal biography, I have arranged every word, every comma, full stop and question mark in a way that perfectly serves me and I know that the pages to follow will be filled with events no longer confined to my dreams." ~ E. Schulz ~ (Seminar Attendee)

~~~.~~~

"Dear Paolo,

I would like to thank you from my heart and soul for allowing me the opportunity of acquiring your given knowledge. And for your beautiful company including the extra time that I was blessed to have with you.

You truly are a gorgeous soul.

It was when I left Jamieson (Victoria, Australia) and was driving down the golden road with emerald trees along the side, some of which having ruby leaves, and hills of smoky quartz with birds sparkling like diamonds in the sapphire sky, that it all really hit me with an overwhelming feeling of love and joy to be alive. I was then aware of my manifestations that started to happen instantly. I am so happy to be living and now knowing that everything is possible, I don't know what to manifest first. My body is tingling with inner power. Blessings." ~ J. Sharman~ (Seminar Host and Participant)

~~~.~~~

The Science of Consciousness

All these life miracles happen when there is a change within us, at the very core of our being. When we change how we perceive ourselves, the world transforms in front of our eyes and opportunities once invisible and hidden surface to the forefront of our conscious attention, ready to be seized, experienced, and enjoyed.

"Everything is energy, and that's all there is to it. Match the frequency of reality you want and you cannot help but get that reality. It can be no other way. This is not philosophy. This is physics." ~ Albert Einstein (Physicist 1879-1955)

PART I:
A NEW PARADIGM

The Science of Consciousness

CHAPTER 1:
A New Paradigm of Understanding

"The key to growth is the introduction of higher dimensions of consciousness into our awareness."
Lao Tzu

HOW THIS BOOK CAN IMPROVE YOUR LIFE, HOW IT CAME ABOUT, AND WHAT TO EXPECT

Welcome to the Awakening Series. It is my goal and great hope that these books will open your mind and consciousness to a new realm of possibility, where nothing can mentally or emotionally affect you, or keep you from achieving your true potential.

It will be a place where you can gain a true understanding of your core self and purpose, and dissolve any feeling of emptiness, sadness, alienation, or inadequacy you might have felt all your life. This is a place where you can learn how to move from being a casualty of your environment to an active creator of your destiny, from a state of barely surviving to truly living.

As you embark on this journey and internalize the messages and insights within yourself, you will be able to leave behind all the unnecessary paradoxes of duality and the illusion of separation that no longer serve you.

Fair warning: Once you begin waking up and revive the spark of life that was buried by old conditioning and dogma, you will not be able to go back to the false, hypnotic version of reality that we as a society have been indoctrinated into. The world will change in an instant, because *you* have changed. You will then truly see the world, yourself, and others in their true beauty and Divine magnificence.

The Science of Consciousness

After all, the hypnosis of separation and duality (as we will see shortly) only works while we decide to identify and play along with it. Until we are convinced that this consciousness-based simulation and our perceptions and assessments are real, we will have no other option than to stay within this limited construct.

To master the game of life, this matrix field, you will need to explore how the game/matrix has been designed, how it works, how you interface with it, and how to actually "unplug" from it.

Some of the paradigm shifts discussed here might be unsettling for you, as they will be new, unfamiliar, and unknown. Unplugging from the matrix, overcoming dogma and old beliefs, can be a shock to the system. For some, this challenges everything they consider true. They may reject the knowledge offered here, through confirmation bias and cognitive dissonance, and might even label it as false, fallacious, awkward, inaccurate, deceptive, abhorrent, irritating, and objectionable.

This is an unsettling task for someone like me, as I would truly love to help and Awaken everyone. But if I am to be true to the task ahead, I need to shake up the old and help you embrace the new. This will require touching on sensitive subjects, sacred cows, and past dogmas. I know that I will not be able to please everyone reading these books. Each word, each sentence, is currently passing through millions of neuro-associations, beliefs, and filters designed to keep people safe from the unknown and plugged into what they have accepted as true all their lives.

Furthermore, I am fully aware that I might even offend and anger some readers with some of what I discuss here. But you cannot have breakthroughs without having break-outs from the old paradigm. If I want to truly help you to become more than you are today, I will have to step outside the boundaries of your comfort zones, of what you think is real and possible, and open your mind and consciousness to new concepts and understanding.

Writing and focusing on what is, at times, uncomfortable, unknown, and challenging, and what most readers have believed to be true for their entire lives, has not won anyone any popularity contests in the past. This would be a risk if my goal was wealth or

A New Paradigm of Understanding

fame. The more you step on people's precious constructs, accepted conditioning, unquestionable dogmas, and developed limited identity, the less the approval and acceptance.

Luckily, I am not here to become anyone's guru or master, or to become popular or make money. I am only here to share my personal experience. Maybe it will help a few people who are in line with this message and transform their lives, as it has done for many attendees of the live events and readers of these works before yourself.

The messenger, the teacher, is irrelevant. It is the message, and the Awakening that it can usher forward, that matters. For this reason, all the PDF versions of the books in this series have been offered for FREE. Furthermore, I give implicit and unconditional permission for anyone to use the materials contained in these books in other texts, audios, and videos for non-commercial purposes. All I ask is that you list where the information came from, cite the author, and if possible, provide a link to the free PDF so that this knowledge can spread around the world. In this way, there will be no obstacles in accessing this material, sharing it by email, at no cost, to anyone that could benefit from this work. Perhaps it may even reach people in countries where only a computer with Internet access is available.

Personally, I wish I had known what is in these books in my teens; it would have made my journey much easier and faster... yet, it was my path and my destiny to live the life I lived, and gain wisdom from my personal experiences, challenges and tribulations.

It is only through sadness that we can appreciate joy, only through darkness that we can understand the light. Therefore, to all the villains, scoundrels, lowlifes, thieves, energy vampires, scammers, egocentrically focused individuals and teachers, impersonators, narcissists, clowns, criminals, adversaries, contenders, saboteurs, betrayers, and to all my enemies, I owe as much gratitude as the heroes, friends, givers, allies, insiders, collaborators, partners, champions, defenders, healers, educators, mentors, teachers, and masters in my life. I love you all, and I am deeply thankful for your participation in my life. You made me who I am today.

The Science of Consciousness

You do not need to wait for someone else to save you, and do the work for you. Knowledge is all around you; you just need to find what best resonates with you and start applying it to your daily life. When you wait for an outside force to do the work, you are delegating your spiritual responsibility, your growth and evolution, to that outside force. This leaves you powerless, helpless, ineffective, inert, paralyzed, and dependent.

This is why there are so many individuals on so many religious paths who have *not* fully awakened, as they are still waiting for someone else to do the hard work for them. On other lineages like Dzogchen there exist tens of thousands of past and present cases of enlightenment, this is because they realized that t*hey* were the person that they had been waiting for. They did not delegate their spiritual power to an outside source. They themselves, their unwavering desire, their unshakable will, was all they needed.

"The Art of Peace begins with you. Work on yourself and your appointed task in the Art of Peace. Everyone has a spirit that can be refined, a body that can be trained in some manner, a suitable path to follow. You are here for no other purpose than to realize your inner divinity and manifest your innate enlightenment. Foster peace in your own life and then apply the Art to all that you encounter." ~ Morihei Ueshiba (*The Art of Peace*)

Other masters, teachers, and educators have come in the past to show us a possible way, a possible path to Awakening and unity; but we are the ones who have to personally walk the path, and embrace the teaching in every aspect of our lives. They cannot do it for us.

Furthermore, in our ignorance, we have often either killed these messengers, teachers, and Awakened masters, and/or treated them like gods — creating more loops, more bureaucracy, more churches, more religions, more middlemen, and more complexities.

A New Paradigm of Understanding

THE EVOLUTIONARY SPIRITUAL JOURNEY

This series is the result of 35+ years of personal research into the field of the unified self and the nature of reality, what Eastern philosophies call enlightenment, or a state of grace, peace, and oneness. They offer a path that can take you from student to philosopher, from philosopher to initiate, from initiate to mystic, and ultimately from mystic to master.

To create context here, let's define each path individually:

STUDENT: A person enrolled in an educational class or institution. It is also representative of someone studying certain subjects in order to attain an understanding and comprehension in regards to a specific topic.

PHILOSOPHER: A person who has a great intellectual understanding of a specific subject. There is a great love for what has been learned but it has not been internalized enough to become a state of being. It is knowledge without application.

INITIATE: A person that has internalized the spiritual knowledge, and transformed it into wisdom, having been initiated (made aware of, Awakened) to a deeper level of understanding. The learning has becoming part of their life, at all levels: in thought, word, and action.

MYSTIC: A person who has had true realizations through a direct experience of the Divine Source; not intellectually, but experimentally. He or she not only knows what, philosophically speaking, being one with all means, but has had a direct experience.

MASTER: A person who has not only Awakened from the slumber of separation (become enlightened), but also has learned how to embody that knowledge and wisdom in every thought, emotion, word, and action as a reflection of this state of unity and grace. They have mastered the laws of reality and can therefore create the miraculous.

The Science of Consciousness

THERE ARE MANY LEVELS OF AWAKENING

When it comes to becoming unified (enlightened), an individual can experience both the sensation of having been turned on like a light, where the entire body is flooded with love, bliss, and comprehension, with an incredible, indescribable sense of unity; as well as experiencing smaller incremental states of openness and oneness.

There are 1,000 levels of unity or enlightenment in the Buddhist and Hindu tradition. This is showcased as the Sahasrara Chakra, the energetic center at the top of your head that has 1,000 petals, each representing a level of realization, most of which happen on small, incremental levels. You are always learning; you are always evolving and perpetually Awakening.

To reach more advance levels of realizations, we will need to reconcile spiritual traditions and secret esoteric knowledge with modern science. Science — especially when we consider quantum mechanics — is the new language of mysticism. Paradoxes will need to be reconciled, the fog of separation and confusion lifted.

Therefore, the reader will find references here to many different spiritual traditions, like the Judaic, Kabbalah, Essenic, Christian, Gnosticism (of various denominations), Hermetic, Chatar, Taoist, Advaita Vedanta, Buddhism, Dzogchen, Egyptian, Greek Philosophy (including Stoicism), as well as various Shamanic traditions.

This is because at their core, when we remove all the dogmas created after the original teaching by the churches, emperors, and the religious/political apparatus as well as the vast level of editing, manipulation, and interpretations, the message is the same.

Let me expand on this further before we move on.

A New Paradigm of Understanding

ALL PATHS ARE JUST INTERPRETATIONS OF THE SAME SOURCE

I will use science models, case studies, allegories, and quotes to explain many of the more abstract concepts. For example, if you look at light passing through a prism, you will notice something peculiar; it breaks up and forms seven distinct colors. This is the same phenomenon and marvel we call the rainbow.

White light goes in, and the seven colors of the rainbow come out: Red, Orange, Yellow, Green, Blue, Indigo and Violet.

Using an analogy, therefore, we could say that if a group of seven friends, all in different locations (for example, Cairo, London, New York, Sydney, Tokyo, New Delhi, Paris) wanted to meet for a wedding in Rome, they will all take different paths relative to where they are. Some will take a train, some will drive, and some, because of the distance, will have to take a plane or two. This would make sense to anyone looking at it objectively.

The same is true with any religious path. Each color could be akin to a place where the language, traditions, and culture are different. Therefore, the interpretation of this pure, unsullied, and undifferentiated "light" would be different, and take on its own spin, characteristics, and religious flavor.

The colors representing different religions and ideologies will seem, from the outside, so far away from each other, and so antagonistic in principle, that conflict might seem the only option between them. Yet, in spite of the differences, all have the same origin, and will eventually lead to the same destination.

Even science could be considered a form of religious belief, where nothing is accepted beside what is believed to be true. This kind of blind belief and narrow-mindfulness is what initially stopped inventions like the radio, flying, and many advance technologies we use today.

The closer you are to the original point of separation, the more the colors fade away and return to be white light. The further away you are from the break point of separation and source, the

The Science of Consciousness

more the colors become solid, more differentiated, stronger, and more intense.

Let us say, you reside in the middle of a red spectrum of a rainbow (e.g. a specific religion), you will not see that the end of your bands in fact integrates and blends in with the other color bands of the rainbow. You will be blinded to the fact that all colors come from the same light source, and will eventually have to return to their origin. If all you see is red, and are open to nothing else, then you will accept "Red" as true and the only reality there is, and reject all other colors as false.

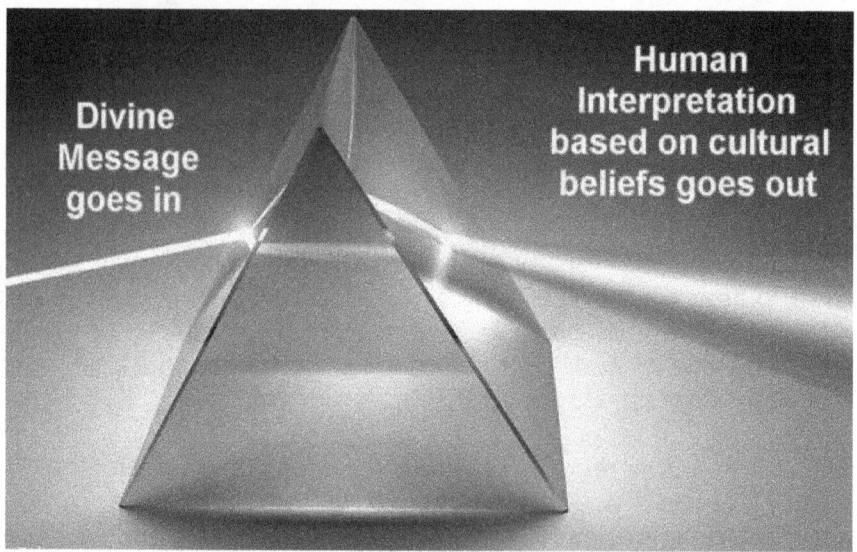

Any extremists in any field, including religion, science and philosophy are guilty of this tunnel-vision. They will only consider their own ideology, which they accept as true, and will fight, rebel against, and discard everything else.

If instead of remaining in one color spectrum, we get closer to Divine unity (no matter what tradition we have come to love and identify with), we will then come to realize that all the external differences in semantics, dogmas, heroes, saviors, and villains will fade away.

A New Paradigm of Understanding

This is why Awakened individuals do not judge. They have a more inclusive, broader, more comprehensive, loving and compassionate perspective of all this.

Enlightened beings never enjoy conflicts. After all, how can a unified being that sees the other as oneself inflict suffering to another?

"There is evil and disorder in the world because people have forgotten that all things emanate from one source. Return to that source and leave behind all self-centered thoughts, petty desires, and anger. Those who are possessed by nothing possess everything." ~ Morihei Ueshiba (*The Art of Peace*)

The more inclusive, open, fair, tolerant, kind, loving, unprejudiced, open-minded, and compassionate a path is, the closer to the original source of Love and Light it is. The more fragmented, exclusive, biased, dogmatic, fanatical, hateful, racist, xenophobic, closed-minded and chauvinistic a path is, the further it is from the source of Love and Light.

Although Jesus Christ was crucified once, his original teachings of compassion, equanimity, kindness, unconditional love, reincarnation, and oneness with God have been crucified multiple times ever since. Some of his teachings were not only suppressed, but also manipulated to a point that in the last two thousand years, they have formed the basis for prejudice, coercion, injustice, control, oppression, as well as crusades, inquisitions, and wars.

Some Gnostic gospels and texts, however, still contain Jesus' original messages, which have escaped the church's manipulation, deletion, and editing. Some of the original teachings and legacies left behind by spiritual leaders and enlightened masters like Buddha, Krishna, Lao Tzu, Moses, and Mohamed have suffered similar fates.

If you examine philosophers, politicians, and leaders, you will find that they all have assumptions, beliefs, biases, and dogmas they promote and cherish. There is always a payout in judgment, indifference, alienation, and prejudice. However, when you look at mystics and masters of old who have achieved a direct experience of the Divine, the facade of separation falls apart. All dogmas become irrelevant; all doctrines superfluous.

People who have accepted borrowed, second-hand knowledge (those identified with a specific color spectrum in the rainbow) are those who start wars, conflicts, and arguments to enforce their own ideology that there is only one path. However, those who have any kind of spiritual or direct mystical experiences, like a deep interconnection and love during meditation, contemplation or prayer, and those who have had near-death and out-of-body experiences, miraculous healing, and psychedelic experiences are those who could truly see the real destination, and understand that there are many paths in the road map to get there.

This is a common experience shared by all great beings, be they Christian Saints, Sufi Masters, Zen Roshis, Hindu Gurus and Sadhus, Taoist Sages, Tibetan Lamas and Masters, or independent mystics.

This is why, in this series of books, I do not wish to destroy, impair, shatter, or diminish your love for your spiritual lineage (if any). Quite the opposite; it is my hope that it will remove the unnecessary clutter and layers of added bias, indoctrination, and manipulation to reveal its original magnificent, beautiful, radiant and loving message. Each path is unique, and if you feel love, connection, and affinity with a specific spiritual message, this a great gift worth embracing as it offers a great opportunity to expand and grow.

You can still walk the green, the yellow, or the blue path or whatever path you choose; but instead of going in the direction of isolation, separation, alienation, judgment, prejudice, and dogma, we are going to move towards the source of *all* paths, *all* lineages, *all* messages.

If you are a Christian, be a Christian of light; if you are a Muslim, be a Muslim of light; if you are a Hindu, be a Hindu of light. Cherish the commonalities between teachings, their core elements, and when examined closely, you will notice that they often build bridges, rather than walls and trenches.

A New Paradigm of Understanding

The original message was never the problem, but it is those who have never experienced the divine, who have altered the teachings to gain control and influence the masses to achieve their own agenda. All religions are based on a secondhand interpretation. Mysticism is based on a direct experiential connection with the Divine source.

True seekers forge their own path based on their own inner truth and experience, while followers follow the crowd consensus. We can talk all day long about what it is like to swim in the sea, how the water feels on the skin, how to coordinate the body and hand movements in the water, the temperature of the water, the techniques to stay afloat... but all this information is of little value until you physically jump in the water and experience swimming yourself.

The same applies when it comes to experiencing the Divine. For this, we need to be still, withdraw from all senses, and go within. We will provide more details on this later.

"And when he was demanded of the Pharisees, when the kingdom of God should come, he answered them and said, The kingdom of God cometh not with observation: Neither shall they say, Lo here! or, lo there! for, behold, the kingdom of God is within you." Luke 17:20-21 (KJV)

"All that is real in me is God; all that is real in God is I; The gulf between God and me is thus bridged. Thus by knowing God, we find that the kingdom of heaven is within us." ~ Swami Vivekananda

"God is within us." ~ Plato

It is only when you start experiencing the Divine *directly* that a door truly opens. That is the difference between a student and/or a philosopher, and a true mystic and/or a master.

"Theologians may quarrel, but the mystics of the world speak the same language, and the practices they follow lead to the same goal." ~ Eknath Easwaran, creator of *Passage Meditation — Original Goodness*

The Science of Consciousness

When you realize that all the paths are there as an expression of human, cultural, social predisposition and acceptance, then you will understand that there are many unique spiritual paths, with infinite approaches and variations. Each one of us, you could say, has a unique relationship with God or the source, including an atheist or an agnostic.

"It takes MORE FAITH to be an atheist than to believe in God." ~ Ruth Bell Graham

In the end, everyone will reach the same conclusions, like all enlightened beings have done in the past, that all paths came from one source and that all students of life, no matter what denomination they have endorsed, identified with, and ultimately chosen, will have to go back "home" to the same original Divine point.

Aside from religions and spiritual paths, these books will cover a wide array of scientific disciplines, including biology, epigenetics, neurology, anthropology, astronomy radionics, optics, astrotheosis, Newtonian physics, and quantum mechanics, just to mention a few. For this reason, many consider this series the unifying bridge, the glue, between ancient and modern spirituality and science.

Although there is a lot of knowledge here that may seem too complex, it has always been my goal to simplify it. For this reason, I will use a lot of quotes, stories, allegories, and parables as mentioned earlier.

CREATING MIRACLES

Some of the contents we will be covering in this work, were originally part of a series of live events and lectures, I conducted, where participants were able to ask questions that were important to them.

Some miracles also occurred at these live events, where cases of instantaneous healing occurred, a broken relationship was mended, a new and better job was acquired, dream relationships attained, a new vehicle was received as a gift, and where money

A New Paradigm of Understanding

was manifested from thin air, etc. I have added some of the participants' testimonials in the Preface, to showcase their personal journeys in one of the three-day events.

It was not I who created these miracles, but the individuals who re-wired their brains on a subconscious level, creating an attraction and coherence that spanned body, mind, and soul. This newfound coherence allowed them to change their mindsets, attract their wanted reality, and ultimately redesigned a new destiny.

When you change your mind at a neurological level and align your heart and soul to your true purpose, your life can change in a moment. It becomes "coherent," in line with the new quantum timeline of potential, and with the new vision you have created. It's that simple.

Consider the example of a symphony. When you know what you want, you send out a clear, harmonious, energetic tune that creates a field of influence and resonance in the quantum field. You become a vortex, a magnet for new potentialities to appear in your reality.

When your desires and beliefs conflict with one another *(e.g., desiring wealth and abundance, while also believing that money is the root of all evil)* you end up creating a conflict within your field of reality, which causes the opposing wave frequencies and forces to be nullified.

Coherent wave frequencies, on the other hand, reinforce and add to each other. This is the same concept we see in constructive and destructive wave interference because our thoughts and emotions create an electromagnetic field of resonance.

Love + Love = More Love
Hot + Hot = More Heat
Hate + Hate = More Hate
Love + Hate = Nullify
Hot + Cold = Nullify

The Science of Consciousness

You can't manifest love in your life if your energy signature is contradictory in nature. More on this later.

The only thing that you would be able to attract with this disorderly field of resonance is more chaos, confusion, and more wanting. Wanting creates more wanting. Your thoughts, and words create physical matter and events, and attract the coherent reality to your field of experience.

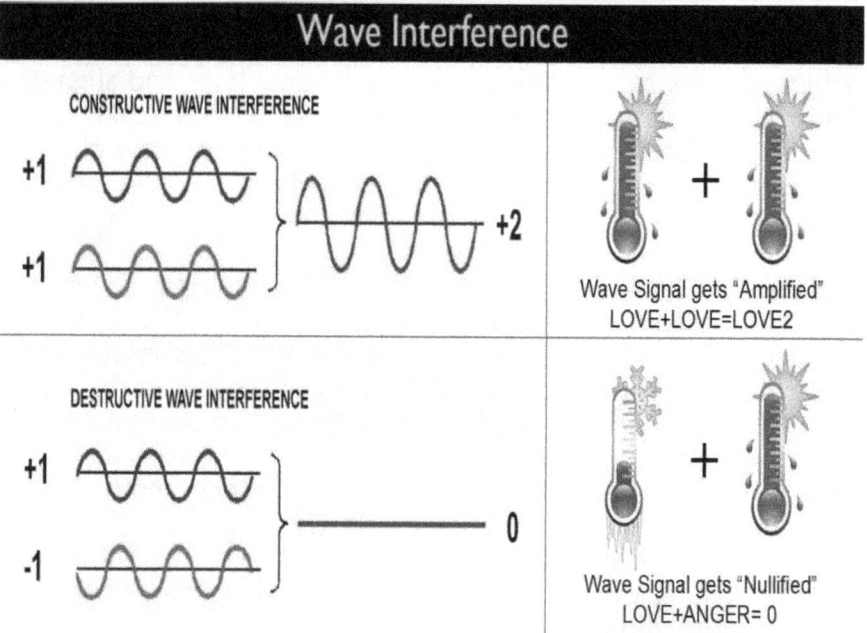

"Thoughts are things; what you feel, you attract; and what you imagine, you become." ~ Joseph Murphy

"Everything is energy, and that's all there is to it. Match the frequency of reality you want, and you cannot help but get that reality. It can be no other way. This is not philosophy. This is physics." ~ Albert Einstein

That's why in Quantum Linguistics and in the Science of Manifestation, we must never use the term "I want..." or "I desire..." After all, new thoughts and emotions create new

A New Paradigm of Understanding

choices, which in turn create new behaviors and experiences that become new destinies.

Negative beliefs, thoughts, and emotions only create, reinforce, and amplify more of the same. Hence, it is so important to dispel the veil of ignorance that has obscured the truth, beyond bias, limiting beliefs and dogma for so long.

This leads me to the topic of gratitude. In gratitude, you feel a strong sense of appreciation and love where anger, hate and resentment cannot co-exist. So when feelings of jealousy, envy or anger arise, focus on gratitude instead and be grateful for the wonderful and special blessings that you have. Put out the fire of discordance with the water of harmony.

Sometimes in life, pain is inevitable. But suffering, like happiness, is a choice. Most sufferings are a mere projection of past memories or future potentialities in your mind that do not currently exist, which are creating your own personal hell. You are the director of your own movie.

If you purely focus on the present moment, you will then come to realize that your personal demons, ghost of the past, and adversaries do not exist in the physical world, but only in your mind. It is your thoughts and emotions that create the personal reality you live in.

Once you realize that you have the power to switch your reality at any moment by making a paradigm shift, then this transformation moves you from a Victim Mentality to a Creator of your own Destiny.

We will learn soon, the science of consciousness and how we can move from the inertia of physicality/matter, to the creative state and fluidity of frequency wave and energy, from the ordinary to the extraordinary, to the natural to the supernatural. For now, please stay tuned to this message, as we build the context and the different knowledge, one page at the time.

After all, clarity leads to power, any breakthroughs are only possible when we let go of old paradigm of understanding.

The Science of Consciousness

> *"All significant breakthroughs are break-WITHs old way of thinking"* ~ Thomas Kuhn (Physicist. 1922-1996)

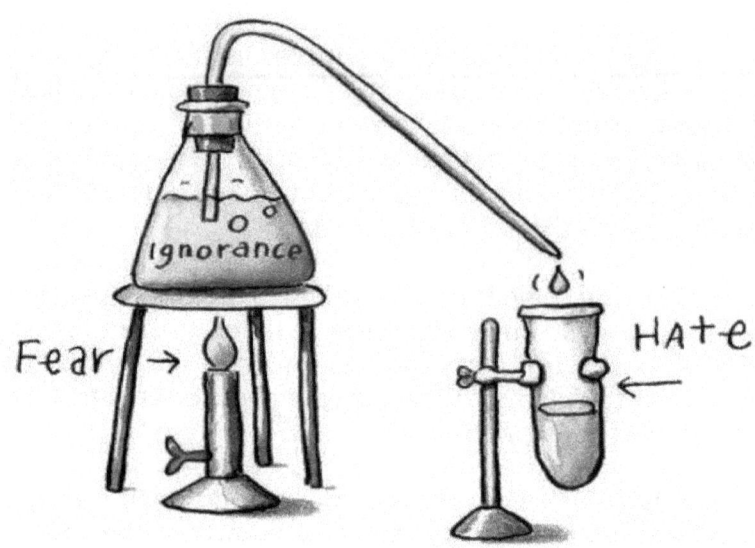

WHAT TO EXPECT

The Awakening Series has been divided into four books.

- **Book One:** *The Science of Consciousness*
- **Book Two:** *How to Create Miracles, a Practical Guide into the Extraordinary*
- **Book Three:** *You Are Light*
- **Book Four:** *Many Lives, Many Lessons, One Destination.*

Depending on when you are reading this book, the rest of the series might be available for you to read and download.

A New Paradigm of Understanding

AN UNFOLDING JOURNEY

I want to take you on a journey of self-discovery with me — like the journey of Neo in *The Matrix*, or the intergalactic quest and personal growth of Luke Skywalker in the original Star Wars trilogy. If you come along, I assure you it will be worth your while. You could say that you have nothing to lose, and all to gain. However, this would be incorrect. Instead, you will lose all the unnecessary layers of limited beliefs, dogmas, and borrowed ignorance that have weighed you down all this time. Only by doing so can you truly soar to new levels of Awakening. The old self needs to be dissolved in order for the new self to emerge.

You see, no one is truly stuck. We are just identified and committed to a certain pattern of behavior, which has greatly served us in the past. However, as we grow and evolve, we must recognize that those behaviors were harmful, destructive, limiting and toxic. The reason why we can't move forward, most of the time, is because we keep projecting the same old thought patterns into the new life we want to create, while expecting a different result.

"Your time is limited, so don't waste it living someone else's life. Don't be trapped by dogma — which is living with the results of other people's thinking. Don't let the noise of others' opinions drown out your own inner voice. And most important, have the courage to follow your heart and intuition. They somehow already know what you truly want to become. Everything else is secondary." ~ Steve Jobs

I will endeavor to make each chapter in these books brief and to the point. However, at times some chapters might be over 10 pages long, as a result of necessary context and information. I will expand and build upon the previous chapters, which will open the doorway to a more outrageous consciousness-expanding principles and concepts.

The first four chapters are of an introductory nature to help build the basis from which all the most extraordinary knowledge can spring.

The Science of Consciousness

For this reason, it is advisable to read these chapters and books in sequence, even if some of the knowledge is already well known or familiar to you. It does not hurt to refresh and reinforce previously held information as it will only support your Awakening.

SOMETHING ALWAYS ESCAPES YOUR ATTENTION THE FIRST TIME

You might have previously experienced that after reading a chapter or book twice, you found that there was so much information that you missed during your first read. This is because as you learn, grow and evolve, so too does your perception of who you are, what your mind absorbs, deletes, ignores, and discards.

As we say in neuro-science (Hebbian Learning): *"Neurocells that fire together, wire together,"* and *"If you don't use it, you lose it!"*

The two main laws of learning, the Law of Association and the Law of Repetition, are, after all, how humans learn. Reinforcing old knowledge helps reinforce the neuro-pathways and your perception of reality. So even if some of this knowledge seems familiar, please keep going.

You will also find that some of the concepts previously discussed are repeated from different angles or different paradigms. This is done purposefully, as it is a way of targeting different parts of your neurology to construct new models of reality, building understanding and developing more useful beliefs within your consciousness. As we will see later, every time you say *"I am"*, you are creating an identity, a box of perception, a program in the field of unified consciousness. These identities, little by little, become ingrained within you through the Laws of Association and Repetition, and form the persona and ego you come to identify with.

You cannot expect to have the same pattern of thoughts, emotions, and responses looping over and over again and expect a different

A New Paradigm of Understanding

result in life. You cannot create a new life, using the old persona, the old ego. A new self needs to be redesigned for a new destiny to unfold.

This is what Book One is all about.

The Science of Consciousness

A New Paradigm of Understanding

CHAPTER 2:
Unifying Science and Spirituality

"The notion that Science and Spirituality are somehow mutually exclusive does a disservice to both."
~ Carl Sagan

THE WHAT, THE WHY, AND THE HOW

In the Western world, most individuals wish to know the "what", the "why," and the "how" of things. This has also been my journey, and one of the reasons I spent most of my life asking questions to crack the code, searching for the true secrets of life and self-Awakening.

Asking the "what," "why," and "how" are what made me perceive science as the new path to mysticism: a form of belief based on inquiry, one where our limited identity, bias, conditioning, and superstitions can be overcome by a new paradigm of understanding through the power of self-discovery and direct experience.

Some of the knowledge and Awakening described by masters in the past now can be understood through physiology, biology, epigenetics, and quantum physics.

If the topics covered here are viewed from various angles, then there is very little room for conjectures, bias, dogma, or superstition. The path then becomes clearer and less convoluted.

Furthermore, by sharing with you the knowledge that was instrumental to some of my Awakenings, I am hoping that the "what" and the "why" will seem incredibly obvious that anyone else can come to the same conclusions if given the same information.

The Science of Consciousness

The allegories, research, case studies and the scientifically beautiful realizations will appear to become self-evident.

THE GLUE THAT UNIFIES SCIENCE AND SPIRITUALITY

I made it my mission to try to unify science and spiritually as much as I could in this manuscript, so that questions are answered and doubts become insignificant and redundant. The knowledge offered in this book series therefore aims to be, as the participants below attest, the "glue" that unifies Science, Spirituality, and Life in general.

Some of the participants of the live event commented that this training is like going to "Jedi School" or "Unplugging from the Matrix." I am honored by such comparisons, being a geek at heart.

For some, it was the pivotal point to overcome depression, the turning point that prevented them from ending their lives; and for others, it was a huge paradigm shift that transformed every aspect of their existence. Sadly, there were also those who did not stop to contemplate or internalize the concepts in the live events. To them, it was just another event, another manuscript, to add to their repertoire, lost in the recesses of their memory. This simply means that it was not for them, or that it was not the right time, which is in perfect accord with each personal journey. All is perfect in its own way. No matter which category you end up fitting into, you are loved either way, and I will be still thankful, humbled, and honored even if you read just a few pages of this book, and get a tiny sparkle of life magic and realization back into your life.

You could spend months, if not years, training to master a skill, but unless you apply that knowledge in your life, it is just another collection of information in your personal memory archive, collecting dust. You might search for many beautiful, exotic and useful seeds that could change lives. But if you have no desire or intention to plant them, after a while the seeds would rot, and fail to sprout, as its life force would no longer be present. Knowledge, like a seed, is useless without application.

The Messenger is Irrelevant

It is my great hope that this work will provide you with a real understanding of who you are, where you come from, why you are here, where you are going, and how to progress in this evolutionary chapter of your existence. In fact, if you are only able to internalize a fraction of this work on a deeper level, your life will be filled with a sense of awe, splendor, excitement, inspiration, joy, freedom, health, compassion, love, and gratitude, as it has been for many others before you, including me.

THE NEED FOR THIS INFORMATION

I started sharing the knowledge in these books after a leave of absence of over nine years from public speaking. It was only after the passing of my friend, Joshua Crook, that I felt the need to get back into sharing on a much larger scale. How the contents of my new live events have been subsequently organized and how these books have come to fruition have all been because of this catalytic event.

Joshua Crook took his own life after the passing of his partner Roxanne five months earlier. Although Joshua tried to make sense of the meaning of life after she passed away, and tried to connect the dots, his depression, bullying from his partner's past lover, and the emptiness he felt inside became too much for him to bear. After we lost Joshua, friends and family asked me to help make sense of his death, explain what happens to a soul after passing, how reincarnation and soul contracts work, the reason why we are here, and so on.

This new understanding prompted me to organize a modified version of my old live event and lectures where reincarnation, soul contracts, and the purpose of life are covered in much more detail in Book 4. Another part that was extended in these books was knowledge designed to move people who suffer from depression to a place of understanding, inclusiveness, and inner peace.

What started as a one-book project shortly became a ten-plus book odyssey, which is now part of four different series: The Awakening Series, The Life Map Series, The Forbidden Knowledge Series, and A New World Series.

The Science of Consciousness

BUILDING THE BLOCKS OF AWARNESS ONE STEP AT THE TIME

The event, and subsequently these books, were designed as an evolutionary process, as a journey of Awakening.

For those of you who saw the 1984 movie *The Karate Kid,* you may recall that the film contained many inspirational messages. In this movie, Mr. Miyagi, a Japanese man in his sixties, decides to teach a young man, Daniel, karate, after witnessing him being bullied by a group of other boys. Mr. Miyagi starts by asking Daniel to wash and wax over twenty old cars, then sand and paint his house deck and his fence — a massive task that would take Daniel many days to complete.

Though this may not seem like a very fascinating movie at the beginning, the viewer soon realizes that Mr. Miyagi is helping Daniel create a neurological muscle memory by repeating certain movements over and over again. This continuous repetition created a subconscious program that became second nature and instinctual.

For example, the hand strokes (like painting the fence) and the upward and downward movement of the wrist can be instantaneously applied to a defense stance when attacked, without having to recall or think about the technique.

"We are what we repeatedly do. Excellence therefore is not an action, but a habit." ~ Aristotle

There are four stages of learning:

1. **Unconscious Incompetence.** You don't know that you don't know. In the *Karate Kid* example, Daniel does not know that one of the main aspects of learning karate or any martial art is to internalize certain movements as muscle memory.

2. **Conscious Incompetence.** You know that you don't know. Daniel discovers that he does not know much about

The Messenger is Irrelevant

martial arts and karate. He realizes that there is much to learn.

3. **Conscious Competence.** You know that you know. After practicing for a while, Daniel has mastered the movements, and knows what they are used for.

4. **Unconscious Competence.** You don't need to think about it; it's just second nature. Daniel's body responds automatically when attacked. It has become an unconscious response.[1]

With any skill, we need to move from the first stage to the last stage. This is the same subconscious process you experience when learning how to drive a car or ride a bicycle. At the start, you always have to be consciously aware of the steps, the rules, the environment, and your hand/body coordination. But after a while, after several attempts and repetitions, the activity becomes a subconscious action, which no longer requires the same level of thought and attention as it did at the start.

You could be driving to work for thirty minutes, thinking about how you will present your ideas at the board meeting that day, and safely park your car in the parking garage without giving much thought as to how you maneuvered your way out of traffic and safely reached your destination. It all happens on autopilot.

This is, in a way, how this book has been designed. We will build on the knowledge of each chapter, so that we can expand your awareness one step at a time, up to a point that you no longer have to be conscious of the process. At times, you may find it odd that certain topics are being covered or explained, but I only ask that you trust the process and the knowledge, as it will all come together in the end.

Some of the concepts (like duality, coherence, frequency, etc.) will be reviewed in different perspectives, so that a deeper

---

[1] To see a video clip of the original version of this movie, see the link at the end of this section.

understanding can emerge. As this work progresses, I believe that your identity will be expanded, your consciousness will be broadened, and your life transmuted for the better.

Then, one day, someone close to you will look at you and notice that you have changed. You talk more calmly, you have become more peaceful, you are happier for no apparent reason, you are more resourceful, you react to life challenges with poise, tolerance, and wisdom, and you have stopped blaming and judging others. On top of that, to the great surprise of the people around you, when you talk about anything, it's like if the wisdom of the ages has opened up, and magic is flowing out of your mouth. This is a normal occurrence, when light, knowledge, and understanding become the new "modus operandi," the new operating system in one's life.

THE ROOT OF MOST PROBLEMS AND SUFFERING

To move from a limited reality to a higher, more expanded reality, you need to broaden your limited self-identification and how you see others and life in general. Self-inquiry, questioning what you have believed to be true and expanding your knowledge and awareness is one of the best tool you can use.

One of the greatest quotes ever expressed by any human is: *"No problem can be solved from the same level of consciousness that created it,"* by Albert Einstein (Physicist, 1879-1955)

If you want a different life, a better life, and are not satisfied with how your life has panned out so far, then the only lasting thing you can do is remodel, widen your mind perceptions and awareness.

It all starts with the Science of Consciousness.

When I coach people from all walks of life, all around the world, one of the common issues my clients face is not understanding how their self-identity and beliefs create a set of boundaries and conditions that affect their life and destiny. Let me expand on this.

The Messenger is Irrelevant

When you look at your hand, you know where it ends and where the environment begins; your skin designates this boundary. What most people are not aware of, is that the same thing happens with your belief system.

Why is this important?

Because you cannot change your destiny or attract new life potentials with the same model of thought or belief systems you initially created. You need to expand the boundaries.

Your belief system creates your field of experience. For example:

You could breakup with your partner to stop a destructive and abusive relationship, but if you loathe yourself and have little self-worth, you would only find yourself attracting the same type of person in the next relationship. The name may have changed, their physical appearance might be different, but the thought patterns and lessons are still the same.

You could start a new business venture with the intention to increase your wealth, but if you feel that you are unworthy, then you would only find yourself losing more money, time and energy. The new business idea may be better, and there might be a bigger market for it, but the thought patterns and lessons are still the same.

This is because your life is a reflection of your inner world.

Your life is trapped within the boundaries of what you know.

If you believe that you do not matter, your life will not matter.

If you believe you are not deserving of love, then lasting and fulfilling relationships will elude you.

If you believe nothing ever works for you, then success, wealth and abundance will evade you. To change your life, you need to expand the boundaries of what you believe to be true.

The Science of Consciousness

What you currently know forms the basis of your life.

What you currently know that you don't know forms your future potential.

What you don't know that you don't know is an unknown hidden potential.

As your boundary expands, so too does your field of influence and awareness.

Many of our problems stem from the belief that we already know what is true. It becomes the law and we live as though it is all we need to know. This creates a cognitive bias, a restricted mindset that does not allow new awareness, knowledge and experience to filter through.

There are three parts to these boundaries:

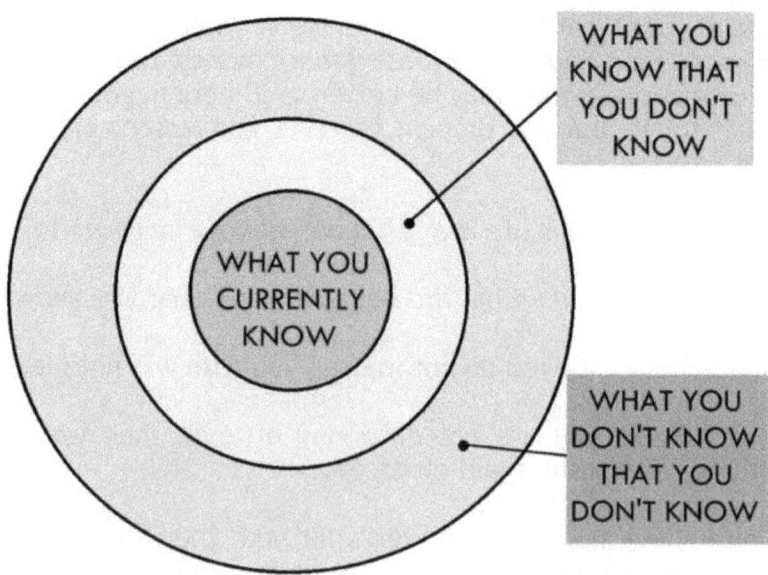

The Messenger is Irrelevant

Just the very fact that our lives do not match the desires we wish for ourselves should be enough to prompt us to review our old belief systems. Our sufferings, disappointments and failures are the best barometers of that.

Imagine your thoughts and emotions like a big net of energy field. When cast into an ocean of potentialities, it will only capture the people, places, things, times and events that perfectly match your vibrational frequency. Therefore, every aspect you have attracted into your life becomes your initiation.

People usually fail to see the limited boundaries that they have created for themselves. This is why a life coaching session is sometimes necessary to help overcome these road blocks and show them how to see the forest rather than focus on one tree.

EXTRA INTERACTIVE RESOURCES

To help further expand your field of awareness and reinforce what you have just learnt, I have included some extra resources for you below.

There are over twenty video clips that were originally shown at the live event; slides related to the topics in the book, extra articles, stories and books in PDF format; Q&As, video interviews and audios. Some of the e-books in the member's area are priced at over $20, so it will be worth your while to register for an online membership.

You will also find that I use a lot of quotes and provide a lot of materials in my work as they help reinforce the knowledge covered and provides more validity and credibility to your cognitive, dualistic mind. But there is also a second reason for this...

Each time you read a quote or view a material, your subconscious mind fires up the new knowledge and realizations you have just gained, which in turn makes the learning more effective and potent. So please bear with me, as there is always a method to my madness.

The Science of Consciousness

> The interactive resources in the **PaoloTiberi.com** website are available here:
>
> https://paolotiberi.com/resources/membership-join/
>
> Cost varies based on the level of resources and interactivity. The materials contain videos, e-books, PDF guides, audios etc., which are all specific to each book and membership.
>
> It also includes a summary and a blueprint version of the manifestation course, which formed part of a $497 live event. Some options include monthly zoom meeting for those readers that would like a more personalized approach.
>
> The amount you donate will help spread this message and help the physical component of this work to continue.

There is also an e-Book with all the quotes in the member's area of **paolotiberi.com**. It is under the link called "Resources".

These resources are for the avid readers and students of the work, who may need a little more than just a bit of ink on a page or a pixelated text on the screen of a smart device. These online resources are not indispensable for your progress and reading, but are just an extra tool available to you.

If you are interested in this first interactive component of this book, which is **Video Number 1**, a movie clip of Mr. Miyagi and Daniel-San titled **"Karate Kid - Wax on, Wax off,"** follow the instructions below.

The Messenger is Irrelevant

> **~ INSTRUCTIONS ~**
>
> 1) To view the video clip, visit: **PaoloTiberi.com**
> 2) Click on the link called "Resources"
> 3) Select "Membership Levels" and how much you would like to donate.
> 4) After payment you will be provided with information on how to access the membership area. Please ensure to bookmark it and save your username and password
> 5) Under Chapter 1 Resources, click on the video called: ***"Karate Kid - Wax on, Wax off"***

If you have no access to the Internet, simply continue reading the book and skip the extra online resources.

The Science of Consciousness

CHAPTER 3:
The Messenger is Irrelevant

"He who has so little knowledge of human nature, as to seek happiness by changing anything but his own disposition, will waste his life in fruitless efforts." ~ Samuel Johnson

THE SOURCE IS IRRELEVANT. IT IS THE MESSAGE THAT COUNTS.

Oftentimes in the past, writers, speakers and spiritual leaders have offered great insights about how to find the elusive mystical connection with the Divine. However, most have done so without providing a scientific background as to how and why certain concepts are valid, or how and why specific practical steps need to be embraced and practiced.

We have often heard concepts like:

"We are all one."
"We are all connected."
"We are light beings living a physical experience."
"Our thoughts matter."
"Our thoughts & consciousness are the base for reality and matter."
And more.

But when inquiring deeper, we are left with: *"You need to trust that this is so."*

It has only been in the last 30 years or so that some great researchers, teachers and masters have come along to help us reconcile scientific evidence with the field of consciousness, mysticism, and spirituality.

The Science of Consciousness

Some might in fact recognize the influence on this book series by the work of: Michael Talbot (*The Holographic Universe*), Fritjof Capra (*The Tao of Physics*), Lynne McTaggart (*The Field; The Power of Eight; The Intention Experiment*), Robert Gilmore (*Alice in Quantumland*), Dr. Candace B. Perth (*Molecules of Emotions*), Joseph Selbie (*The Physics of God*), Ellen Langer (*Counter Clockwise*), Dr. Bruce Lipton (*The Biology of Belief*), Joseph Ledoux (*The Emotional Brain*), Deepak Chopra (*Quantum Healing*), Neville Goddard, Caroline Myss, Santos Bonacci, and the works of Ramtha, J.Z. Night, Dr. Joe Dispenza, Esther & Jerry Hicks (*Abraham*), RA (*The Law of One*), Neale D. Walsch (*Conversation with God*), David Wilcock, Sadh Guru, Ram Dass, and other great authors like Nassim Haramein and Gregg Braden.

There are many others, too many to mention, who have influenced the way we think of life and reality. Some of these authors and their works will be mentioned in this book series. To these authors I will be forever thankful.

Each author, teacher, and master have their own "flavor," their unique vibrational blend of knowledge, light-frequency signature, experience, understanding, and Awakenings, that makes him or her resonate in tune with a specific type of student. In the theosophical esoterical path, these flavors are also called "Rays" and "Sub-Rays."

All paths, therefore, are necessary. As we evolve, our taste for the type and quality of information changes. We start seeing that our questions evolve, our perceptions become expanded, and because of this, it becomes necessary to have a different experience and oftentimes a different type of teacher.

Our acquired "Tribes," and the individuals who are in the same path as us, change as we grow and evolve. For a while, they become our soul family as we walk a similar path, until we are ready to move even further and adopt another tribe, in alignment with our new and expanded level of understanding and realizations.

When you find people who don't judge you for who you truly are or have become, but welcome you with an open heart; when they not only tolerate your quirks and peculiarities, but also celebrate them with glad cries of "Me too!" and look at you as part of their network, clan, and spiritual family, make sure you cherish them. These individuals that the "programmed" and "conditioned" society call weirdos, outcasts, loners, eccentrics, and broken are truly your soul tribe!

These individuals are Awakening or have Awakened, and that's why they no longer fit into standardized society.

We shouldn't force ourselves to fit into a world where we never truly belonged — a world where elected leaders cherish money, influence, and power over nature, life, and people's rights.

As we grow spiritually, we realize that if we don't fit into this world, it is not that we are bad, wrong, or broken, but rather because we have come into this plane of existence to help create a new world, a new way of doing things and a new way of being.

Don't be afraid to be unique or different; be afraid of being a copy, a replica of everyone else. As you expand, you will naturally let go of the ordinary and embrace the magic and splendor of this path and life. When you do, you will see that the larger part of society is living in a zombie-like reality, where constant gratification makes them spin around a never-ending hamster wheel of conditioning.

The masses are asleep. The media tells them what to believe, and they follow blindly. They are the true walking dead. They are too busy being entertained, seeking pleasures, and/or a false sense of security, while fighting for a few fictional political parties controlled by the same hidden powers.

It has become so obvious. Wherever you look, you can see the dim light in people's eyes, and wish you could somehow shake them, awaken them from this social conditioning slumber. But it's hard, as oftentimes these individuals lost in their own personal dramas are on two completely different paradigms of understanding. You can't have a conversation with someone who is asleep. This is one of the reasons why a lot of individuals suffer mental health issues like depression. Life seems like a trap with no light, justice, or

The Science of Consciousness

hope in sight. The way most people live today does not make sense from a spiritual perspective.

This sense of alienation, isolation, separation, withdrawal, antagonism, exasperation, irritation, resentment, anger, bitterness, and cynicism is what makes people want to end this life journey, and why we need this information like never before.

We wake up, go to work, and make a living, and go back home to rest — just to start all over again the following day. We buy more things that we have been conditioned to believe will make us happier, just to become mired deeper in the debt trap. We start to believe that happiness is only attainable by outside stimulation, or new shiny objects and gadgets. By believing this, we get sucked in into more liabilities, commitments, and responsibilities. Life ends up seeming to be purposeless.

We live to work and barely survive, rather than working to live, grow, love, and thrive. It's time for transformation, to help Awaken those who are ready to transfigure from the caterpillar to the butterfly.

You cannot talk butterfly language with caterpillar people.

The Messenger is Irrelevant

They simply cannot understand, as they have not gone through their own metamorphosis and internal transmutation. How would you explain what it feels to fly? What it is like to see the world from above, instead of having "leaf tunnel vision"? How would you explain what nectar tastes like? Or how to pollinate a flower, and how this act can make a generous contribution to the wheel of life, and help the sustainment and growth of all beings small and large?

A university professor would not be suitable candidate to teach young kindergarten audience, and vice-versa.

The path, the teacher, the master, is irrelevant. I, Paolo F. Tiberi, the author of these works, am irrelevant to your journey. We are all one on a higher-consciousness level; any separation is, after all, an illusion of this three-dimensional reality we live in.

If you picked this book, it means that on a deeper level, YOU needed this information. Not the author, not his personality, just the information. It is the message that matters; the rest is irrelevant.

If I were not around to provide this knowledge to you, the intelligent universe, the source field, made of an infinite ocean of energy, frequencies, and potentialities, would have looked for the closest match to your energy specificity and "vibrational resonance and signature" (more on this later on in this series) and sent you another messenger. This could have taken the form of a manuscript, a video, a person, or a teaching to provide you with the same type of information and potential for Awakening that you are consciously or subconsciously requesting.

Again, the source is inconsequential; it is just another name, face, personality/identity that was sent to you by your desire to learn and to be provided with the relevant information you seek. It's a tool (the book) or/and the actor (the author) in your play of consciousness. All that matters is you and your path to Awakening. If we use the example of the caterpillar and the butterfly, we can learn something else that is very powerful.

All our life lessons, as in the case of the caterpillar, are based on overcoming lessons and boundaries. While we are caught within these boundaries, even if they are limited and of painful nature, we might feel at home with them, and might have a sense of comfort and familiarity. We might even think that it's better "the devil that we know" than the one we don't know, and therefore want to stay in these defined states; yet soul progression always pushes us to learn new lessons, and to break the boundaries of self-imposed limitations.

These lessons — losing money, a destructive and abusive relationship, or others — keep coming back, poking, shaking, and shocking us into a new paradigm of understanding, a more boundless and more advanced state. That's nature; that's the innate and instinctive process of the soul evolution desiring to go back home, to reconnect and unify itself with the source.

Nothing stays frozen in time forever. Everything moves, evolves, breaks through. It just a question of time. At one point or another the caterpillar has to stop and dream the dream of becoming a butterfly. It must liquefy its own body and recreate a completely new being. The old has to go, so a new form and identity can be formed. This is evolution.

EVERYONE AND EVERYTHING IS YOUR TEACHER

As we are going to spend some time together, I think it is necessary to introduce myself a bit further. Not because I matter in the scheme of things, but because I want you to give credibility to the message contained in these book series. I need to befriend your ego, to allow some of the more outrageous information to get through the layers of conditioning and judgment. So here it goes:

My name is Paolo F. Tiberi, and all my life I have searched to become closer to what some call God or the Divine presence. I have visited over 30 countries in this quest, and tried nearly everything to expand my awareness, knowledge, and Awakening. In my quest for a more direct hands-on approach, I also became certified in many alternative medicine practices, learning from some of the best minds and teachers on the planet. A more

The Messenger is Irrelevant

detailed reference of this training can be found at the end of the book.

As my investigations into consciousness and unified states progressed, I broadened my source of information and experience. In this journey I spent seven years in the Egyptian esoteric school in Rome; studied Judaic and Christian gnostic teachings (including the Essene tradition) for five years; practiced Advaita Vedanta and different types of Yogas for over eight years; Shamanism for four years; as well as studying Hermeticism, Kabbalah, Greek Philosophers, Taoism and Buddhism.

Additionally, a lot of my information and education came from live events of different types, and other earthly and disincarnated teachers, (including NDEs, dream states, and channeled sources).

It was hard to find individuals who had embodied their progress and could not only talk the talk, but also walk the walk. Most of what I found was a charade, and a play of mirrors and tricks. This was the reason why my search continued. It was my insatiable thirst for knowledge that knew no boundaries that made me travel so extensively. I looked for any teacher from any cultural, sociological, religious, or spiritual background who could help me Awaken — anyone who seemed to have "cracked the code" that was not just knowledge, but was also a living example of its own truth.

In this journey everything and everyone become my teacher, until I stared at myself in the mirror and realized that I am my biggest and most relevant teacher.

This realization helped me see that, my life is my map to enlightenment, and my initiation. I also understood that I am the biggest asset in this journey, and also the biggest antagonist.

INFORMATION AND KNOWLEDGE IS EVERYWHERE

In a modern society where information is freely available, ignorance is a choice. In our earthly existence, everything and everyone is a messenger for learning and change when you are truly open to grow. In my journey, I kept an open mind and heart, and cherished what resonated with me, while discarding what was not in alignment with my level of understanding and consciousness.

Some of the teaching was kept and integrated, some was left behind. Some of the best knowledge and experiential wisdom I have gained in these 35+ years are parts of what I will share with you, within the body of this book.

It is, in a way, my interpretation of the unified *field of consciousness*. Yet it does not eliminate the need for personal change, and for doing the inner work. Think of this field of consciousness as an ocean or (if you have seen the movie, The Matrix) the matrix of life. It is a consciousness-based program that works behind what you perceive as your reality. This matrix program can't tell you who you truly are; you have to go within and cut out all the white noise and distractions to do that.

In the end, no matter how much philosophy or knowledge you obtain, a direct action must be taken in order to transform ourselves from the student to the initiate, and from the mystic to the master.

"Wisdom is the daughter of experience." ~ Leonardo da Vinci

"Knowledge is of no value unless you put it into practice." ~ Anton Chekhov

The goal for all beings is to raise our consciousnesses to a higher level, and then help those who are struggling or are seeking guidance. This is an ongoing process as we climb "Jacob's Ladder" towards unity and reawaken our Divine essence. Any awakened master would tell you that he or she is still someone else's student, forever learning, growing, and expanding. We are all students; mastery is just a state of ability, comprehension, familiarity, know-how, and expertness that one develops in a particular field. To someone who hasn't yet awakened, the extraordinary may be perceived as a miracle, but to an initiate or a master, it is simply spiritual science that has been applied practically.

The Messenger is Irrelevant

Often, we take life mastery for granted. Perfectionists take years to perfect even a simple task. It takes on average seven years of apprenticeship in top Japanese restaurants to be consider qualified and knowledgeable enough (a master of the craft) to make the right rice consistency for sushi.

Filtering water using straw, charcoal, and sand would be seen as wizardry just few millennia back. If Greeks from 2,000 years ago could see us now speaking on the phone, flying in helicopters or airplanes, or shooting down enemies with a shotgun at a great distance, they would have probably perceived us as gods.

"Man is the most insane species. He worships an invisible God and destroys a visible nature, unaware that the nature he is destroying is the God he is worshiping." ~ Hubert Reeves

"Men create Gods after their own image, not only in regards to their form but with regard to their mode of life." ~ Aristotle

We are the masters and the teachers of the people with less awareness than us, and we are also all students of those who have Awakened and realized more. It is a beautiful cycle that will never end.

CHAPTER 4:
Confirmation Bias

"Don't let the noise of others' opinions drown out your own inner voice." ~ Steve Jobs

THE BUDDHA STATUE WITH THE HIDDEN SECRET

The Thai Golden Buddha statue is believed to date back to the Sukhothai kingdom, more than 700-800 years ago. It was common, in that period, to cover sacred statues in plaster to disguise their true value from invading armies. When it arrived in Bangkok during the reign of Rama III (1824-1851), the statue was still covered with this clay-stucco decoration, and little value was assigned to it except for its antiquity value.

With nobody realizing the true value, it was housed in relative anonymity at the temple of Wat Phrayakrai. When that temple eventually fell into disrepair and was abandoned, the statue was offered to various temples in Bangkok. Due to its plain appearance, no one wanted it as it was too common and unattractive.

With nobody else wanting the statue, the abbot at Wat Traimit decided to construct a building at the temple to house the statue. It wasn't until 1955, when the Buddha statue was ready to be moved, that the forgotten secret was finally revealed. During transport to the new building, the plaster on the statue was damaged. On closer inspection, the abbot could see something shining below the stucco and stripped it away to reveal the full beauty of the Golden Buddha.

The Golden Buddha's value at the time of this writing is roughly USD $300 million for its 5.5 tonnes (194,007 troy ounces) of pure gold.

The Science of Consciousness

We go through life thinking that we are just a physical being made of only flesh, without fully realizing that we are much more than that. We are energy beings, light beings (as we will discover in the *You Are Light* book) in a physical shell living a three-dimensional life. You just have to stop identifying with the clay body-mind shell and start seeing yourself as a shimmering, beautiful being of light.

"Most of the shadows of this life are caused by standing in one's own sunshine." ~ Ralph Waldo Emerson

Confirmation Bias

Most of us live our lives thinking that we are not enough, that we don't belong here, and that no one can truly understand what we are experiencing. This creates a sense of alienation, solitude, emptiness, guilt, shame, and depression. Most of us will never discover our true nature and purpose, and therefore will continue to live in a state of forgetfulness.

Hopefully with these books, all of this is about to change.

> *"If you ever felt that you did not fit in this world, it is because you were sent here to help create a new one!"*

THE BLACK PLAGUE AND LIMITING BELIEFS

"We first make our habits, and then our habits make us." ~ John Dryden

We go through life wearing colored glasses made out of our belief systems, opinions, and understanding. Sometimes these beliefs become laws so ingrained in our society that there is no space for innovative thinking or a different perspective. This destructive "head in the sand," "follow the herd blindly," "don't question" approach is continued until the evidence is so overwhelming that there are no more places to hide.

So, let us start with a simple example of negative and destructive belief systems. This will be used throughout the book series to remind us how damaging limiting beliefs and a closed mind can be.

One of the best examples of how limiting beliefs can have destructive effects in society was the "Black Death," or "Bubonic Plague."

This was a devastating pandemic that first struck Europe in the mid- 14th century (1347-1351). It killed approximately 60 million people, though some say there were as many as 200 million deaths, or as much as 60% of Europe's entire population. A conservative estimate is that one in three Europeans died. Everyone knew someone who directly or indirectly died of the Black Plague.

The leading cause of the Black Plague was *Yersinia pestis*, an enzootic bacterium found in populations of fleas carried by ground rodents, including marmots. Due to climate change in Asia in mid-century, rodents began to flee the dried-out grasslands to more populated areas, spreading the disease.

But was this the main reason why the Bubonic Plague spread through Europe?

Well, the answer is a bit complicated. Some would argue that it was the absence of natural predators that caused it. Let me explain.

It was the belief of the general populace at the time — especially the clergy — that cats in general, and specifically black cats, were connected to the occult and to devil worshiping. So people of all types and backgrounds went on a rampage and killed these beautiful felines in an attempt to eliminate the presence of evil in their villages and cities. It is presumed that hundreds of millions of cats died.

But there is a significant problem with this limiting type of thinking. What species of animal would be most likely to hunt, kill, and eat rats, and keep their populations in check?

Cats.

If you kill the cats, you will have a rodent infestation. If you have a rodent infestation, you produce more carriers for infected fleas. You are involuntary spreading the plague.

Which locations were most affected by the Black Plague?

Convents and monasteries. They lost 80% or more of their occupants. Most of the priests, monks, and nuns died. This was also where this limiting belief of killing cats was most pronounced. A limiting, destructive belief caused the deaths of 60-200 million people.

Confirmation Bias

The fact is, belief systems are the makers of history, and **a closed mind can truly have dire consequences.** Winners re-write history (and hide facts that portray them in a negative light) to match their side of the story, their belief systems, their bias.

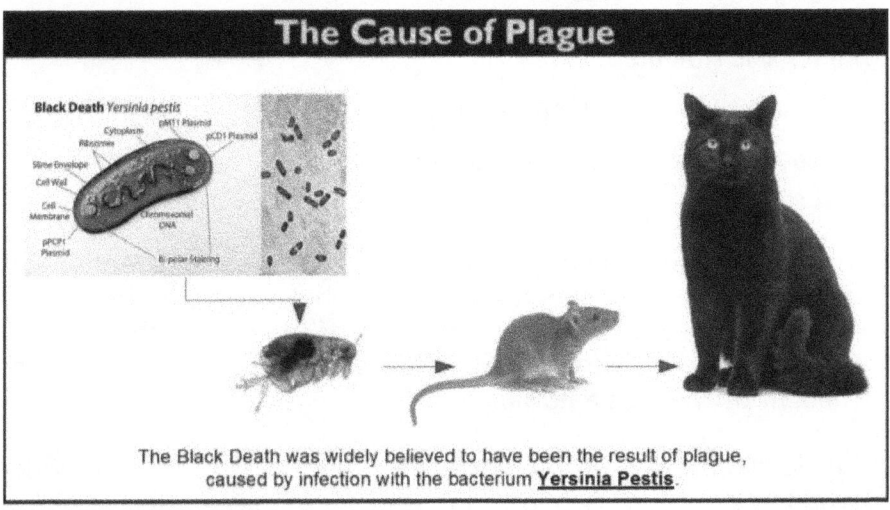

This is a recurrent human behavior. The winner controls the narrative. The winner embellishes, romanticizes, and adds, distorts or deletes parts of the story to make themselves the hero.

Winners control the narrative,
the history we have been fed and
as a result, they have controlled
the beliefs and opinion we have formed.

There are many other great examples of limited thinking, like the invention of the radio. Before radio was invented, people thought the idea of sending voices and music through space was an absurd concept. If they could not touch it with their own hands and see the radio waves with their own eyes, that meant they did not exist; therefore, it was ridiculed. Today no one would question it!

THE THREE STAGES OF TRUTH

According to German philosopher Arthur Schopenhauer, truth goes through 3 major steps:

First, it is ridiculed.

Second, it is violently opposed or ignored.

Third, it is accepted as self-evident.

This was what happened with radio, and more recently with mobile phones. You may not know this, but when the first mobile phones came out, they were the size of bricks and the chargers were the size of a small ice chest. People laughed at them, and thought of them as a nuisance.

Blockbuster Video Rental executives laughed at the idea of video streaming, and missed the opportunity to buy a 100% stake in Netflix for $50 million. Today Netflix is worth billions and Blockbuster is out of business.

YOUR THOUGHTS & BELIEFS CREATE YOUR REALITY

"Whether you think you can, or you can't, you are right." ~ Henry Ford

You are right because whatever you believe to be true will manifest in your reality as self-evident, and everything that does not match your assumptions and belief system will be discarded as false — just like with a computer operating system. That is why *"No problem can be solved from the same level of consciousness and mind that created it,"* as Albert Einstein put it so well.

So, if I am truly serious about helping you change your life, then I need to make you see how your mind has been working and has been misleading you all this time. No change can happen in your life unless you take full ownership of your mind, belief system and happiness.

> *Change your Mind, Change your Life,*
> *Keep Your Mind, Keep your Life!*

"Reality is merely an illusion, albeit a very persistent one," said Albert Einstein.

If you think something is impossible, it will be impossible for you. Only when you break the barriers of what you think you can achieve do you open the doors to possibilities. Your mind and beliefs are the biggest obstacles.

You can either be the victim of your circumstance, or the creator of your own destiny. In both cases, *you* decide. You can give control away to something or someone else, or you can take control.

"Life begins at the end of your comfort zone. You won't find glory at the center of safety, but at its edge. You won't find love at a place where you are safe, but in a space where you are exposed. You gotta take some risks. Life is not long enough to spend it on the sidelines." ~ Neale Donald Walsch

THE WORLD AS A REFLECTION OF WHO YOU ARE

If you don't believe that you will amount to anything, because that is what you have been programmed to believe since a young age, then that is what you will experience. All the great opportunities in your life will pass you by, without even being noticed.

Do you believe that you are unworthy of being loved? Then even if you find your perfect match in front of you, you may think: *"It's too good to be true; he is just faking it to sleep with me,"* or *"It would never last; why would a man or woman like him/her love me?"*

You get the point. You are creating your reality every moment based on what you have accepted as true, as what happens with the placebo and nocebo effect. In the wrong hands, this could create an Orwellian society, as whoever can control perception — how we see reality — can control our behavior, life and destiny.

"As soon as you're born you are given a name, a religion, a nationality and a race. You spend the rest of your life defending a fictional identity" Anonymous

If you do not like yourself, you will not like your life. How you see life is an interpretation of how you perceive yourself. It's a mirror image, in fact.

"All that we are is the result of our thoughts." ~ Gautama Buddha

---
*You don't see the world as it is,
you see the world as you are.*

You see, your contentment (or a state of lasting inner happiness) is a state of mind; it is a choice. Respect for yourself and others is also a choice. Which emotional states you decide to endorse, from anger to forgiveness, is a choice. Whatever choice you make makes you. Therefore, you need to learn how to choose wisely.

"Finding yourself... is not really how it works. You aren't a ten-dollar bill in the last winter's coat pocket. You are also not lost. Your true self is right here, buried under cultural conditioning, other people's opinions, and inaccurate conclusions you drew as a kid that become your belief about who you are. Finding yourself is actually returning to yourself. An unlearning, an excavation, a remembering who you were before the world got its hands on you." ~ Emily McDowell

Confirmation Bias

> *You see... the sky is not the limit,*
> *what you believe to be true, is.*

The problem is that many of us fight vigorously to maintain the mind prison we have created for ourselves. We argue to maintain and protect our limitations.

FIGHTING TO KEEP OUR BELIEFS EVEN WHEN THEY ARE NOT RELEVANT AND TRUE

When these beliefs and dogmas become unquestioned laws, we miss the opportunity to grow and learn. We stay within our one spiritual color, using the prism analogy, and cannot accept that there is anything else except for what we can perceive.

"Sometimes people hold a core belief that is very strong. When they are presented with evidence that works against that belief, the new evidence cannot be accepted. It would create a feeling that is extremely uncomfortable called cognitive dissonance. And because it is so important to protect the core belief, they will rationalize, ignore and even deny anything that doesn't fit in with the core belief." ~ Frantz Fanon

Cognitive dissonance is very powerful. It is how we defend, protect, and fight for our limitations. Unfortunately, it is human nature to fiercely attack anything that goes against what has become part of our accepted belief system. Anything that makes us feel threatened and pushes us towards a new paradigm of understanding is negated as false, even in the face of modern scientific discovery. The shame of having believed something for most of our life that has been proven not only to be limited, but incorrect, is too much for some to face.

So why is this book going to be any different? How is it going to be able to bypass the rigorous barriers imposed by our preconceived ideas and, at times, limited thinking?

The Science of Consciousness

I will endeavor to do this by opening the door of consciousness (through knowledge and scientific research) little by little, so that you will be able to review the concepts with an open mind and a healthy skepticism. In this way, your mind can allow a new wave of light in.

But I am also fully aware that the more I challenge your accepted views, beliefs, and old paradigms, the more chances I create for you to reject this entire book and its message. It is a risk, but I think it is time to shake things up. Otherwise, nothing will ever change for you or this earthly society.

A lot of hidden knowledge, once revealed, will make complete sense; and it will, for many, become so obvious that it will make you question how you could have not have seen or recognized it before. This oftentimes happens as a result of lifting the veil of all the filters that we have put in place to protect our reality.

"We are addicted to our beliefs, and we do act like addicts when someone tries to wrest from us the powerful opium of our dogmas." ~ Yale Surgeon Dr. Bernie S. Siegel.

That is why I have moved slowly through this book. Again, this is all about perception; for some, we have gone at quantum speed down the rabbit hole in the unknown already!

The mind, like a parachute, works better when fully open. So all I ask of you is to keep an open mind, as the most important assumptions that I will offer you in this book will be followed by some kind of research, peer-reviewed case studies, and/or scientific evidence that should clarify any possible objection of a skeptical mind.

Real scientific data teaches to follow the data even if it appears to be strange, bizarre, and at times so far-fetched that it touches the boundaries of the impossible. So we will do exactly that.

CONFIRMATION BIAS

This, of course, does not mean following "confirmation bias," where you find a creative way to interpret the data and come up with evidence to prove your desired outcome.

This is what happened in the tobacco industry after the first World War until the 1970s. There were even doctors promoting smoking during the 1940s, 1950s, and 1960s, or telling the public that asbestos was safe in our homes, or that mercury dental fillings did not pose any health treats, or that mercury in vaccines is safe. The U.S. EPA's safe level for mercury in drinking water is 2 ppb, while some vaccines contain up to 51,000 ppb. Some countries are now banning mercury in vaccines, as well as other toxic compounds present in other prescription medications.

I guess *conspiracy* is often just another word for inconvenient truths.

The same was true for DDT, and many more cases where multinational companies used media propaganda and confirmation bias to manipulate public opinion.

This is still done today to promote toxic pesticides (glyphosate) that in independent research (not sponsored by the company producing that compound) has proven not only to effect bees and bee colonies around the world, but also human health.

Think about it: your gut flora (bacteria) is responsible for your ability to digest and absorb the nutrients in your food and if through antibiotics and pesticides you kill these bacteria in your stomach and intestine, you will end up unable to digest those foods associated with the specific bacteria you have damaged or killed off.

If you destroy lactose bacteria, you will all of the sudden become lactose intolerant. If wheat full of pesticides is ingested regularly, you will soon become gluten, wheat and grain intolerant. This is the main reason food allergies have gone through the roof in the last years.

The use of fracking and many other practices include cases of confirmation bias. The pharmaceutical industry is the most renowned for this form of fabrication, manipulation of data, and suppression of results that could jeopardize their financial bottom lines. Whenever new, independent research disproves their false data, they come up with 10 more fabricated studies to prove the opposite, confusing the public and swaying opinion.

Using sponsored research to prove a false hypothesis is what confirmation bias is all about: Favoring evidence that supports your pre-existing beliefs, while ignoring evidence that doesn't.

Please do not do this with this book. Keep an open mind.

Confirmation Bias

We will review and deconstruct many of the tenets we use in everyday society that have limited our lives, so that we can rebuild from a completely different point of view.

As each chapter opens new realms of understanding, through acceptance, the brain creates new neural pathways that redefine how we see life and what opportunities become visible and accessible to us.

"The lips of wisdom are closed, except to the ears of understanding." ~ The Kybalion

This concludes the introductory aspect of this book. Now we can start truly reveling in the extraordinary.

PART II
THE SCIENCE OF CONSCIOUSNESS

CHAPTER 5:
Everything Is Consciousness

"You are not IN the universe, you ARE the universe, an intrinsic part of it. Ultimately you are not a person, but a focal point where the universe is becoming conscious of itself. What an amazing miracle." ~
Eckhart Tolle

YOUR CONSTRUCT, YOUR CREATION

It is my greatest honor, privilege and blessing to be able to share some of the body of knowledge that helped me awaken to a higher level of awareness. For this I am humbled and forever grateful to you. Let's start!

Everything you consider true e.g. your beliefs and assumptions, creates a blueprint or virtual construct that defines your entire life. Therefore, we could say that your construct is not only your creation, but it also becomes your experiential reality.

You might reject this by saying: *"Hell no! I have not created my abusive childhood, nor my financial struggles, and certainly I have not chosen my parents!"*

Some might also say that their construct was and still is influenced by outside forces. In part, this is correct. In fact, a lot of society's hidden programming is done through "preemptive programming" or "social conditioning" through the use of movies, TV show, news, political agenda and policies, as well as social media.

That's why we call the shows on TV "programs." It's all programming.

The Science of Consciousness

However, if you see these from the perspective of reincarnation, soul contracts, and evolutionary learning (as we will see in Book Four in more details) then it becomes a life designed by you in order to grow and progress.

The First Law of Thermodynamics states: "Energy cannot be created or destroyed, only converted from one form to another." This also applies to consciousness in the form of a higher self and soul moving from one level, state, or density through reincarnation to another.

Your soul has an idea of all the challenges and tribulations and even the characters that will be relevant in your future life, even before birth. Your body, your parents (or lack of), your handicaps, etc. are all chosen to teach you specific lessons. This, and the concept of free will and predetermination, will be covered in detail in later books of this series.

For now, I just want you to keep an open mind to the fact that your reality is not only a field of learning for the soul, but also a construct: A CONSTRUCT OF YOUR OWN MAKING.

If your life is your own construct, then it means that your reality, your life, can be redesigned, and redefined. ALL of it. I know this can be one of the hardest concepts to accept right now. After all, this is the world that has become your routine, draining the life out of you. The dead-end job with the arrogant boss who has no clue how hard and time-consuming your position truly is. The job that requires you to work like a dog for the same measly pay — payday by payday, month after month.

We think that these situations or people in our lives can never change, right? WRONG! All of it can be changed! Past students, even those with incredible life challenges and significant health issues, have proven this over and over again.

So you may be thinking that I'm talking to you about some theory of visualization and mind power, right? Not quite.

EVERYTHING can be redefined. Quantum physics, quantum biology, epigenetics, and extraordinary events like miraculous healing,

The Energy Field & Consciousness

Dissociative Disorder (Multiple Personality Disorder, as it used to be called), remote viewing, inedia (not eating at all), and other supernatural occurrences have proven this statement beyond any reasonable doubt.

The question, however, is, *how is our subjective reality constructed?*

To answer this question, we need to delve into the reality of brain wave states.

CONSCIOUSNESS EXPRESSING THROUGH "MATTER"

Before we move on to how the mind, your thoughts, and emotions create the nature of your reality and destiny, I want to share with you a story that will establish the vibrational setting for all the books in this series.

To provide some context around this, let's just say that *Physics* is the science related to what we can see and perceive with our physical senses, whereas *Quantum Physics* is the science of the very small world of subatomic particles, which are invisible to our physical senses.

Many scientists and philosophers have realized that matter and physicality are not what they seem.

"There is a spirit (consciousness) manifest in the laws of the universe, a spirit vastly superior to that of man" ~ Albert Einstein, genius, theoretical physicist (1879-1955)

"All matter originates and exists only by virtue of a force. We must assume behind this force is the existence of a conscious and intelligent Mind. This Mind is the Matrix of all matter." ~ Max Planck, the father of Quantum Physics (1858-1947)

"What one man calls God, another calls the laws of physics." ~ Nikola Tesla - Genius, Inventor, electrical and mechanical engineer (1856-1943)

The Science of Consciousness

"Physics is the study of the structure of consciousness. The "Stuff" of the world is mind-stuff." ~ Sir Arthur Eddington, English astronomer, physicist, and mathematician (1882-1944)

"The universe begins to look more like a great thought than a great machine" ~ Sir James Jeans, English astronomer, physicist, and mathematician (1877-1946)

"Matter derives from mind, not mind from matter." ~ Tibetan Book of the Great Liberation

"The world you perceive is made of consciousness; what you call matter is consciousness itself." ~ Sri Nisargadatta (1897-1981)

"The laws of physics is the canvas God laid down on which to paint his masterpiece." ~ Dan Brown

"Consciousness sleeps in minerals, dreams in plants, wakes up in animals, and become self-aware in humans." ~ Rumi

Stories, allegories, and parables are one of the best ways to communicate directly to the subconscious mind and bypass most of the analytical, judgmental, capricious, and dualistic mind. It is a direct way to the heart and soul. For this reason, you'll find many stories in this book series.

This specific story will show that what we perceive as life, is just a personalized interpretation, and that matter is not physical at all, but something much more beautiful and inspiring. The first part of the story has been taught in many esoteric schools, while the second part of the story is part of a NDE (Near Death Experience). I have merged the two stories to create a better flow, as the two stories complement each other.

In this story, the word "God" is used. You can interchange this term with "Source Field," "Divine Intelligence," or other terms that you are more comfortable using.

Back to the story:

ICE, WATER, GAS, CONSCIOUSNESS, AND THE NATURE OF REALITY

"A boy brought to his mother a piece of ice and asked: "What is this?"

The mother answered, "It's ice."

Again the boy asked, "What is ice made of?"

The mother thought for a moment and then answered: "It's made of water."

The boy, desiring to find the water in the ice, procured a hammer, pounded the piece of ice into little bits, and exposed it to the sun. The ice soon melted and changed into water.

The boy was grievously disappointed, for the ice that the boy thought contained water had disappeared.

The boy said, looking up at his mother: "Where is the ice that once contained the water?"

So it came to pass that the mother felt compelled by the child's persistent questioning to say: "The ice, in reality, is just water; there is no such thing as ice; Ice is what we have called water when is in a state of solidity. That which we call ice is really only crystallized or frozen water. If you put a glass of water into a freezer, it will turn to ice. Ice," she continued, "is just water in a different (denser) state."

The boy understood.

As he grew up, the child became a young student interested in the nature of things. He approached his biology teacher and asked, "What is water? What does it contain?"

The teacher answered, "Water contains two atoms of hydrogen and one atom of oxygen, H_2O. In their singular state, both are gases. But when bound together, they form what you call water."

The Science of Consciousness

She then explained how the two gases might be separated and set free by using heat and catalysts.

The young student put the water into a pot and heated it up with a steady flame from the biology lab until all the water transformed into vapor and no water was left.

The student asked the teacher, "Where is the water that once held the gases? Where did it escape?"

The teacher was then compelled by the student's persistent questioning to answer, "There is no such thing as water. Water is just gases in a denser state. Water itself is the product of those two individual molecules, the two atoms of hydrogen and the atom of oxygen. Both are gases in their natural state. What you perceive as a liquid, what you call water, is just the union of those two gases."

The student therefore asked the teacher, "Does this mean that water is both ice and vapor?"

"The phenomenon you call water, although real on one level, disappears when the union of these gases is broken by a higher frequency state which we produce by exciting the atoms through the flame's heat, as you have observed — or when you lower the atoms' speed by freezing water. Water is just a state of combined hydrogen and oxygen molecules in interaction."

The student understood.

The student became interested in the nature of things and read all the texts he could on the matter. One night, after a long day at his university, although completely exhausted, the young man decided to ride back home on his motorbike. On a narrow stretch of road, he hit a turning truck that did not put on its indicator. His young body was thrown many meters away on the nature strip by the impact. While his physical body was still unconscious, his soul lifted up above the tree and his wrecked motorcycle. He floated up farther and farther above, and wondered if this was a near-death experience (NDE), or if he had died.

The Energy Field & Consciousness

As he pondered this, he saw a beautiful light being coming towards him. It smiled with unconditional love; and before the young student was able to ask, the entity replied, "This is not your end; you will be back in your body soon." The entity also transmitted telepathically that while he waited, the young man could ask any questions he wanted.

He thought for a moment, and then asked, "Please tell me, what are these atoms behind the gases, we call oxygen and hydrogen, truly made of? I think I have an idea, but I want to know more."

The light being said, "There are no such things as elements like hydrogen or oxygen, just differing numbers of electrons, protons, and neutrons in a geometrical formation. The geometrical shape of these smaller particles creates the illusion of elements. The shape, weight, appearance and description of all matter might change, but at the core of it all, everything is made of the same substance."

"So are atoms and their components the base of all that exist?" asked the young man.

The light being smiled, then continued, "At the core, if we go deeper, there are not only these small particles, but others much, much smaller, the subatomic particles. The more energy you apply, the less dense the subatomic particles are, and the freer they are to become something else."

The young man nodded.

The light being asked: "And if you reduce the amount of energy applied, the more solid the element will become: gas will become water which will become ice. If we go deeper into this higher state, smaller than the subatomic level, then is it possible that at the base of all this is pure energy? A wave of energy or a cloud of potentiality, waiting for an intent to crystallize it into a denser form, like a particle?"

The young man thought for a moment, and then he replied: "Yes, that's the basis of quantum physics, an observer collapsing the *wave function, or manifesting matter out of the sea of potentiality. But then, what is this wave energy made of?"*

"Your scientists have called this string theory, but these are just sections or parts of the wave. Imagine a wave composed of millions of strings. The unexpressed waves, at all levels of frequency and density, or the ocean of energy, which your scientists call the void or empty space, is the body, the substratum, the 'prima materia' of all that exists and what all creation is made of. Both void and matter are, at the core, made of the same substance. The void is not empty, as many of your people think, but is full of creative energy: a sea of pure, virgin potentiality waiting for an intent to respond to. What you call physical matter is this wave or potentiality coagulated in form. What you call dark matter, the void, is the womb of creation," answered the light being.

Then the young man asked, "What then, is this sea of energy, this void, these waves that compose the body of the universe made of?"

The light being replied, "These same waves, gases, atoms, or principles are what compose the body of what you call God or Divine Intelligence; for God and the universe are one and the same. There is nothing that is not God, as all is one."

Confused once again, the young man asked, "Then, please, may I ask, what is spirit and what is matter?"

And thus answered the light being: "As ice and water are one, just at a different stage of density, and as water is one with the two gases, hydrogen and oxygen, just at a different stage of density, so too are spirit and matter one, just in various stages of frequency and density. All there is... is consciousness in different vibrational states. The different phases and manifestations in the molecules of the Divine body, that is, all the levels of density, expression and physical reality, as you call it, are caused by intent — a dream of being. A desire, if you wish, to keep what the Divine Intelligence desires in form. Thus, this form is the Divine Intent expressed through thoughts and emotions clothed with matter. The Divine Source's love is what you call strong atomic force and

The Energy Field & Consciousness

gravity; it is what holds reality together. Without this love and intent, Creation would fall apart. Each creative form, be it a child, a man, a flower, a rock, or an insect has the power of intent. Intent is the creative force moving into motion the Laws of Creation. In a way, it is a seed of a potential outcome we wish to create and experience."

Now the young man felt bold, and asked: "Is my blood, then, identical with thy blood in composition and Divine essence?"

And the light being said, "Yes, thou art one with God. All is one. Any form of duality or separation is an illusion. You are living in a consciousness-based simulation where your thoughts, emotions, and intent create the nature of your reality. What you think and feel, you become. All of that you see before you, and all that you can't see or perceive, has been made for you to learn, experience, grow, and become perfected."

"So is this the purpose of life?" asked the young man.

"It is one of many, as it is through the expansion and expression of God in all its Creation that it can experience itself!"

The young man understood, and said: "Now my eyes are opened, and I perceive that, when I walk, I walk in God; when I eat, I partake in the body of the Divine; when I drink, I drink God's rivers of life; and when I breathe, I breathe God's spirit. As all that exist is within God's being."

To be continued...

The young man's name was Paolo. This was my NDE experience.

This dialogue and NDE experience continues, and will unfold as we progress in our Awakening journey. Through the unfolding of the knowledge contained in this near-death experience as well as the other content in these books, I will help you reconnect to your authentic heritage and unveil the illusions of separation.

You'll soon realize that what you call reality is just a construct based on your belief and understanding. This construction of reality, as quantum physics tells us, (the observer and the collapsing of the wave state) happens on a moment-by-moment basis.

All is one, all is source, all is light, and all is a form of love coagulated through thoughts, emotion, focus, and intent into what we call life and matter.

THE LOVER AND THE BELOVED

The reason for creation is the expression of love. Love is the coagulant of manifestation, the force behind gravity, and light is the substance of which reality is formed. Love and light therefore are conjointly, intrinsically, and inseparably combined.

A beautiful poem by Meher Baba showcases this concept beautifully.

*"God is love.
And love must love.
And to love there must be a Beloved.
But since God is existence, infinite and eternal,
there is no one for Him to love but Himself.
And in order to love Himself,
He must imagine Himself
as the Beloved Whom He as the lover imagines He loves.*

*Beloved and lover implies separation.
And separation creates longing (and duality);
and longing causes search.
And the wider and more intense the search,
the greater the separation
and the more terrible the longing.*

*When longing is at its most intense point,
separation is complete,
and the purpose of separation,
which was that love might experience itself
as lover and Beloved, is fulfilled;
and union follows.*

The Energy Field & Consciousness

*And when union is attained,
the lover knows that he himself was all along the Beloved,
whom he loved
and desired union with;
and that all the impossible situations that he overcame
were obstacles which he himself
had placed in the path to himself.
To attain union is so impossibly difficult,
because it is impossible to become
what you already are!
Union is nothing other than knowledge
of oneself as the Only One."
~ Meher Baba*

CHAPTER 6:
Is Physicality an Illusion?

"Atoms are mainly empty space. Matter is composed chiefly of nothing." ~ Carl Sagan

WHAT YOU PERCEIVE IS A PERSONALIZED CONSTRUCT

Before we start looking at how you have created your reality through the lenses of your belief system, how your emotions work and affect your body, life and destiny, I need to introduce you to what reality truly is, as until now, most of us have believed that what we experience is physical in nature.

> *"...when paradigms change, the world changes with them."* ~ Thomas Kuhn (Physicist, 1922-1996)

By the end of this chapter, my goals are to have shown you that:

1. There is no physical matter.
2. That all that you sense, feel, taste, see, touch, and smell is just your brain interpreting and decoding the sea of frequencies in your experience.
3. Solidity, resistance, mass, and weight are just illusions of your conscious mind.
4. We are all surrounded by a "Force Field" that permeates everything and gives us the sensation and impression of mass and weight in all things. There is no emptiness, but rather a field of raw potential, energy waiting to be utilized and expressed.
5. You are not separated, but one with this field.
6. This life is a CONSCIOUSNESS-BASED LIGHT SIMULATION.

The Science of Consciousness

What you perceived in a sensory way, like smell, touch and vision, is simply not what is "real". It might seem real to you, as all your life your senses have been trained to interface, interact, and identify with this field of energy. But it is only as real as the identification a virtual character would feel in a simulated reality. It feels real while you remain an active participant in the simulation. The feeling of "real" and "physicality" has been programmed into the simulation.

It is only when you remove the 3D goggles you are wearing that you realize you were and still are just a consciousness-based character in a Divine simulation. You are not the goggles, and you are not your virtual character, but something much more beautiful and powerful. We will cover why we feel physicality, density, weight, and mass in this chapter in more detail.

So, how can I say that this is a simulation?

Well, there are many ways to come to this conclusion. For now, let's examine one: Physicality.

This subject will be covered in much more detail in Book Two, where we will immerse ourselves in the realm of energy, vibration, and resonance, and discover many more secrets in regards to the science of manifestation. For now, we need to lift the veil on what you believed until this moment to be true, solid, real, and physical.

So please stay with me, as in this chapter and the next, we are going to have a momentary swim in the ocean of quantum reality. This chapter is one of the most technical chapters in this book, but is necessary to give you some context. So, in an effort to simplify a complex subject, I will add some interesting facts, allegories and stories.

Let's get into it!

MASS, MATTER, AND ENERGY

Albert Einstein proved that matter and energy are equal. This is demonstrated in his world famous equation, $E = MC^2$, where (E) Energy = (M) Mass times (C) the Speed of Light, squared.

In physics, mass-energy equivalence states that anything that has mass has an equivalent amount of energy. Every physical object, all matter, is nothing more than a conglomeration of atoms, particles combined into a geometrical shape; or in a nutshell, all matter is condensed energy.

> *"All matter is energy, in different states of frequency and density."*

This 3D reality we call "life" represents less than 1% of the electromagnetic spectrum, and less than 1% of the acoustic frequency range.

What is "reality"?

"What we have called matter is energy (light), whose vibration has been so lowered as to be perceptible to the senses. There is no matter." - Albert Einstein

Nassim Haramein, a world-renowned physicist and one of the greatest minds of our time, mentioned in one of his lectures that if all the matter in the universe could be condensed in one space, it would fit in a small cube that could easily sit on the palm of your hand!

IF THERE IS NO MATTER, WHY DO WE FEEL PHYSICALITY?

If matter is an illusion, as many spiritual traditions like Hinduism, Buddhism, Jainism, and Sikhism have told us, as well as present scientific evidence, then why do we experience solidity, density, tension, resistance, and physicality?

The Science of Consciousness

If you kick a rock, you will experience the impact, and if your kick was strong enough, you will also feel pain. If you drink a cold glass of water on a hot day, you will feel the cold liquid easing your body heat and discomfort as it goes down your throat. Solidity must be real; otherwise how could I type these paragraphs without having my fingers atomically merging with the keyboard?

This physicality, after all, forms the basis of our sensory experience. So why is it perceived as a very obscure, convoluted, complex illusion or consciousness-based simulation, when we can sense it, feel it, smell it, touch it, taste it, and see it? How do we explain how we can bump into things, touch and lift objects, and feel like a separate entity, when an atom is 99.9999999999999 empty space?

This, of course, is a question that must be answered before we progress!

So let's first examine what an atom and a particle really are. An atom is the smallest constituent unit of ordinary matter, which at the basic level (an atom of hydrogen) contains one proton and one electron. As each atom grows in complexity, it has more protons, neutrons, and electrons.

The main reason why atoms are different from each other, although containing the same type of particles, is related to the number of protons in the nuclei of the atom. This is the main factor that differentiates the elements from each other. For example, a hydrogen has only one proton, while a gold atom has 79 protons, lead has 82 protons, and an atom of iron has 26 protons.

This is why alchemists of old believed that by purifying and transmuting liquid mercury, they could obtain the "Red Lion" or, in modern terms, the Elixir of Eternal Life. One of the reasons is that mercury has only one more proton than gold. Move one proton away from its bond with mercury, and voila, your flask full of mercury would transmute into gold. However, I would not try this, as mercury is a very dangerous poison that can be ingested and absorbed by the skin.

Mercury can damage many parts of your body, including your lungs, kidneys, and nervous system, which includes the brain, spinal cord, and nerves. It can also cause hearing and vision problems. How serious the damage is, depends on how much mercury you're exposed to. It can even cause death.

This is also why Isaac Newton, who was not only a physicist but also an initiate and alchemist, died from mercury poisoning. When his body was moved after burial, it was discovered that Newton had massive amounts of mercury in his body.

Many mercury-related poison deaths have been reported for centuries in Chinese culture. The official "Twenty-Four Histories" records numerous Chinese emperors, nobles, and officials who died from taking mercury-based elixirs in order to prolong their lifespans. The first emperor to die from elixir poisoning was likely Qin Shi Huang (d. 210 BCE) and the last was Yongzheng (d. 1735). Despite common knowledge that immortality potions could be deadly, fangshi and Daoist alchemists continued the elixir-making practice for two millennia.

In the natural, holistic medicine world, mercury is known as the "great mimicker," because it can mimic many different chronic diseases, including Alzheimer's, dementia, nervous system dysfunction, and even cancer. It also worsens the effects of a variety of conditions like ADHD, autoimmune diseases, heart disease, and gut problems.[2] As it can influence many systems, mercury-related diseases are misdiagnosed daily in doctor's offices around the world, as very few doctors investigate the role and presence of mercury while treating people. These patients are treated symptomatically and are given medications for the rest of their lives, without ever knowing that mercury toxicity could be at the root of the problem.

A way to test for heavy metals, like lead, mercury, aluminum etc, as well as fluoride in your system, is to have a test done. I was

---

[2] http://www.sciencedaily.com/releases/2008/04/080424120953.htm

able to find two tests you can do from home for yourself and your loved ones online: https://amzn.to/2RnTZzk or https://amzn.to/2RdcBlP.

If we move up in the periodic table, we find lead with 82 protons and bismuth with 83 protons, three and four protons more than gold. This is one of the main reason why most alchemy focused on transmuting Lead into Gold. So, is this fact or fiction?

Using the LBNL's Bevalac particle accelerator, in 1980 David J. Morrissey was able to transmute bismuth into gold. Glenn Seaborg, who shared the 1951 Nobel Prize in Chemistry for his work with heavy elements, was the senior author on this study and reported that: *"It would cost more than one quadrillion dollars per ounce to produce gold by this experiment."* Although by removing protons, you could potentially transmute one element into another, it is evident that the alchemists of old found a more cost-effective way to perform this transmutation.

At the time of this writing, 118 separate elements have been identified. The entire universe, our earth, and all animate and inanimate things and beings are formed by the arrangement of these 118 elements (and possibly others not found yet) in various combinations.

Between the proton, which forms the nucleus, and the electron, which resides on an outside orbit, is a large amount of empty space. The distance of an electron from the nucleus of a hydrogen atom is about 50,000 times the radius of the nucleus. To visualize this, if you made a proton the size of our sun, then the electron would be only visible if you traveled 21.62 billion miles (34.8 billion kilometers) away. Furthermore, the electron would appear to be only the size of a basketball!

To understand, then, how we can feel physicality and the separation between us and other objects, people, and things, we need to look at the dynamic way an atom behaves. The electrons in an atom travel at around one percent the speed of light, or 1,800 miles (2,896 km) per second. While just reading this entire paragraph, for example, an electron would have traveled around the nucleus of its atom trillions of times.

Traveling that fast creates a cloud of energy called the electron cloud. This cloud creates a nearly impossible-to-break membrane, field of energy, or bubble if this helps you visualize it.

Although electrons can be stripped from an atom, leaving for example a proton of hydrogen alone for a brief time, nearly instantaneously this empty orbit will be filled by another loose electron, therefore re-establishing a form of balance and its original force field.

This electron transfer is a process by which an electron moves from one atom or molecule to another. This is easily observed in chemistry reactions where one reaction partner loses electrons (oxidation) while the other gains electrons (reduction).

Breaking, or smashing, the actual particle is much harder. As... wait for it... drum roll... there is no *real* particle, there never was. What is actually there is a concentration of energy in a field, which we have come to call particles — because the idea of matter as a cloud of energy concentrated in one specific area seems a very hard concept to stomach and accept. Instead, we have continued to use an old paradigm of physicality to explain something that, in reality, has no physicality whatsoever. However, a particle can, at times, *act* like a bullet rather than a wave, as in the famous slit experiment reviewed in Chapter Nine.

IMPORTANT: Therefore, whenever we discuss "particles" in any form, please realize that we're talking about a concentration of energy, and not an actual physical particle.

When we breakdown the atom further, we find that a proton is an energy concentration in the positive spectrum, while the electron is an energy concentration in the negative spectrum. A neutron is a neutral energy concentration.

Billions of dollars have been spent to create the Large Hadron Collider (LHC) at CERN in Switzerland, which is huge in comparison to the original one developed in 1929 by Ernest O. Lawrence of the University of California, Berkeley. The CERN particle physics laboratory is an international research center located on the

Swiss-French border, formed by a coalition of 19 European nations. The Large Hadron Collider has helped us in studying and investigating the building blocks of matter, including particles that are millions of times smaller than the atom.

What these particle accelerator/collider experiments have proved is that all atoms are a dynamic vibration of force fields that seek to keep their balance. In the LHC, you are not colliding particles, but force fields. When the force field (particle) equilibrium is disturbed or lost, a new balance is sought. This concept of a particle as an excited, vibrating field of energy is known as Quantum Field Theory, or QFT.

Through experimentation, physicists have been able to build a "Standard Model" of particle physics consisting of sixteen different forms of matter and energy. Twelve of these sixteen represent what we perceive as matter, and four represent force carriers. If we take a closer look, we can see that, out of these sixteen, six are quarks (which make up protons and neutrons), six are leptons (which includes the electron) and the last four are force carriers that communicate forces though space, like a photon (a particle of light) does.

Okay, back to why we feel solidity, density, tension, resistance, and physicality.

Everything in life, from a flower, to a drop of water, to our skin and any other physical object, has the same configuration of atoms (force fields), each with their impenetrable shield of electron clouds. If you push one surface with another (for example, one hand touching a table or the surface of water), the electron cloud shields will oppose each other, forming resistance.

This resistance is what allows you to feel the separation between you and your seat, or to stand on your feet, or feel the bed supporting your body while you lie down. Although matter is pretty much all empty space, the resistance you feel is what has been translated by your mind as solidity, matter, and physicality, when in reality there is none. All there is, are clouds of energy in each atom creating resistance against other atoms.

The Energy Field & Consciousness

The difference in tactile sensation between, for example, a silk garment, sandpaper, and pizza dough is just the configuration of this resistance, and the mental and emotional associations we have given it. All of the sensations of physicality we experience are nothing more than the electromagnetic forces of the electron clouds opposing each other and keeping objects restrained in a specific position, separated from other objects.

SENSORY EXPERIENCE AND FREQUENCY

The perceptions of colors, and the feeling or the sense of matter and physicality, are merely the brain's three-dimensional interpretations of light frequencies. Sound is a light frequency and smell is a light frequency, as is everything else. Not to mention, at least 95% of the matter and energy in the universe is unmeasurable and unseen, what scientists call "dark energy and dark matter" or the void.

Our ears detect sounds that vibrate between 20 and 20,000 Hz. Bats and other animals can perceive much bigger ranges, topping over 200,000 Hz. The reason why you can't see atoms (apart from the extremely small size!) is because they vibrate as high as 10,000,000,000,000 Hz, well beyond our human capabilities. Once something vibrates fast enough to pass our range of visual capabilities, it disappears from our sense of sight. It is still there, but it becomes invisible to us.

You might have observed that cats, dogs and even infants sometimes seem to see and follow things that are not visible to us; that is because they can see what we cannot. Spirits, as we will see in one of the book in this series, vibrate at a different frequency than visible light, and therefore are invisible to us.

> *"Our separation from each other is an optical illusion of consciousness." ~ Albert Einstein*

The Science of Consciousness

So scientifically speaking, all perceptions of matter are a mental construct (like in the Matrix movies).

"With the advent of quantum theory, it was found that even these minute subatomic particles were themselves far from solid. In fact, they are not much like matter at all—at least nothing like matter as we know it. They can't be pinned down and measured precisely. They are more like fuzzy clouds of potential existence, with no definite location. Much of the time they seem more like waves than particles. Whatever matter is, it has little, if any, substance to it." ~ Peter Russell (M.A., D.C.S., F.S.P.)

"Remember how electrical currents and 'unseen waves' were laughed at? The knowledge about man is still in its infancy."
~ Albert Einstein.

"The day science begins to study the non-physical phenomena, it will make more progress in one decade than in all the previous centuries of its existence." ~ Nikola Tesla

Before you discard these above concepts (of matter being space or a cloud of potential) as total nonsense, you need to understand that many technologies we use every day are the result of these exact same findings, e.g.:

- Transistors
- Semiconductors
- Computers
- Smartphones
- Lasers
- Telecommunications
- Atomic clocks
- Global Positioning Systems (GPS)
- Magnetic Resonance Imaging (MRI)
- Wi-Fi
- Other frequency based technologies

Just type into any search engine: "Technologies that use quantum mechanics" to delve deeper in this subject.

WHY DO WE PERCEIVE GRAVITY, WEIGHT, AND MASS?

Earlier on, we broke down the atom into smaller subatomic particles. The standard model of how subatomic particles interact can be applied to many things, including electricity, magnetism, and radioactivity.

But there was a problem, as there was no way to understand why these subatomic particles, and particles in general as clouds of energy concentration, could have different masses, or no mass at all! For example, photons, neutrinos, and gluons have no mass whatsoever (as they are force carriers), while quarks and leptons do. The mass is quantified as the electron-volts of energy they contain.

To overcome this issue regarding mass, in 1964 a physicist by the name of Peter Higgs and his team of colleagues proposed that an energy field existed that permeated and surrounded the entire universe. This energy field came to be called the "Higgs Field." This could be also called the Source Field, the Sea of Energy, the Field of Consciousness, etc.

Some of us who are geeks at heart might also be familiar with the Jedi Master Yoda's interpretation of the Higgs Field as "The Force" in Star Wars (Episode V, *The Empire Strikes Back*). There, we get a description of what this force field is. While Luke Skywalker tries to lift his spaceship from the water...

Luke Skywalker: *"I can't. It's too big."*

Yoda: *"Size matters not. Look at me... Judge me by my size, do you? Hmm. Hmm. And well you should not, for my ally is the Force. And a powerful ally it is. Life creates it, makes it grow. Its energy surrounds us, and binds us. Luminous beings are we... (Yoda pinches Luke's shoulder) ...not this crude matter. You must feel the Force around you. (gesturing) Here, between you... me... the tree... the rock... everywhere! Yes, even between this land and that ship!"*

The Science of Consciousness

To see a video clip of this movie, visit the member's area or YouTube.

Like The Force in Star Wars, the Higgs Field permeates all things and all space, and is believed to be what imparts mass to all particles.

Painting and Copyright by unknown artist

So how does this Higgs Field explain mass? In his theory, Peter Higgs postulated that bigger subatomic particles (or bigger concentrations of energy) would have more mass then smaller ones. When a particle passes through the Higgs field, it interacts with it.

The displacement of the energy in this field by particles passing through it excites the field, and is what he used to then calculate the mass of a specific particle. The more it interacts with the field, the more mass it has.

To better understand the idea, we can use the analogy of seawater, dolphins and whales. In our analogy, the water will serve the role of the Higgs Field.

A dolphin, similar to a low-mass particle, being supremely streamlined and light, will interact only slightly with the water tension and field, and can swim through it very easily at high speeds.

The Energy Field & Consciousness

A whale, on the other hand, having a larger size and a bulkier body (a high-mass particle) would have more difficulty swimming through the water, as its mass would displace more water.

The swales (sunken areas in the field) and indentations in the Higgs Field are caused by this displacement of mass.

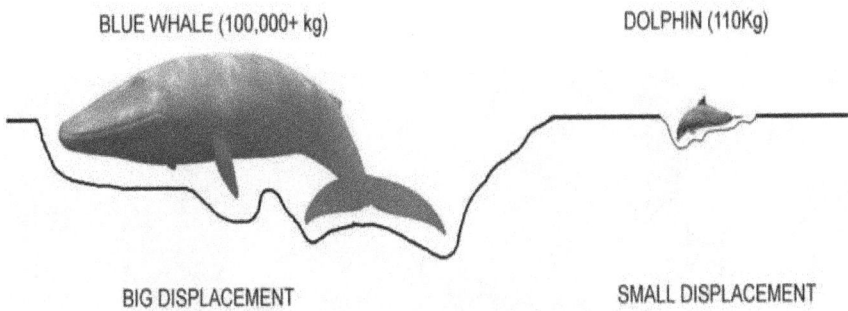

Using the particle accelerator collider, scientists have found that this excitement in the field can be measured, because the Higgs Field forms a three-dimensional grid. The intersection in this energetic force field grid is made by the Higgs Boson particle. Stay with me, as we're close to the conclusion.

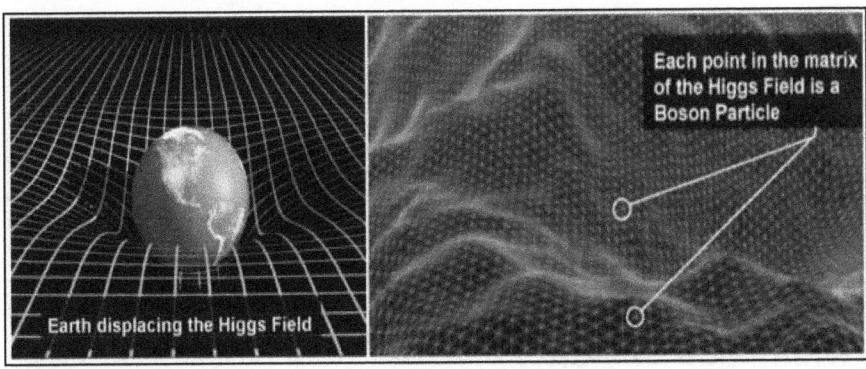

All particles are in fact excitations of fields.

Before the recent confirmation of the Higgs Boson (which some physicist call the God Particle), physicists had no proven way to

The Science of Consciousness

explain why one field of energy (subatomic particle) would have more "mass" than another.

In nature this excitation can be seen in the phenomenon of bio-luminescence visible in oceans around the world, where light is emitted by a living organism. It is a form of chemiluminescence. When an object or surfaces touches the living organism, in this case plankton, it excites it and it emits light.

In Image 1 above, the plankton gets excited by the interaction with the gravel and sand on the seafloor, making the breaking wave glow. In Image 2 the interaction is with the pillars of the jetty, and in the third image, the excitation was made by throwing a rock in the water.

This is not dissimilar from the excitement of the Higgs field, which instead of creating bio-luminescence, creates valleys (when not excited) and swales when activated by the mass of a particle.

Now that we have a visual, let's go back to the Higgs Boson, which is an excitation of the Higgs Field. By finding the Higgs Boson, quantum physicists have been able to prove the existence of this theoretical force field.

WHAT ABOUT WEIGHT?

If you are confused about mass and weight, a simple explanation is this: Mass is the measurement of the amount of matter in an object or container (e.g. volume of water or air in a container), while weight is the measurement of the pull of gravity on an object (e.g., how much that same container weighs in respect to the gravity present). In this view, then, weight becomes relative to gravity.

An empty glass full of air has the same mass of a glass full of water; however, the weight will be different, as water weighs more than air.

To visualize this, think about how much you weigh right now; walk and feel the pressure of your weight on the floor. Now, if all of a sudden you went to Virgin Galactic or NASA in one of their Zero-Gravity Environments and training rooms, you would not weigh anything; you would start to float in midair, because in those special rooms, gravity has been eliminated. Because the moon's gravity is one-sixth of the Earth's, if you weighed 200 pounds (90 kg) on Earth, you would only weigh 33 pounds (15 kg) on the moon. That is why astronauts can jump instead of walking on the moon's surface; they are much lighter.

CONCLUSIONS

So how does all this talk about quantum physics and subatomic particles and Higgs Fields and bosons relate to consciousness?

As long as you think that what you are experiencing is physical in nature and that solidity is an actual thing, you will have difficulty grasping and accepting the reality that THERE IS NO MATTER — that all you sense, feel, taste, see, touch, and smell is just your brain interpreting and decoding the sea of frequencies in your experience.

What you call the experience of the physical senses is just your consciousness decoding frequencies.

Solidity, resistance, mass, and weight are just illusions of your conscious mind. **What you call physicality is just an interpretation of your experience of the force field.**

We are all surrounded by a force field that permeates everything and gives the sensation and impression of mass and weight to all things.

We are all connected. This life is a consciousness-based light simulation.

THIS WAS WELL-KNOWN BEFORE

That is why many spiritual traditions (e.g., Hinduism, Buddhism, Jainism, and Sikhism) have called this reality an illusion (Maya). It is not that the world is not real, it's just that its reality is based on consciousness rather than the sense of physicality and matter.

Matter is not what it seems.

"That which makes the unreal appear as real, and the real appear as unreal is Maya." ~Sri Vishwanath

"If you believe illusions to be real, and reality to be an illusion, you will never achieve inner peace." ~ Anonymous

"Reality is merely an illusion, albeit a very persistent one." ~ Albert Einstein

"The visible world is the invisible organization of energy." ~ Heinz Pagels, Former Executive Director of the NY Academy of Sciences (*Cosmic Code*)

"Matter is a light-show illusion made of vibrating energy." ~Joseph Selbie

Soon we will review scientific case studies of people who have "unplugged from the matrix" and are able to play with what we call reality and change their physical bodies at will. This includes making scars, moles, allergies, and diseases appear and/or disappear, and eye color to change in matter of seconds. This is well-known and proven in medicine. You just have to look at Multiple Personality Disorder (what is now known as Dissociative Disorder) to see how this is possible, or how people have miraculous remission through belief in placebos or by believing in higher powers, and in the process making cancers and tumors disappear in days. We will see how blind people with no physical eyes have been able to see using echolocation (like bats and dolphins) to perceive frequencies, and much more in the next book.

All of this is possible when you stop identifying with your body and cease seeing it as a solid, unchangeable bag of flesh and matter.

Moving from MATTER to WAVE perception will be the topic of the next chapter. For now, you just need to realize that any "physical changes" are only possible if you fully realize that everything around you, including yourself, is made of energy, vibration, and light. At its core, everything in life is different aspects of consciousness.

Consciousness, then, is the causation of what we perceive as matter. Change your mind, change your life and body. Your perception becomes your biography and biology, as we will see in this book in the Awakening series.

Consciousness is not based in the brain. The body is just a marionette that we use to live this physical existence.

It is the mind that changes the energetic field that we have called, until today, the physical body.

> *"Looking for consciousness in the brain is like looking inside a radio for the broadcasting station announcer."* ~ Nassim Haramein

This has been proven scientifically all around the world, and will become more self-evident in the next chapter. For now, let's reinforce what we have learned though a familiar dialogue in the movie *The Matrix*.

The Science of Consciousness

BLUE PILL OR RED PILL?

The world I am going to show you later on in these manuscripts is a world where rules of physical reality, the Newtonian physics that you knew so far, means very little — if anything at all. Energy, light, vibrational resonance, and coherence are not only fundamental key concepts, but a scientific reality.

In Newtonian physics, life happens to you; you are a victim of your circumstances. In quantum physics, you, the observer, are the creator of your own reality. That's a shift each of us can make.

That's also the difference and allegory in *The Matrix* movie between the blue pill, continuing living in a simulation based on Newtonian physics, and the red pill, waking up as a creative force in the realm of quantum potentiality, and unplugging from the matrix.

Below are some of the dialogues between Morpheus and Neo in the movie.

Morpheus: I imagine that right now you're feeling a bit like Alice, tumbling down the rabbit hole? Hmm?

Neo: You could say that.

Morpheus: Let me tell you why you're here. You're here because you know something. What you know you can't explain. But you feel it. You've felt it your entire life, that there's something wrong with the world. You don't know what it is but it's there, like a splinter in your mind driving you mad. It is this feeling that has brought you to me. Do you know what I'm talking about?

Neo: The Matrix?

Morpheus: Do you want to know what it is? The Matrix is everywhere. It is all around us, even now in this very room. You can see it when you look out your window or when you turn on your television. You can feel it when you go to work, when you go to church, when you pay your taxes. It is the world that has been pulled over your eyes to blind you from the truth.

The Energy Field & Consciousness

Neo: What truth?

Morpheus: That you are a slave, Neo. Like everyone else, you were born into bondage, born into a prison that you cannot smell, taste or touch. A prison for your mind.... Unfortunately, no one can be told what the Matrix is. You have to see it for yourself. This is your last chance. After this there is no turning back. You take the blue pill, the story ends, you wake up in your bed and believe whatever you want to believe. You take the red pill, you stay in Wonderland, and I show you how deep the rabbit hole goes... Remember, all I'm offering is the truth, nothing else.

The Matrix – Red or Blue Pill Scene.
Image courtesy of Warner Bros & Village Roadshow Pictures - ©

VIDEO RESOURCE:

To view this powerful lesson, a video clip can be found on PaoloTiberi.com. Go to "Resources", then "Science of Consciousness Membership" to log in. Look for Chapter 6 and the video titled: "The Matrix - The Pill scene."

The Science of Consciousness

So let's unplug ourselves from the matrix. Let's raise our consciousness above the play of consciousness and duality. When we do this, we will be able to access a new world of quantum potentiality, where miracles will start to be known as advanced science. There, anything and everything is possible and happening!

This may sound a little like New Age hocus-pocus, but believe me when I say this: it is as true as the sun rising every morning.

"If you wish to understand the Universe, think of energy, frequency, and vibration." ~ Nikola Tesla

This knowledge is yours for the taking.

So the question is: do you want to continue with the illusion of separation, or are you ready for a new paradigm shift? This translates in visual terms in *The Matrix*. "Do you want the red pill or the blue pill?" You can see the video clip by following the link below, or you can skip it.

If you have not seen the first Matrix movie in its entirety, I would recommend doing so. If you *have* seen it, you might want to watch again after reading these books, as it will put this movie into a different prospective for you.

CHAPTER 7:
The Energy Field & Consciousness

"Every feeling is a field of energy. A pleasant feeling is an energy which can nourish. Irritation is a feeling which can destroy. Under the light of awareness, the energy of irritation can be transformed into an energy which nourishes." ~ Thich Nhat Hanh

Before we further review how this mental construct is experienced, how consciousness started as an experiencer, how you as a creative force can affect reality, and how the science of consciousness and its functioning can manifest things at will, I must introduce the concept of energy fields.

This is how you experience the **perceptions** created by your senses of smell, touch, sight, and taste, as well as things like weight, gravity, and mass. To clarify this, I will start first with the Chinese discovery of magnetic fields and the compass.

If we go further back in time, based on Veda texts and the Greek Platonists, Thoth Trismegistus' description of Atlantis, and archaeological findings, we can see that technology and civilizations have risen and fallen for at least 30,000 years. Each time a great technologically advanced society has fallen because of misuses of technology or destructive decisions made by egos desiring absolute power and control, humanity has returned to a primitive way of life. The world is, after all, a soul school; if you remove the basic Divine gift and covenant of creative free will by reducing human rights and freedom, nature resets the scales. This has happened over and over again. Most of these lost societies, along with their technological prowess, culture, greatness, and dismay, have gone missing in the vastness of time and the memory of our species.

The Science of Consciousness

Just one example: the ancient Egyptians were able to move objects that we, today, cannot move with the largest cranes. They were able to cut through solid granite with a precision possible only using current laser technology. They had sophisticated engineering skills, allowing them to place pyramid blocks so close to each other that not even a human hair could pass in between them.

When we travel back in time, we can only refer to the last 5,000 years or so. For this specific story, we will start by traveling to China. A keen individual in China during the Qin dynasty (around 200 BC) discovered that a magnetized object would always align itself with the Earth's magnetic north and south poles. The first object used for this alignment was a magnetized spoon. This instrument became known as the compass.

In the same way that everything is consciousness, and consciousness is energy and frequency, everything also has an energy field, with a negative and positive charge. In particle physics, a magnetic monopole is a hypothetical elementary particle that is an isolated magnet with only one magnetic pole, but this still remains unproven. So far, we know that in life, you can't have energy without positive and negative poles. This dichotomy is present in all aspects of life: Right/Left, Light/Darkness, Female/Male, Good/Bad, as we will see from a Gnostic prospective (the Seven Hermetic Keys) later on.

The Energy Field & Consciousness

Everything from our planet (with its south and north poles), to our physical bodies, individual cells, atoms, and even photons display this polarity. Each thought and emotion we experience also creates an energy field. Our thoughts create an electrical charge, and our emotions a magnetic charge, producing an electromagnetic field of resonance and influence around us. Positive and negative thoughts and emotions create charges related to their polarization, as their names (positive/negative) suggests.

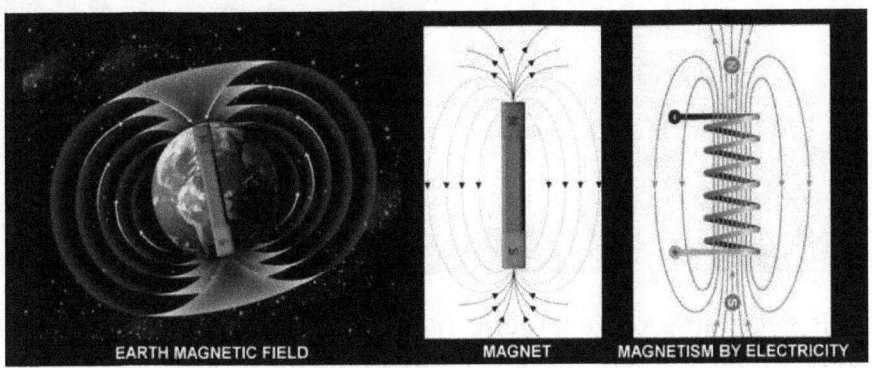

EARTH MAGNETIC FIELD   MAGNET   MAGNETISM BY ELECTRICITY

When someone is in a heightened emotional state, like depression or love, they emanate a strong field of resonance and influence that most people can intuitively feel. In fact, when human electromagnetic fields come in close proximity with each other, they start to interact. For most people, this field extends to about five meters (16 feet) from their body. It has been said that it takes less than a second to form an opinion about someone. Maybe this is the time it takes for the subconscious mind to decode the energy field of another person.

"A series of experiments by Princeton psychologists Janine Willis and Alexander Todorov reveal that all it takes is a tenth of a second to form an impression of a stranger from their face (and energetic fields), *and that longer exposures don't significantly alter those impressions (although they might boost your confidence in your judgments). Their research is presented in*

their article "First Impressions," in the July issue of Psychological Science." ~ Eric Wargo.[3]

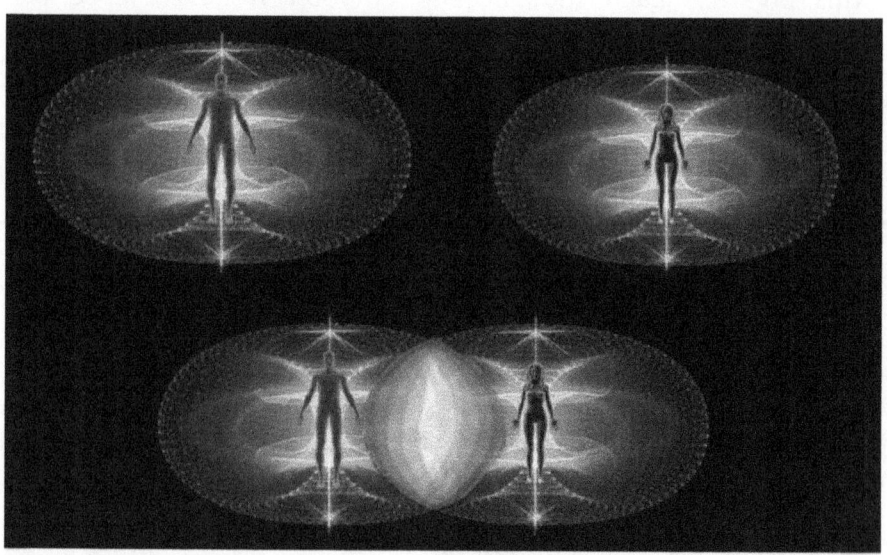

This is because our energetic fields interact before we even lay eyes on each other. There is a large amount of interaction going on that most people are unaware of.

CHANGING THE FIELD FREQUENCY IN AN ENVIRONMENT: A PERSONAL STORY

To paraphrase Buckaroo Banzai, *"No matter where you go, there you are"*. Therefore, wherever I am, becomes my training ground. For over 15 years, I worked as cabin crew for two major Australian airlines. For me, working there was like going to Jedi training. I would do counseling, healings, and readings for other crew, and affect the energy fields of individuals and larger groups.

---

[3] https://www.psychologicalscience.org/observer/how-many-seconds-to-a-first-impression

The Energy Field & Consciousness

Knowing the power of free will, at the start of each day I would say: *"Let this day be full of life, light, love, joy, learning, wisdom, and abundance. I set my intent today to inspire and transmute those energies and people that I have been sent to help, and shield the others that need their darker state of being to move them to a higher level of frequency and understanding. May I today breathe, think, talk, and act in resonance and within Divine light, wisdom, and grace."*

Duality is present in all aspects of life. Love can sometimes be destructive, possessive, and suffocating, while anger can sometimes be the freeing emotion that breaks the shackles of limitation and moves the person towards a positive change. Like knives, emotions have two edges. They can be used for good (as a surgeon wields a scalpel to save lives) or for evil purposes (as a tool to kill someone).

As limited individuals, separated from the Divine source, we cannot know the extent of a person's life design (reincarnation, soul contracts, planned learning, challenges scheduled, etc.) and why they have attracted pain and suffering in their lives. Therefore, we have to trust, and help the other person as much as we can within the boundaries of their free will. This is why I start my day with the above statement of intention. This is also the reason many Biblical prayers finish with: *"Not my will but yours be done"* (Mark 14:36 and Luke 22:42)

Going back to working as a flight attendant:

During times of delays or disruptions, when life got in the way, and passengers would enter the aircraft with a dark cloud over their heads and bodies, I would initiate a transmutation process. Let me explain.

I could see and feel their darkness, their anger, frustration, sadness, and sense of powerlessness. Most of the other crew looking at the situation anticipated a very tiring and confronting day. I would try to change their energy by telling the cabin supervisor and the crew that we are all "alchemists," healers of the sky. We are there mainly for the safety of our passengers, of course, but also to help people transform their attitude and energy, transmuting darkness into light.

I would challenge myself to change the frequency of an entire passenger plane (175 to 275 people) full of overworked, tired, depressed, angry, anxious passengers by pulsating light, love, compassion, and kindness, and expanding my field to include the entire aircraft and all the people present.

On some unpleasant days, full of disruptions and delays, passengers would come in with an angry, negative attitude. Because they felt we were part of the problem, causing their stress, they wouldn't even acknowledge the cabin crew's presence or our greetings, and at times, even gave us angry stares.

People are usually stuck in their own bubbles. They don't realize that some of the cabin crew are experiencing their own dramas, have had to reorganize their lives, opted to work overtime, and leave their families behind, to help them get to their destinations.

The darker the atmosphere, the more my desire to transmute it. As my level of light and unity increased, I was able to help more and more people. After entering as a resentful, spiteful, anxious, stressed, angry mob, the passengers would end up leaving with a different energy and state of mind. They become chatty, joyful, with genuine smiles across their faces, even commenting on how great the flight was and how relaxed they felt.

I can see it in their expression: *"What just happened?"*

We need to realize (as we will see in this chapter and the ones after), that every thought and emotion we have, when paired with intent, can have a powerful effect not only on us, but on the entire universe. All is consciousness, all is energy; all thoughts and emotions create ripple effects.

We are not bodies moving through space and time; we are energy fields interacting with an ocean of different energy, interfacing, integrating, and exchanging information at all times. We are all one at a certain level.

It does not matter where you are, or what job you are doing; every thought, word, or action can become an act of light, love, gratitude, and compassion. This is true even if you work with garbage or clean toilets for a living.

Everything can become a Divine meditation.

Gnostic teachings would tell you that positive emotions, thoughts, and intent are "white magic," as all are for the betterment of the other person; and that any negative emotions, thoughts, and intent are "black magic." In this context, we are all white and black magicians, with great responsibility for how we use our free will and creative powers.

If you think about it, when one creates light, it is of service to others; darkness is performed in service to the self. So in a way, magic is a form of energy and frequency, when you understand the science behind it.

THE CORONA COVID-19 PANDEMIC

We can find light and opportunity even in the darkest moments. As I was finalizing this book around the end of February 2020, the COVID-19 pandemic erupted around the world.

Virgin Australia went into voluntary administration and 10,000 workers, including myself, were stood down. I pondered deeply on what this life event meant for me. What was it that I could learn from it? How I could re-invent myself? How I could make a living and continue to make a contribution towards our household expenditures and commitments?

The books I am writing now, as you know, are free of charge in PDF format. Making a profit on these books was never on the radar. So I had to look elsewhere to not only survive, but also thrive.

How could I manifest wealth and abundance in this black hole of global despair? Then it occurred to me that this was perhaps the best opportunity to put back into practice the science of consciousness and the laws of manifestation I was previously using on a smaller scale to reinvent myself and turn my life round.

Like everyone else, I had a choice to make. I had the option to either find new streams of income, take a break, or succumb to fear, anxiety and frustration. After having had my security blanket (12 years with Virgin) pulled away from me, I knew that this was a time for change and a time to reinvent myself. I had to set aside the feelings of anxiety, the fear of the unknown, and instead began focusing on the life that I desired through active manifestation.

So I intently visualized the outcome I wanted, as well as the range of emotions that I would experience once I have achieved it. I knew that the details on how to set the wheels in motion were not as important as the end outcome, so I did not worry about the 'how'. Instead, I attentively focused on the mental imageries and emotions of people telling me how much they appreciated my help and knowledge, that I have exceeded their expectations and that the money they have spent was the best investment they have ever made. I did this for a few days.

Then lo and behold, a business owner that I previously created a website for in 2015 called me out of the blue and asked, *"Are you still doing branding, websites and self-publishing for people? As you know, there is a transition happening from direct dealings with clients to online services."*

"Yes, I am", I said, a little surprised by the call as I had put all my energy towards book writing for the last few years.

"Your phone must be ringing hot! If you have time, I have a client that would love to use your service! I told him what a great job you did for me, and he wants to have a chat with you! Do you still offer your no obligation, no pressure strategy calls?"

"Yes of course! I can organize a free session for him." I replied with excitement.

The Energy Field & Consciousness

I was delighted. I did not know how the income and opportunity would come. All I knew was that the universe, this field of potentiality, would know how to get the ball rolling for me.

To those who are interested in this process, I have a more detailed guide in the member's area called: *"The Manifestation Blueprint"*.

Everyone has something worth sharing, everyone has a voice, a message and a legacy that could help others. The source field tuned into my desires, tapped into the skillsets I already had, found what I could offer and how I could be of service to others, and it unfolded an opportunity that was in direct alignment with my mind's creation.

I began offering complimentary sessions with individuals that wanted to make an impact in this world, who had a message that truly needed to be heard. So I suppose this is still a form of spiritual work, except it has taken on a different flavor.

I sensed that majority of the clients that have approached me felt voiceless and overwhelmed. Some have spent sleepless nights wondering how they could cast their name, brand and unique legacy out to the world. Though some of them were new entrepreneurs, struggling business owners and aspiring book authors, they all wanted the same thing......to have a voice, to have their message heard, and to make a living out of their knowledge, experience and skillsets.

So I redesigned a side business that laid dormant for a few years and created a turnkey system to remove the pain, stress, and frustration out of digital branding, market presence, website creation and self-publishing. This business, I called Summit Business IQ.

Every person's journey, whether they be striving for financial success, spiritual awakening, emotional and physical well-being, is a path to the peak of a mountain, the Summit.

INSECTS SEE THROUGH FREQUENCES AND ELECTOMAGNETIC FIELDS

On a smaller scale, flowers have electromagnetic fields that display their energy and frequency signatures, which are often dependent on the insect they are trying to attract. For example, the flowers can spread their pollen, and the bee and its colony get to eat. This type of arrangement is called "mutualism," and is a win-win scenario.

When a bee looks at a flower, it does not see what we see. It sees it in a completely different light. Literally. It sees the flower in ultraviolet light, as shown on the next page. Scientists from the University of Bristol have recently discovered that bees can also sense a flower's electromagnetic field.

Observation suggests that bees can tell how much energetic charge is left on the flower by simply observing the pollens' energy field, and will avoid a flower that has already been used and depleted by other bees.

"Bumblebees, Bombus terrestris *(Clarke et al. 2013) and honey bees,* Apis mellifera *(Greggers et al. 2013), have been shown capable of detecting weak electric fields, each in different behavioural contexts, using different sensory mechanisms."*

"The sensory basis for e-field detection in bumblebees appears to rely on mechanosensory hairs, which are mechanically deflected by an applied electric stimulus (Sutton et al. 2016). The mechanical deflection of these hairs in turn elicits neural responses, conveying information to the bee's central nervous system. Using laser Doppler vibrometry (a technique that measures nano-scale vibrations), the deflection of a series of dorsal hairs in response to applied electric fields reveals a collective sensitivity covering a range of stimulus frequencies."

"Bumblebees can use electric information to discriminate between rewarding and unrewarding flowers (Clarke et al. 2013). They can also learn colour discrimination tasks faster when colour

cues are paired with electric field cues similar in magnitude to those surrounding natural flowers."[4]

Flower images courtesy of Dr. Klaus Schmitt, Weinheim, Germany

Since the bee experiment, this capability to see electromagnetic fields or life-force has also been observed in hummingbirds, worms, ants, other insects of different kinds, and even algae.

MRI & EEG: MONITORING ELECTRICAL AND MAGNETIC IMPULSES AND FIELDS IN THE BRAIN

Humans might not be able to perceive ultraviolet light or electromagnetic fields, but our brains have been built to feel them. Even on a smaller scale, like our neurons, the brain's

---

[4]"The bee, the flower, and the electric field: electric ecology and aerial electroreception," by Dominic Clarke, Erica Morley, Daniel Robert. *Journal of Comparative Physiology* September 2017, Volume 203, Issue 9, pp 737-748. https://link.springer.com/article/10.1007/s00359-017-1176-6

storage rooms of information and memories have tiny electrical currents, just like a magnet.

In fact, these energy fields and electromagnetic currents inside the brain are what current medicine use to observe the brain energetically.

An electroencephalogram (EEG) is used to analyze electrical currents, which produces a graph of the different brain frequencies and a Magnetic Resonance Imaging (MRI) is used to monitor and observe magnetic fields in the brain – see the comparisons on the next page.

THE ENERGY FIELDS IN THE BODY

At the beginning of the 1900s, there was a great deal of medical interest in the body's energetic fields. One of the pioneers in the field was Harold Saxton Burr, a professor at Yale School of Medicine. He searched for the energetic fields emitted by plants, animals, and humans. It seemed to him that all living cells and molecules changed, adapted, and grew based on the instructions and specifications of the field in which they were positioned.

After years of research, Burr came to the conclusion that a biological organism is not the *cause* of an energetic field, but rather it is the energetic field that reassembles and organizes the cells, molecules, and atoms of a body into a coherent orderly fashion. This is why stem cells or T-cells, which are undifferentiated cells, can adapt and change their functions specific to the field they are been placed in.

Burr wrote: *"Something like this... happens in the human body. Its molecules and cells are constantly being torn apart and rebuilt with fresh material from the food we eat. But, thanks to the controlling field, the new molecules and cells are rebuilt as before, and arrange themselves in the same pattern as the old ones."* ~ Burr, *The Fields of Life*, 1943, pp. 12-13.

The Energy Field & Consciousness

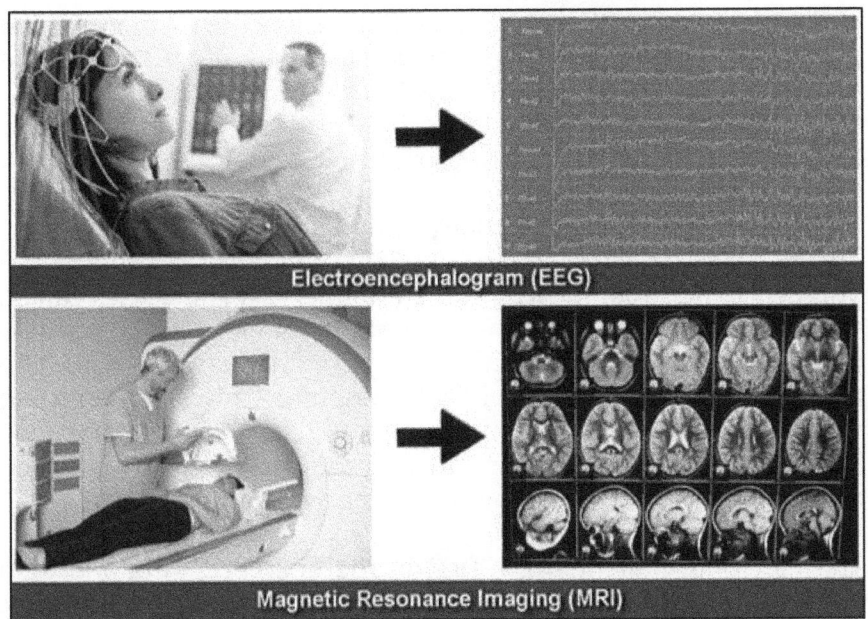

Burr went on to experiment with salamanders, and found the egg had two different voltages, one the strongest at one point and the other 180 degrees opposite to the first reading the weakest. When the egg developed and hatched, the part that had the greatest amount of energy developed into the head, and the one with the lower voltage developed as the tail. This differential frequency and voltage made him suspect that each part of an organism's body has a different frequency signature.

In a study published in 1947, Burr moved on to observe human frequency resonance and fields. He realized that diseases and sickness also have frequency specificities, and that women with uterine cancer have a different energy signature than healthy women.[5] He then tested a random group of women that did not have any signs of uterine cancer, and found that some had the

---

[5] Langman, L., & Burr, H.S. (1947). Electromagnetic studies in women with malignancy of cervix uteri. *Obstetrical and Gynecological Survey* 2(5), 714.

energetic frequency signature of the cancer, even if none was present yet. The women who had the signature of the uterine cancer developed the cancer at a later date, proving that before a physical ailment is coagulated into physicality and matter, it appears in the energetic, vibrational field first.

"Change the field and you change the matter." ~ Dawson Church

This also means that most, if not all, ailments and diseases can be cured with frequency and vibration alone, making nasty prescription medicines with tons of side effects and the pharmaceutical companies of today obsolete. This is probably one reason why some of the information in this book are not well known to the public, and why there has been a war on consciousness and energy-based alternative medicine.

The fact that ailments form first in the energetic field and then in the physical body is another confirmation that we are light frequency-based individuals living a physical experience.

AILMENTS, FREQUENCIES, SOUNDS, AND GEOMETRY

Each ailment produces a frequency signature, which produces a geometry and sound that can help us visualize and understand the difference between a healthy cell and an unhealthy one.

There are some great videos produced by CymaScope and Dr. James Gimzewski showcasing, for example, how a healthy cell (FIG 1, left) has a nice thunder-like sound with a geometrical pattern, while the frequency signature of a sick cell (FIG 2, right) is scratchy and incoherent.

> ### *VIDEO RESOURCE:*
> Two videos showing this effect, as well as, the sound and geometry of a beating heart, and a Tibetan bowl, can be found in the Member's Area.

The frequency nature of the human body has been well-known for centuries by Chinese acupuncturists as meridians and energy channels, and in India through the knowledge of chakras and auras. In fact, an ancient saying in Chinese medicine states: *"The mind controls the Qi (life force/energy), and the blood follows the Qi."*

ANCIENT ACUPUNTURE

In total, there are over 400 jingmai (points of energy), the majority of which run along the Twelve Primary Meridians. These are the primary meridians through which qi flows. It is believed that the Chinese discovered acupuncture 2,200 years ago, yet one archaeological find related to the Otzi Iceman suggests that this knowledge of plants and acupuncture points is much more ancient.

As the ice melted in the Ötztal Alps near Hauslabjoch on the border between Austria and Italy in 1991, an incredibly well preserved mummy of a man in his forties was discovered by two German tourists, at an elevation of 3,210 meters (10,530 ft). Ötzi the Iceman, as he was named, is believed to have been murdered about 5,300 years ago. He may have consumed medicinal herbs and had a treatment similar to acupuncture prior to his death.

Albert Zink, head of the Eurac Research Institute for Mummy Studies in Bolzano, Italy, shared these findings with *Live Science*: *"The ancient society of the iceman most likely already had a considerable knowledge about medical treatment. It seems that they used different forms of therapy, including physical treatment and using medical plants. This definitely requires a certain knowledge of the human anatomy as well as how diseases arise and develop."* ~ Albert Zink.

The Science of Consciousness

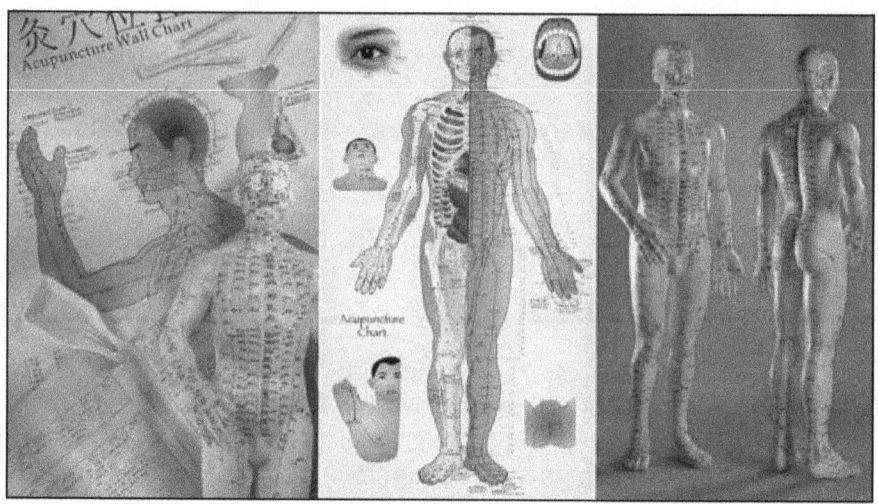

Since the discovery, scientists have scrutinized almost every aspect of the man's life. Physical analysis had revealed that Ötzi had a host of ailments at the time of his murder (by a blow to the head), including arthritic knees and rotten teeth, a likely case of Lyme disease, and signs of stomach ulcers, as reported by *Live Science* [Mummy Melodrama: Top 9 Facts About Ötzi the Iceman].

"What is most incredible is that the iceman was inked; Ötzi was covered in 61 tattoos. The tattoos were all simple stripes with two crosses, so they didn't seem to be decorative, but rather seem to suggest a more practical purpose, like showing areas of pain and location of energy centers.

"The tattoos are all located at body regions where the iceman had some health issues and probably experienced periods of pain. For example, he had degenerative diseases of his hip, knee, ankle joints and lower back. Most of the tattoos are located [on] the legs and the lower back; some of the inked spots corresponded to traditional acupuncture "pressure points," suggesting to some researchers that the iceman underwent a form of acupuncture. Also at the time of his death, the iceman had a "medicinal mushroom" known as birch polypore in his digestive system. Birch polypore is thought to have anti-inflammatory and fever-reducing properties.

The Energy Field & Consciousness

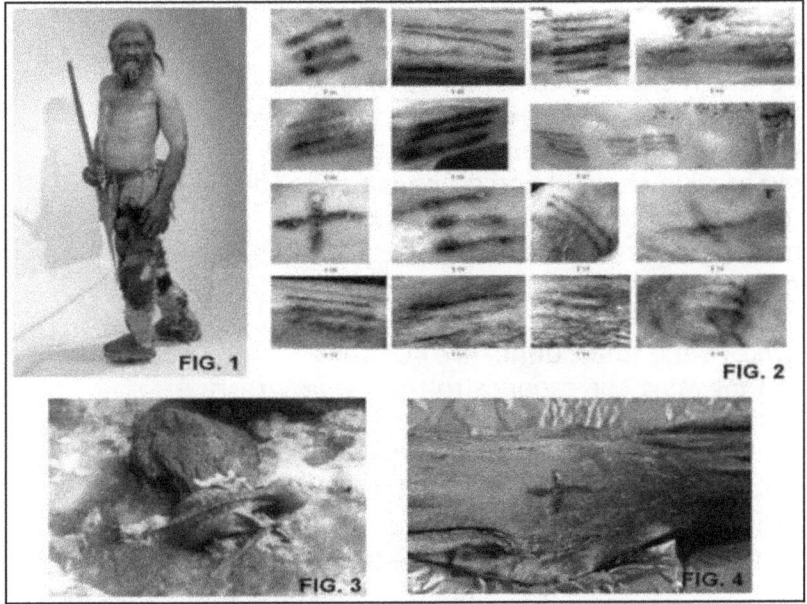

FIG 1 credit: By Thilo Parg - Own work, CC BY-SA 3.0, https://commons.wikimedia.org/w/index.php?curid=35621968; FIG 2 Credit: EURAC/M. Samadelli/M. Melis; FIG 3 and 4 Credit: South Tyrol Museum of Archaeology.

"Ötzi had also consumed ferns, which could have been either a primitive food wrapper that Ötzi mistakenly ate or a treatment to kill off the parasitic worms that plagued the iceman," Zink said.

MERIDIANS, AURAS AND CHAKRAS

As mentioned in one of the first chapters of this book, all truth is the same, just decoded and translated through the language, ideology, traditions, beliefs, and filters of each culture. Both Chinese and Indian culture have observed the flow of energy/life-force in the human body. In the same way as Chinese have the Qi as the circulating life force (moving through the meridians), the Indians have the Prana, which is seen as a universal energy which flows in currents in and around the body. Because breath is considered a form of life-force, the Indian culture consider the oxygen Meridians related more to the energy centers of 12 organs in the body, including:

Primary Yin (feminine-water) Channels:
Arm Tai Yin channel corresponds to the Lung
Leg Tai Yin channel corresponds to the Spleen
that we breathe as Prana as well.
Arm Shao Yin channel corresponds to the Heart
Leg Shao Yin corresponds to the Kidney
Arm Jue Yin corresponds to the Pericardium
Leg Jue Yin corresponds to the Liver

Primary Yang (masculine-fire) Channels:
Arm Yang Ming corresponds to the Large Intestine
Leg Yang Ming corresponds to the Stomach
Arm Tai Yang corresponds to the Small Intestine
Leg Tai Yang corresponds to the Bladder
Arm Shao Yang corresponds to the San Jiao
Leg Shao Yang Channel corresponds to the Gall Bladder

While the Chinese focus on the correlation between the organs and the life force (Qi), expressing itself as a cold, wet feminine energy called YIN, and a hot, dry masculine energy called YANG, the Indians focused on the energy emanated by the channels related to the human endocrine glands.

The endocrine glands are the ductless glands of the endocrine system that secrete hormones (e.g., adrenalin as a hormone for fear) directly into the blood. The major glands of the endocrine system include the pineal gland, pituitary gland, pancreas, ovaries, testes, thyroid gland, parathyroid gland, hypothalamus, and adrenal glands.

The first energy center or chakra, Muladhara, is connected with Sexuality and relates to the gonads, like the ovaries and testis.

The second, Svadhishthana, is connected with Survival, associated with the adrenal glands and the sacrum.

The third, Manipura, is connected with power, which associated to the pancreas and solar plexus.

The Energy Field & Consciousness

The fourth, Anahata, is connected with Love and Relationships through the thymus gland and the heart.

The 12 Meridians
- Lung
- Large Intestine
- Stomach
- Spleen (Pancreas)
- Heart
- Small Intestine
- Bladder
- Kidney
- Heart Governor
- Triple Heater
- Gall Bladder
- Liver

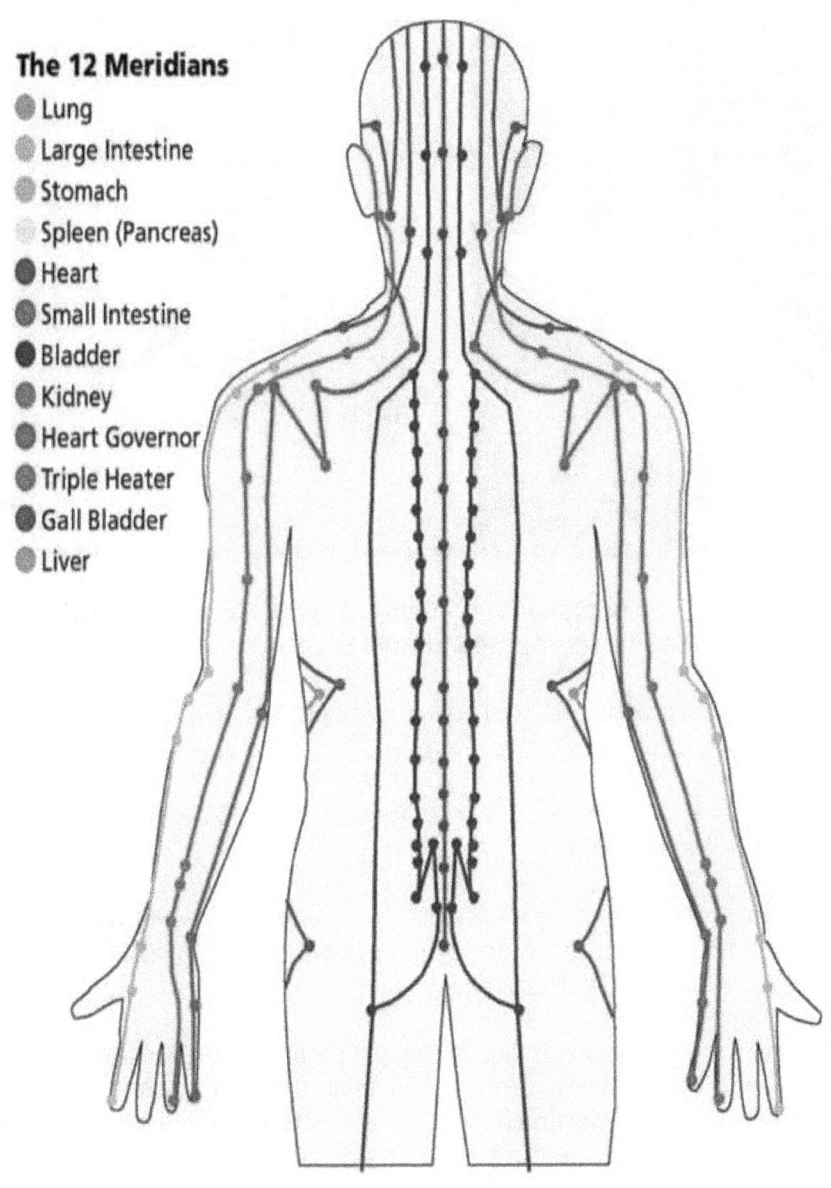

The Science of Consciousness

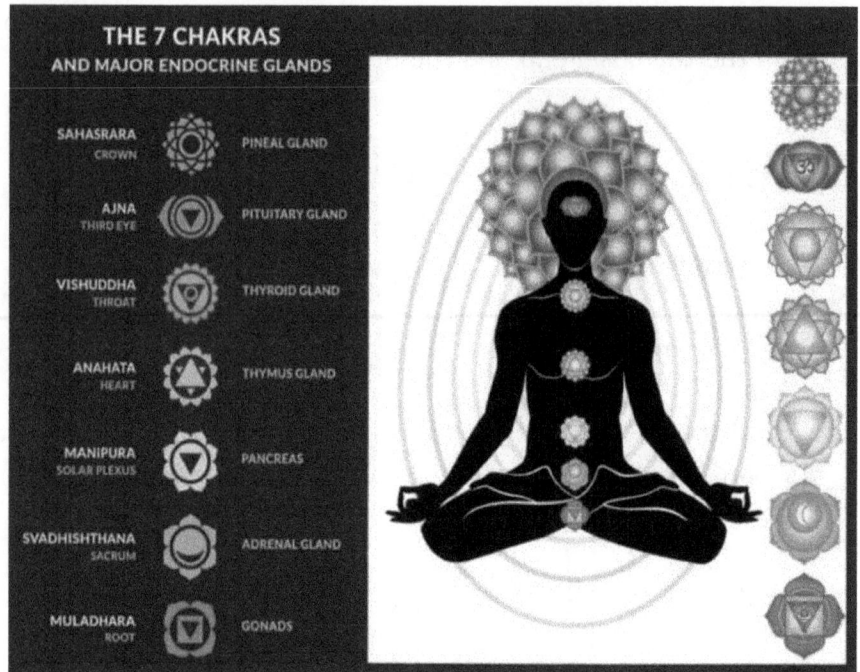

The fifth, Vishuddha, is connected with Communication and Creativity via the thyroid gland and the throat.

The sixth, Ajna, is connected with Intuition, Perception, and the pituitary gland.

The seventh, Sahasrara, is connected with Unity Consciousness and the pineal gland.

We will see how these chakras and glands are related to our process of soul evolution and reincarnation progression in the book *Many Lives, One Destination*.

Chinese medicine and Ayurveda, as well as many other nature-wise traditions, have long known that different plants resonate and reinforce or diminish certain aspects of the energetic body system, and prescribe Ying and Yang plants as tonics and relaxants, laxatives, diuretics, detoxification agents, for healing and well-being.

CHAPTER 8:
Consciousness and the Physical Body

"A human being is part of the whole, called by us 'Universe,' a part limited in time and space. He experiences himself, his thoughts and feeling, as something separated from the rest — a kind of optical delusion of his consciousness."
~ Albert Einstein

HOW THE BRAIN DECODES INFORMATION

If everything written here is correct so far, this means that consciousness is not limited to human beings. As discussed in previous chapters, everything contains consciousness, including our cells. But how can we prove this? How can we prove that consciousness is an energetic field of coherence that can hold memories and information? This is what we will try to achieve in this chapter.

Consciousness is not located in the brain, as proven by many Near Death Experiences (NDE) and studies in the field of neurology. The brain is important, but only as a decoder of information not dissimilar to a radio, computer or a mobile phone. It receives information, which is translated into something you can see, touch, smell and taste.

"Looking for consciousness in the brain is like looking inside a radio for the announcer." ~ Nassim Haramein, physicist

This is what we call a *transponder* in telecommunications. A transponder is a device that, upon receiving a signal, emits a different signal in response. Your mobile, radio, and television are all transponders; they receive electromagnetic waves and decode them into sounds and visual images. Every one of your senses is also a transponder, visually translating light into color and images through your eyes, chemical signals of different foods into taste through your tongue, and sound waves into decoded words, music, or noise through your ears.

Everything is aware at some level, even a rock; and there is nothing that is not part of consciousness.

"The stones are alive. It has not been so understood by the [people] of your culture." ~ Elkins, Ruechert, and McCarty, *The Law of One*, Session 2, question 4.

We think of ourselves as individuals, because our perception of identity is that we are the body. Our coherence and influence is the strongest "Voice" in our physical body, and therefore we perceive it as our identity. In truth, it is the leader of a trillion cells, each able to communicate and interact with other cells. Just because we do not hear the inner conversations of these cells does not mean such communication is not occurring.

The body's function, after all, is always to respond to the commands, impulses, caprice, and whims of the greater voice — the fearless, and at times, incompetent leader. Every now and then, however, we put the body in such a crisis that it needs to communicate with us.

"You are overworking; this is lowering the immune system, putting you at risk of potential viruses and diseases. You are over-stressing your neurons, damaging the brain circuit, which is causing headaches and disrupting sleep. Go and rest", says the body.

"You need to drink and eat; you have not done that for over eight hours. We will send you some cravings to remind you!" demands the body.

"You have been toxic, angry, resentful of everything. You think everyone is an idiot and is a waste of your time! You feel you don't deserve to be happy. Very well, we will show you how your thoughts create your reality. Don't be surprised if you start having digestive intestinal problems and you become full of... shit!

Consciousness and the Physical Body

Maybe then you will take action!" reacts the body, tired of being in a toxic environment.

This mind-body interaction will be covered in greater detail in the *Biology of Self* in the Life Map series. For now, you need to understand that although your consciousness is being hosted by your physical body, this is like a radio announcer broadcasting through the radio. The announcer is not the radio. This communication happens on all levels of the body – physical, emotional, mental and spiritual. For instance, a heart organ has a field of coherence made up of a specialized group of cells that have a mind of its own.

How do we prove this? This has been demonstrated thousands of times though organ transplants.

CASE STUDIES: ORGAN TRANSFERS

"Your mind is in every cell of your body. The way our brain is wired, we only see what we believe is possible. We match patterns that already exist within ourselves through conditioning. The chemicals that are running our body and our brain are the same chemicals that are involved in emotion. And that says to me that... we'd better pay more attention to emotions with respect to health." ~ Dr. Candace B. Pert, neuroscientist, pharmacologist, and author of *Molecules of Emotion*

If this is so, then if we were to transfer a body organ, let's say a heart, from one donor to a recipient, then we are not only transferring the actual organ, but also some aspects of that person too. Correct?

Dr. Paul Pearsall collected accounts of seventy-three heart transplant patients, and sixty-seven other organ transplant recipients, and published them in his book *The Heart's Code: Tapping the Wisdom and Power of Our Heart Energy*.

I will discuss two of these case studies here.

The Science of Consciousness

Case 1: Murder mystery involving a donor is solved by an organ recipient

An eight-year-old girl who received the heart of a murdered ten-year-old girl began having recurring vivid nightmares about the murder. Her mother arranged a consultation with a psychiatrist, who after several sessions concluded that she was recalling actual physical incidents. They decided to call the police, who used the detailed descriptions of the murder (the time, the weapon, the place, the clothes he wore, and more) provided by the little girl to find and convict the man in question.

The perpetrator was apprehended, and because of the overwhelming evidence and the police having found the murder weapon, the murderer confessed to the crime and was convicted.

Case 2: The gender transplant

After receiving a heart transplant, the patient exhibited very strange changes in her usual eating habits and personality behaviors. The heart donor's mother reported:

"My Sara was the most loving girl. She owned and operated her own health food restaurant and scolded me constantly about not being a vegetarian. She was a great kid — wild, but great. She was into the free-love thing and had a different man in her life every few months."

The recipient reported: *"You can tell people about this if you want to, but it will make you sound crazy. When I got my new heart, two things happened to me. First, I hate meat now. I can't stand it. I was McDonald's biggest money-maker, and now meat makes me throw up. Actually, whenever I smell it, my heart starts to race. But that's not a big deal. My doctor said that's just due to my medicines.*

I couldn't tell him, but what really bothers me is that I'm engaged to be married now. He's a great guy, and we love each other. The sex is terrific. The problem is, well... I'm gay. At least, I thought I was. After my transplant, I'm not... I don't think, anyway... I'm sort of semi or confused gay. Women still seem attractive to me,

Consciousness and the Physical Body

but my boyfriend turns me on; women don't. I have absolutely no desire to be with a woman. I think I got a gender transplant."

Each cell includes a blueprint of the entire body. A cluster of cells like the one within an organ (e.g., a heart), has the power to change the whole subconscious programming of a person, including their likes and dislikes.

BOOKS LINK RESOURCE

Molecules of Emotion by Dr. Candace B. Pert

AMAZON: https://amzn.to/37uLqbp

BOOK DEPOSITORY: https://tinyurl.com/u3t4plu

The Heart's Code: Tapping the wisdom and power of our heart energy. By Dr. Paul Pearsall

AMAZON: https://amzn.to/2uELV3V

BOOK DEPOSITORY: https://tinyurl.com/r4krdpq

Each cell is, in a way, a holographic representation of the whole system. This is why you can diagnose illnesses by looking at the eye, for example, by using Iridology or Reflexology, or by examining your blood, just to name a few options.

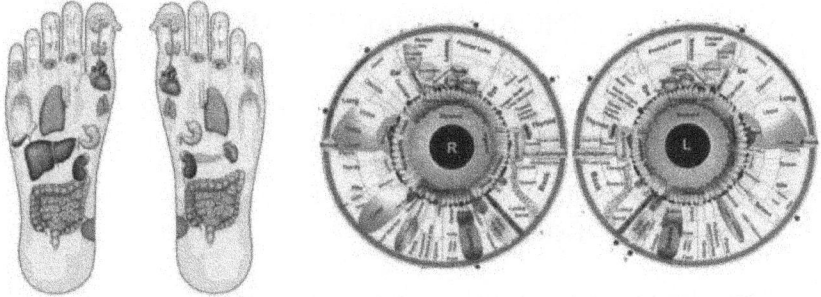

Image of the eyes (iridology map) on the right courtesy of Phil Harris

The Science of Consciousness

Each organ has a different electromagnetic field (the heart has a field 5,000 times stronger than the brain), a different frequency signature, but still the same blueprint on a cellular level. If the field and the blueprint is strong enough, it will be able to affect the donor and influence his/her behavior, thoughts, and emotions.

Coherence fields are what allow stem cells and T-cells, which are "blank", unsullied cells, to take the identity, form, characteristics, and attributes of a specialized cell the one in your liver or heart. This consciousness-based field of energy in our cellular makeups should prompt us to take a closer look at our thoughts, intent, beliefs, and emotions.

There is another beautiful video showing the power of frequency. A crying infant who has lost his mother. Many strangers tried to console the baby without avail. It was only when the man, the recipient of the mother's donated heart, held the baby that the baby stopped crying. The baby recognized the frequency, energy and beat of his mother's heart.

VIDEO RESOURCE

To view this video, simply login to PaoloTiberi.com. Under Resource Area, Chapter 8 you will find "HEART COHERENCE: Infant crying until Heart Transfer recipient holds the baby".

MICROTUBULES: THE ANTENNAE OF OUR CELL TRANSPONDERS

Found at the base of your cellular structure, microtubules are like optical fibers that conduct information and frequencies around the body. Microtubules are hollow, allowing them to resonate and vibrate like a percussion instrument.

In their book *Mathematics and Computers in Simulation*, Hameroff & Penrose describes how microtubules can quantum superimpose and perform computation tasks. A copy called: "1998

Consciousness and the Physical Body

Hameroff Quantum Computation in Brain Microtubules: The Penrose Hameroff Orch OR Model of Consciousness" can be downloaded in the member's area.

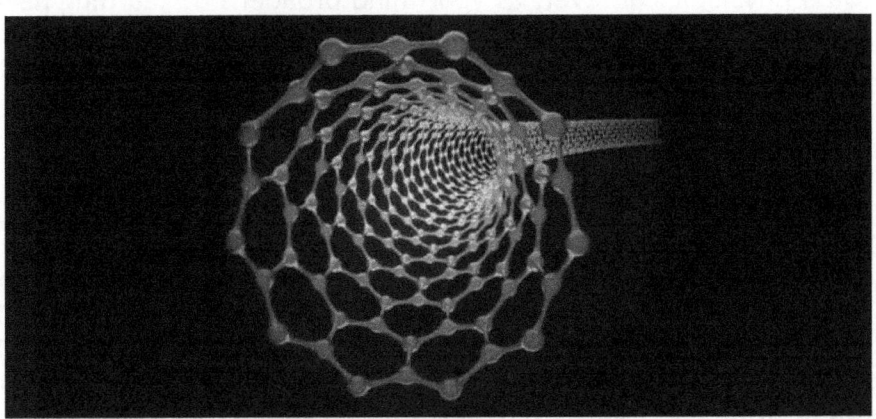

The microtubule is the smallest transponder in the body that we know of, always ready to receive information and take action based on the command received. Frequency, resonance, light, and electromagnetic forces seem to be the way microtubules communicate with each other.

Let's use an analogy. If you go to the gym and do some weight training, the muscles you engage will become bigger as more blood and oxygen are pumped through them. As damage in the muscular tissue is created and more energy is put into a specific muscle, it grows, specifically to deal with the extra workload and stress.

The same happens with your brain. As you focus more on one aspect of life, your neurons (the memory and information centers of the brain), become bigger and more capable of interacting with other neurons that are in resonance and related to them. The more you spend time practicing a skill, or learning a subject, the more you become it.

Going back to the microtubules, the more they play a certain vibration or tune, the more they are going to become resonant to that state. This enables neurons to communicate with each other based on resonance fields, like a symphony of instruments (cells) communicating in unison through harmonic fields of resonance.

On a physiological level, as your mind broadens by learning new knowledge and expanding your beliefs and world views, your brain changes. As you do, you create a different music, a different harmonic coherence.

USE IT OR LOSE IT

On November 5, 1998, *Science,* one of the world's most prestigious research journals, published an article titled: "New Leads to Brain Neuron Regeneration" (M. Barinaga, 1998; *Science* Vol. 282 Issue 5391, page 1018). In this article, the two teams that had originally discovered stem cells, led by Evan Snyder at Harvard Medical School and Ronald McKay of the NINDs, share their discovery on the adaptability of the brain — which, according to their research, can add new neurons even late in life. This means, contrary to previous belief, that your brain never stops growing while you are learning and being stimulated.

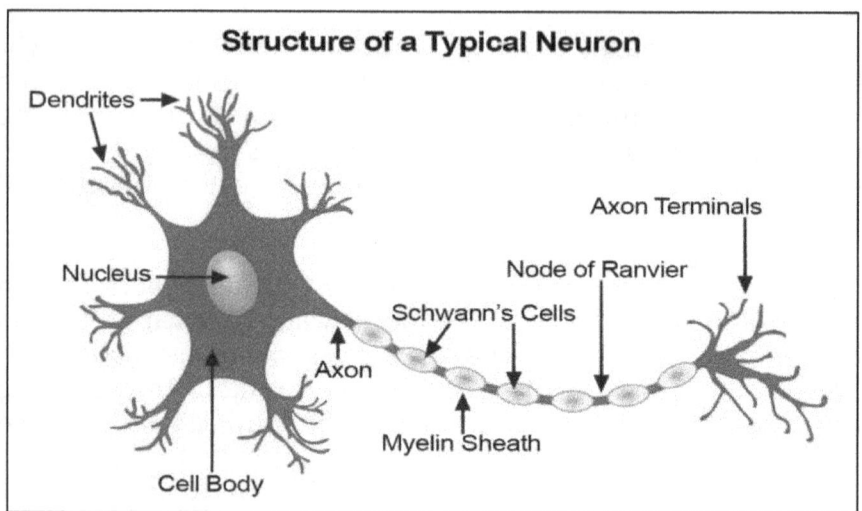

Without even knowing it, you are directing your brain to create new neural connections, new centers of memory, knowledge, and information, and new frequency freeways (axons in the neurons)

Consciousness and the Physical Body

for this data to travel through. As you do so, your brain adapts and starts more and more to match your overall state of being, not just physiologically, but also on a frequency and resonance level. As you learn, new knowledge enters into your mind, creating new pockets of understanding, possibility, and light.

Your transponder/radio/mind is then upgraded to the new perception, thoughts, emotions, intention
and beliefs, and without even realizing it, your life is altered and your destiny transformed. You no longer see things the way they were, but the way you have become.

Each time you learn, your brain creates new circuits and data/memory sensors in the form of neurons to encapsulate what you have learned. As nothing goes to waste in the brain, if these new realizations, knowledge and beliefs are not exercised, within a few hours and days, they will lose strength and little by little fade away (the circuits disconnect). In neuroscience, this is called pruning. In other words, if you don't use it, you lose it.

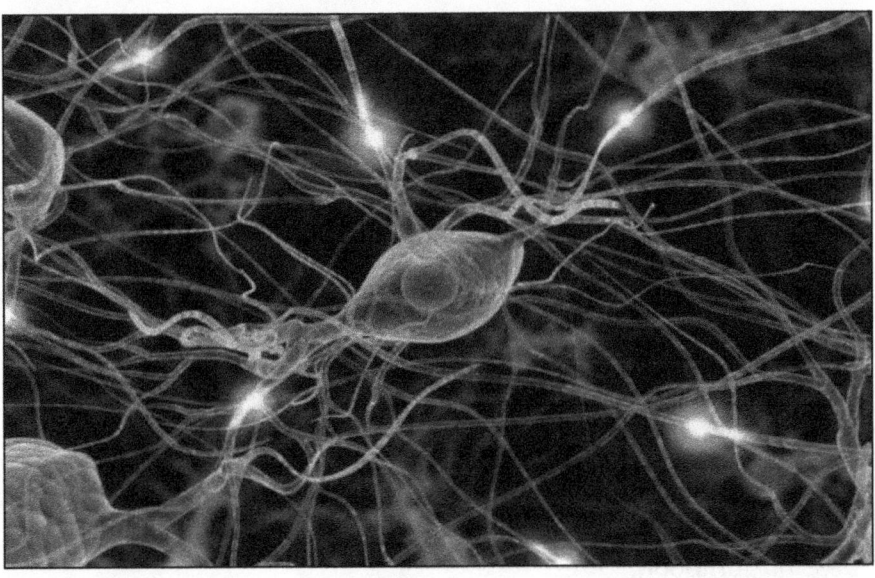

As proven by Nobel Prize-winner Eric Kandel, a world expert in neuroscience, if you continue to stimulate the newly-formed areas in the brain, the synaptic connections can double in just one hour, rewiring concepts, ideas, and beliefs within the brain. On the other side of the equation, neuroscience suggests that if you don't entertain, think, repeat, and review what you have learned, those newly-formed neural connections get pruned within hours and days.

When you lose the magic, the connections, the inspiration, the vibrancy of the new understanding; you lose the future potential you had just able to access and unveil.

Your consciousness is like a field. As you keep cultivating the soil, and nourish the seeds of thoughts, emotions, and understandings, these grow into a new and perfected state of being. This was well known by the Essenes and the Greek Therapeutae ("Healers" or "Attendants"), Jewish and Greek sects (respectively) consisting of healers, speakers, and ascetics that closely resembled each other — as seen in the Gnostic teachings of Jesus, Mark 4:3-9, and Mark 4:10-20, where words become the seeds sown in one's consciousness.

This is why in my live events; I always ask the audience to vocalize what they have learned to the person next to them so the data centers of their brain can create new neuro-connections.

The more you reinforce a concept by remembering, vocally expressing and articulating it to another person, you are essentially nourishing a new seed, a new program into your being. As this new concept becomes part of you, you will subconsciously begin to make different choices, take on different paths, and have different experiences.

Now imagine your consciousness as a vibrational field of beautiful, vibrant light. This light does not reside in your brain. The brain is just the operating system of your physical shell, a marionette, a puppet of sorts that you are using in this life to navigate physical reality. This will be self-evident in the *Many Lives, One Destination* book.

Consciousness transmits information through frequencies, coherence and resonance, which send instructions to the physical brain (the hardware) so that the limited senses you have become

Consciousness and the Physical Body

accustomed to can be engaged and stimulated. Your senses create the illusion of separateness. Returning home to a unified field and self, where the divided mind, the bubble, can be popped, is the path of the initiate.

Think of this bubble as container for your identity, and your belief system as a binocular with different lenses. If your belief system is limited, you will only see a partial view of reality. A limited belief system is exemplified in the illustration below as a dry, scorching desert, with no signs of hope in sight; but if you were to expand how you perceive yourself, life and reality, you will begin to see a lush field of potentialities and opportunities unfold before you.

When the knowledge is applied, aligning your thoughts with your intent and behavior, then your body and mind, has no other option than to adapt, engage, endorse, and identify with a new potential. This opens up different choices, experiences, and destinies.

When this happens on an emotional level, you will experience elevated states of emotions such as love, gratitude, joy, compassion, empathy, freedom and abundance. On a physiological level, your body responds by releasing chemicals and activating positive gene expressions (while deregulating negative ones) in line with the new beliefs, intent, and experience. In this way, the body starts to energetically, chemically, and genetically reflect the new mind.

The Science of Consciousness

The new state of being creates an energetic field that attracts the matching (resonant) reality to your field of experience.

You will find that synchronicities are not random events, but rather your resonant field are attracting to you people, places, things, times and events that match your frequency signature, intent and desires.

As you internalize the knowledge it becomes part of you. Not only is it fully integrated in your mind, but also in your field of energy.

You don't need look for love anymore as there is no craving, no longing, no yearning, because your soul, mind, heart, and every cell in your body has become love. You emit, exude, radiate love. You become the spring of your own love, light, inner peace, compassion, abundance and wisdom.

"This is how common people around the world are beginning to do the uncommon. In doing so they are transitioning from philosopher to initiate to master; from knowledge to experience to wisdom; from mind to body to soul; from thinking to doing to being; and from learning with their head to practicing it by hand and knowing it by heart." ~ Dr. Joe Dispenza (*Mind to Matter*, p. xiii)

These elevated states then become effortless, peaceful, serene, flowing, uncomplicated, automatic and natural. You have transmuted theoretical knowledge into a practical skill and then a state of being. In doing so, you have moved from being the philosopher to the master of your own domain, from the ordinary to the extraordinary. But there is more.

Your heart and mind are not a static magnet. They are more akin to a Wi-Fi router, able to wirelessly transmit and receive information from the consciousness field. This has been shown in many experiments dealing with consciousness as we will see shortly.

But before we look at case studies on conscious intent to affect matter, we need to first answer a profound question: Is the Universe and a single particle, self-aware?

CHAPTER 9:
Is the Universe or a Particle Self-Aware?

"You must unlearn what you have learned."
~Yoda, *Star Wars*

REDEFINING REALITY

If this reality we perceive as real is actually an interpretation, a consciousness-based simulation of sorts, then we can conclude that each of us has a personalized world-view map of this matrix construct. It is not hard to conclude that consciousness plus energy (emotions) and intent (coherent thoughts) would create the nature of this reality.

"There's a one in billions chance that this is base reality." ~ Elon Musk, 2016 Code Conference

"Base reality" is what Elon Mask calls physicality and matter. He believes that we live in a consciousness-based simulation. But the only way for this reality to be a construct would be if this entire reality, universe(s), matter, and even subatomic particles were truly based on consciousness. Consciousness also requires SELF-AWARENESS and INTELLIGENCE.

Can even subatomic particles or an energy field have an intelligence, thoughts, and emotions? If this were the case, it would not only have an effect on reality, but it could also imply that this self-awareness (intent, thoughts, and emotions) could be at the base of the universe's programming language, code, and expression.

So how can we scientifically prove that even a subatomic particle like a photon (a light particle) is aware, thinking, and interacting with the rest of creation? To do so, we have to immerse ourselves in the world of "panpsychism." This weird and funky term describes the idea that the Universe is the ultimate intelligent organism, capable of thinking, creating, and interacting with its own creation — what most religions call 'God'.

In his book, *This Book Will Change Your Life*, Ben Carey calculates the odds of life starting on earth, and showcases that without this thinking, problem-solving, and evolving cosmic consciousness, there would not be life on any level.

"There is 1 chance in 140 trillion that the Earth should exist. There is 1 chance in 795 billion that life should have evolved on earth. There is 1 chance in 89 billion that life should have evolved into mankind. There is 1 chance in 12 billion that mankind should have created the alphabet and thus civilization. There is 1 chance in 6 billion that your parents should ever have met and got together. There is 1 chance in 90 million that you should have been the lucky sperm that fertilized your mother's egg..." ~ Ben Carey

---

BOOK LINKS

To view or buy the "This Book will change your Life" by Ben Carey, please click on the links below:

AMAZON: https://amzn.to/37tmXTH

BOOKDEPOSITORY: https://tinyurl.com/yx6ct9e7

Just looking at the odds should be a clear indication that there is an intelligent consciousness that is expressing itself through this universe. But let's go a bit deeper.

FROM WAVE TO PARTICLE

Quantum physicists and other researchers are coming more and more to the conclusion that we live in a participatory universe in which each subatomic particle has consciousness and the ability to think and react. This is not dissimilar to the functions of the cells in a body, which also have brain-like functions as well as social interaction skills and even digestive processes, as we will see later.

Scientific materialists, who believe that life is the result of randomness and that everything can be explained through the concept of energy and matter, are left with a great paradox. They can't refute the evidence of quantum physics that involves an observer and consciousness, and yet are not willing to embrace it or even engage it with an open, unbiased mind.

We know science is full of ideas that seem hard to believe, but as new scientific discoveries spring forward and our technological prowess increases, our life is more and more resembling a sci-fi TV series like *Star Trek* than anything else. This is hard for some to accept.

Take quantum mechanics. In this strange world of subatomic physics, a particle is in a wave state until an observer influences its state. This fluid potentiality, as many scientists are discovering, is not based on a roll of the dice, i.e., randomness, but seems to be the result of a conscious, thinking and feeling mind/consciousness controlling the subatomic world. This cosmic mind could be what makes the universe be and respond.

We encountered the analogy of the prism and different ideologies earlier on. Now we are going to see how light can be both a particle (what we perceive as matter) and a wave (a cloud or force field of potentiality, waiting for an intent to manifest). But as already discussed earlier, matter is an illusion. A particle is an erroneous term to define a concentration of energy in a localized spot. It is still a cloud of energy, just localized.

Therefore, if we could visualize the difference between a "Particle/Matter" and a "Wave/Potential" in its true form, then we will be able to see it as a widespread sea of wave-like potential, or as a localized condensation of energy. The next illustration shows how it would appear.

The Science of Consciousness

The main difference between these two states is that in the one on the left, the "WAVE" state is still a sea of potential waiting to respond to a conscious intent, while in the other, the "PARTICLE" state, in which the wave has collapsed, is a condensation of localized energy, thought and intent made manifest as a denser state of energy (which we call matter). The radiating circles on the particle are just a visual representation of the electron potentiality in space.

If we take this a step further, we can say that there are three levels from WAVE state to PARTICLE. The first state is where there is only the ocean of energy, in a neutral floating state, full of waves of potentiality.

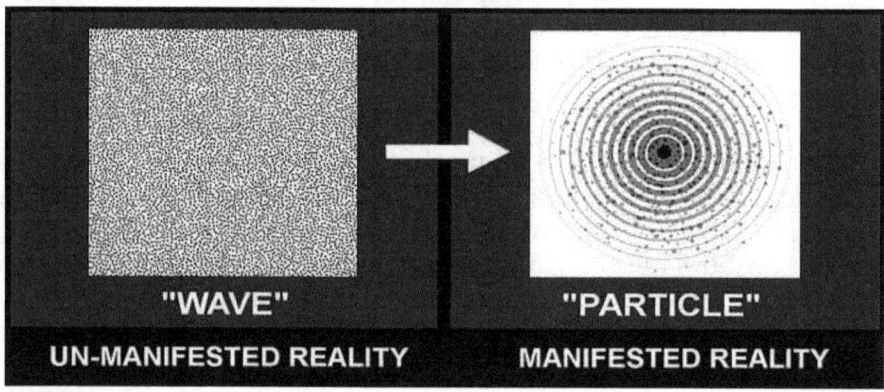

As consciousness imprints a desire (coherent intent), through a thought (direction of the energy and outcome) and emotion (energy), this wave state starts to condense little by little (level two) from wave to concentrated energy, or what we have come to call a physical state (level three).

Is the Universe or a Particle Self-Aware?

"You can show mathematically that electrons lose and gain energy constantly from the Zero Point Field in a dynamic equilibrium, balanced at exactly the right orbit. Electrons get their energy to keep going without slowing down because they are refueling by tapping into these fluctuations of empty space. In other words, the Zero Point Field accounts for the stability of hydrogen atom — and, by interference, the stability of all matter. Pull the plug on zero-point energy, and all atomic structure would collapse. What this implies is a 'kind of self-generating grand ground state of the universe', which constantly refreshes itself and remains a constant unless disturbed in some way. It also means that we and all the matter of the universe are literally connected to the further reaches of the cosmos through the Zero Point Field waves of the grandest dimension." Hal Puthoff — "The energetic vacuum: implications for energy research," *Speculation in Science and Technology* 1990; 13: 247-57. Also *Scientist*, 2 December 1989

This is what David Bohm postulated in the 1980s when he coined the ontological concepts for quantum theory of implicate order for un-manifested reality in a state of wave fluctuation, and the explicate order for the manifested "physical reality." This can be better understood via the next image.

Why is this relevant to consciousness or even your day-to-day life?

Because as conscious beings, we are manifesting our reality using our thoughts and emotions all the time. We are collapsing the wave function, coagulating energy into experience every day.

What you entertain, think and feel, you become. What you become, you attract.

The universe does not speak English, Chinese or Russian, but frequency and resonance. From a monocellular organism to a complex system like the human body, and even a tree or a particle of light, all beings use electromagnetic fields, light, energy, and frequency to communicate.

The Science of Consciousness

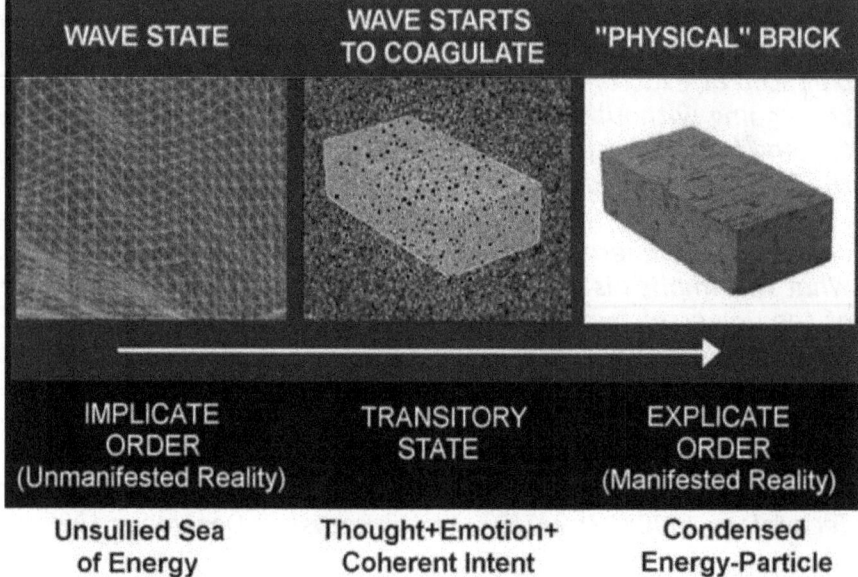

The issue is that we live without awareness of how life, consciousness, intent, and our thoughts and emotion really works. The other problem, as we will see later, is that our intent, thoughts, and emotions are incoherent and scattered, which means we cannot manifest and attract what we desire in our life. How can the universe, the implicate order, the sea of infinite energy and possibilities give you love, for example, when you believe that you are not worthy of happiness? How can the universe, the implicate order, the sea of infinite energy and possibilities give you wealth and abundance if you hold a belief that money is dirty, and the root of all evil?

Without understanding the inner engineering of consciousness, you will always be like a boat without rudder, or a leaf in the wind: powerless, lost, confused, ineffective, helpless, and dependent on someone else's creation. If you don't actively create your destiny, someone else will do it for you. Your life will look random, but it is only that way because you allow external people, places, times, and events to control your outcomes.

If you fully understand what we have discussed so far, you will not be able to refute that there is an intelligent observer or

Is the Universe or a Particle Self-Aware?

consciousness that somehow is integral to the formation of matter, physicality, and the reality we are experiencing.

We are told that we have been made in the image of God. This could have many meanings; the least probable is that this Divine intelligence has chosen a feeble-looking human body to represent the vastness, the limitlessness, the splendor of its being. It is more likely that being made in the image of God means that what we have the same potentiality and capabilities for expression and creation.

This is, after all, the idea of the "Prodigal Son" in Christianity, and the gift of FREE WILL. That allows us as conscious beings to create by freely using our thoughts, emotions, and intent, through the dualistic aspect of reality: learning to appreciate light through darkness, joy through sadness, love through anger.

It is only when we overcome the paradoxes that we can find unity, peace, unconditional love, and a grace not moved by the storms of life. More on all of this will be covered later in this series.

Back to "reality," or how consciousness expresses itself. If we use the example of ice, water, and vapor, we can clearly see how the more "physical" the energy is, the more solid it becomes.

The atomic bonds become more fixated as the condensation of matter becomes more intensified.

The freer the state (vapor) the more the energy contained is able to become something else. The more fixated the state (ice), the less energy is available for change, as the bonds in the atoms are more firmly attached to the form.

WAVE/PARTICLE DUALITY

For thousands of years, researchers, seekers, philosophers, and scientists have debated about what light is. Most religious faiths, in fact, are based on the creed of light and the Sun, as we will see in *The Path of the Initiate* in this Awakening series.

In the late 1600s, Isaac Newton proposed (in his *Treatise on Opticks*) that light was a stream of particles or corpuscles. But in 1864, James Clerk Maxwell discovered that light is an oscillation of electromagnetic fields, meaning it is a type of wave.

Electromagnetic fields; does this sound familiar? It seems more and more that we are light-based beings communicating through light-based fields.

Confusion arose. Is light a wave, or is it a particle?

Later on, Albert Einstein stipulated, based on his equations and realizations, that light can *also* be a particle through the photoelectric effect.

Is the Universe or a Particle Self-Aware?

Eventually, as all experiments proving that light was a wave *and* a particle could be proven without any doubt, it was concluded that light is in fact both a wave and a particle, giving rise to the Wave/Particle Duality Paradox.

Light, it seems, can be anything and is everything.

Physicist Louis De Broglie, in his 1924 Ph.D. thesis, proposed that this duality did not end to light and its related particle, the photon, but could also be applied to electrons, neutrons, and virtually all matter. That is, all particles, all things are both waves (as a potential waiting to unfold) and particles (a concentration of energy that has manifested and unfolded in this reality).

To better understand this duality of Wave and Particle — which forms the basis of all creation and all things, as we saw in the previous pages — we need to consider the famous Double Slit Experiment.

Thomas Young (1773-1829) performed the first Double Slit Experiment, but later on, this experiment was repeated by many researchers around the world, all coming back with the same results and conclusions. One of the most renown tests was conducted in 1927 by Davisson and Germer. They demonstrated that electrons show the same behavior, which was later extended to atoms and molecules by De Broglie.

Two great videos showcasing this experiment can be found by typing into YouTube: "Dr. Quantum, Double Slit Experiment" (https://www.youtube.com/watch?v=DfPeprQ7oGc); or you can view this video in the member's area, as well as The Original Double Slit Experiment review.

This is an experiment so simple that you can even do it at home!

For those without access to the internet, I will try to explain this through words and illustrations, in a similar way as it was shown in the documentary *What the Bleep Do We Know?*

The Science of Consciousness

This is important, as consciousnesses and light is the foundation, the prime matter (*prima materia*), of all that exists. So please stay with me for the next couple of pages.

STAGE I: HOW PHYSICAL MATTER RESPONDS TO THE DOUBLE SLIT EXPERIMENT

Let's say we have a paintball gun that can shoot towards a screen that has two vertical slits in it. Some paintballs will hit the sides of the panel without going through the slit, while others will go through and hit the second panel behind the first, creating two lines of paint stains. This is the response we would expect when dealing with matter as particles.

However, when light is used instead of paintball, the results become very, very interesting, as it opens the door to a new and uncomfortable topic in physics: consciousness.

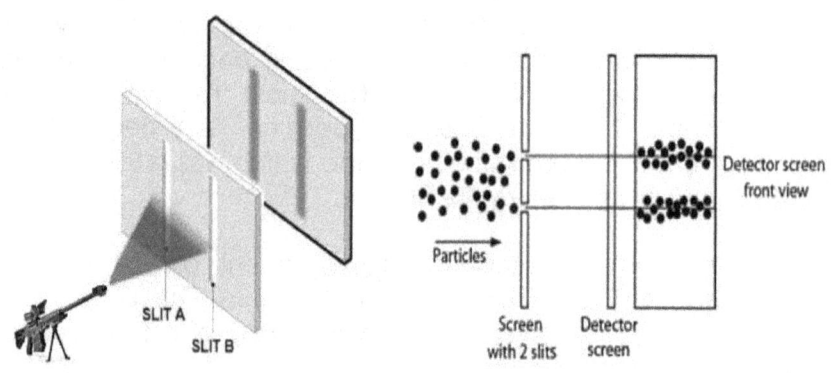

STAGE II: HOW LIGHT RESPONDS TO THE DOUBLE SLIT EXPERIMENT

If we use a laser to emit light (instead of paintballs) in this experiment, two things can happen, depending upon whether an observer is present or not. If an observer is *not* present, light acts

Is the Universe or a Particle Self-Aware?

like a wave, creating both constructive and destructive interference on the detector screen. It is, in a way, like wave in the ocean. As a wave it is also neutral, a potential waiting to be expressed.

In that way it is like a blank canvas waiting for a painter (the observer) to express their creativity. This is what is called "collapsing the wave function" in quantum physics. Imagine two ripples in a pond amplifying (constructive interference) and disrupting (destructive interference) parts of the combined wave created. We saw this concept earlier through Hate plus Hate, generating more Hate, and Hate plus Love nullifying each other.

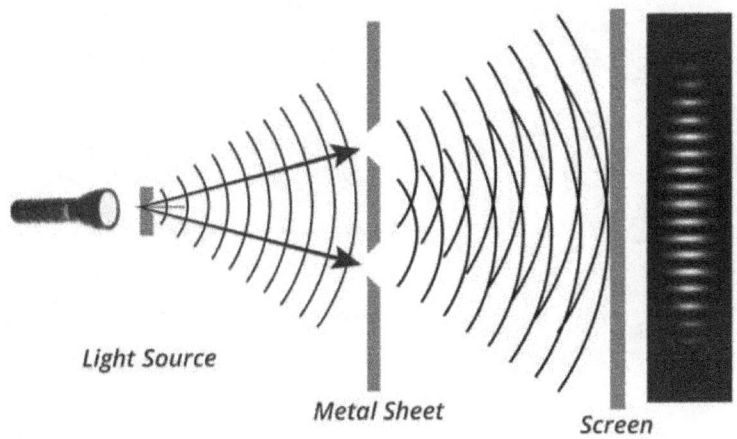

Now, let's consider the implications of this behavior when the slits are so small that only one photon can pass through at a time, and only one photon is emitted at a time. Logic would dictate that these photons would leave a pattern of two stripes on the detector wall (one for each slit) as it did with the paintball example. However, this assumption is wrong, because they mysteriously paint a band of stripes, creating a wave pattern. This phenomenon could only happen if one photon goes through both slits *at the same time*: in other words, the one particle (remember, only one particle is emitted each time) is in two places at once. This is called superpositioning.

The Science of Consciousness

As shown in the next illustration, the other possible interpretation (Bohmian Mechanics) is that the particle has gone back to a wave state, and what we are observing is an interference pattern created by the wave state (present without an observer) rather than superpositioning. My personal mystical experience seems to align with the last theory. Light is, at its core, a wave; and as such, it has no physicality, no time or space. We saw earlier that has a force carrier it also has no mass. It is a wave of potentiality; it is present potentially at all places simultaneously, like a sea of potential, but because we see the wave and forget the sea, it gives us the illusion of superpositioning.

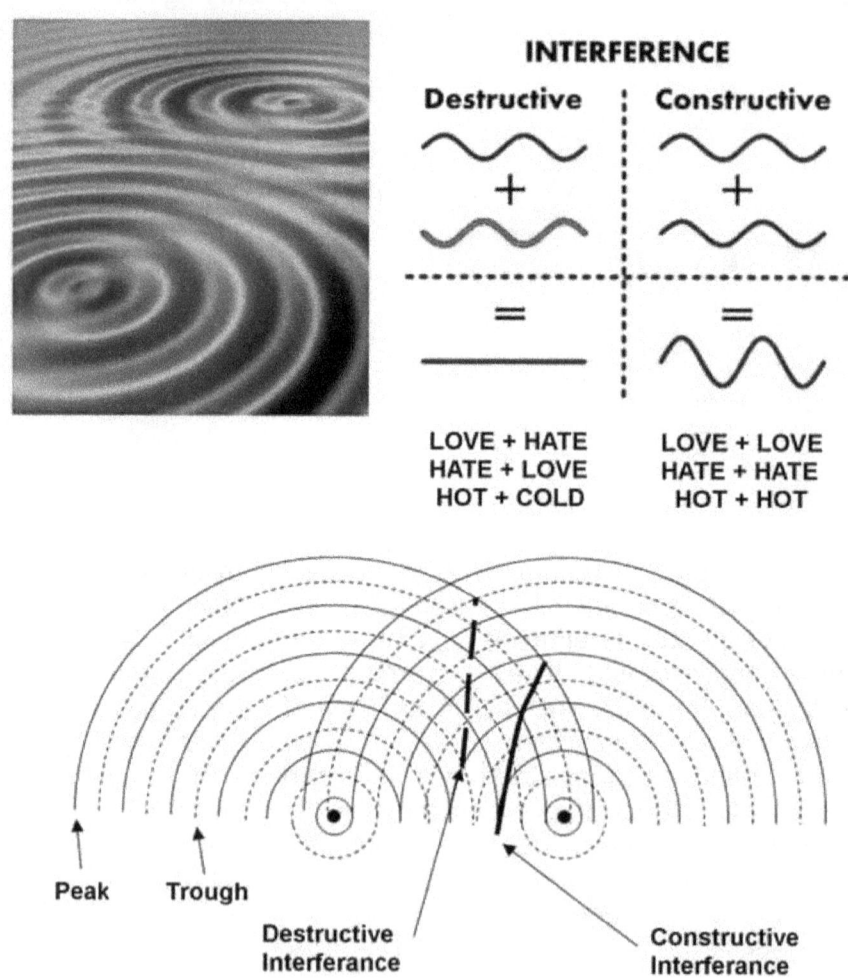

Is the Universe or a Particle Self-Aware?

The strangest thing of all is what happens when you put an observer next to the slits. When the photons are being watched, the wave pattern disappears, and you end up again with the behavior of a particle and matter, resulting in two stripes!

This means that an observer has the power to condense energy into physicality, or a wave into a particle. The wave, the infinite sea of potential, disappears, and what you are left is a particle, matter.

Light acts the same way as the paintballs did before (see next picture) — meaning the light being observed has collapsed its wave function and can now be perceived as a particle, and no longer a wave.

Someone merely observing the wave has made the light behave like a physical particle!

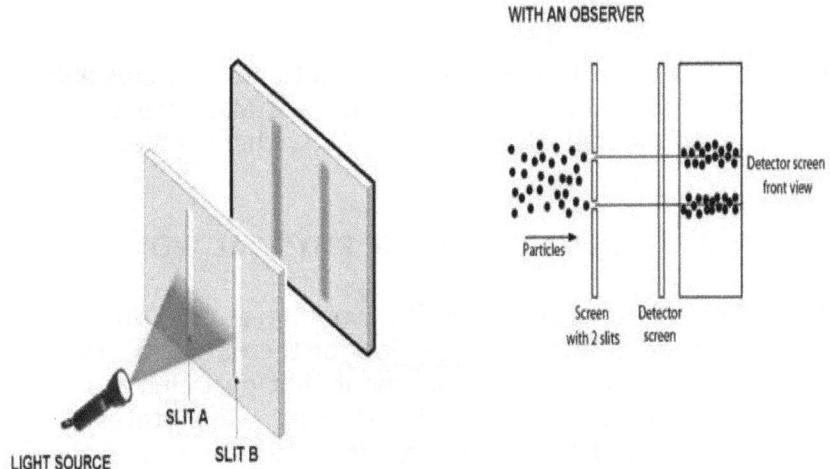

If you take away the observer, the wave pattern comes back. This proves that we can change the way reality behaves just by looking at it. Consciousness has an effect over reality, physicality, and our overall experience. We are left to conclude that without an

The Science of Consciousness

observer, there is no manifestation in the explicate order (the world we live in), reality, and physicality. Consciousness is therefore at the basis of what we call matter.

NO OBSERVER= NO COLLAPSE OF THE WAVE FUNCTION, which means NO OBSERVER = NO MATTER OR PHYSICALITY

Without conscious observation, all of reality would be in a state of wave potentiality, meaning there would not be a planet, a rock, a physical body, cars, or anything that you could touch, taste, smell, or see.

The intent of the observer, focuses the interference of light photons (this sea of unlimited potentiality) into a coherent pattern, we call a particle or matter. This could mean that when the observer is not present, that the light particle is potentially everywhere at the same time (superpositioning) but also that this sea of potentiality as waves are free to interact and interfere with each other (Bohmian Mechanics), and therefore forming an interference pattern.

But is this effect of the observer on subatomic particles only part of the field of quantum physics, or does it also affect our more fixed reality, the one that is supposedly unchangeable?

WAVE/PARTICLE DUALITY IN THE PHYSICAL WORLD

Renown physicist Anton Zeilinger, working at the University of Vienna, wanted a better explanation for the nature of reality. He knew from the double-slit experiment that particles are nothing more than clouds of potentiality in their wave states, but he wanted to transfer this understanding to the world of the very large, the world of physicality we live in.

So in his research, Zeilinger adapted the slit experiment using fullerene carbon molecules, which contain 60 carbon atoms. These are not subatomic particles or photons, but carbon, one of the main constituents of matter. In fact, humans are carbon-based life forms. It would be impossible for life on Earth to exist without carbon. Carbon is the primary component of sugars, proteins, fats,

Is the Universe or a Particle Self-Aware?

DNA, muscle tissue — pretty much everything in your body.

Zeilinger heated up the fullerene molecules to 1,158 Fahrenheit (900 Kelvin; 626 Celsius), so that they would create an intense molecular beam, and then fired this beam through the double slit, creating the same interference pattern as with photons.

He then tested the same hypothesis using a fluorinated molecule containing 70 carbon atoms and another containing 100 atoms called teraphenylporphyrin, a derivate of the bio-dye present in chlorophyll. Again, the result was the same, suggesting that even at the largest scale of life, physical matter exists in a malleable state.[6]

This proves that even what we consider stable, fixed matter in our physical world is nothing more than a cloud of potentiality waiting for a coherent intent to assemble it into a final state of being.

SCHRÖDINGER'S CAT AND THE OBSERVER

If a tree falls in a forest but no one is there to hear it, does it still make a sound? If no one is looking at the moon, does the moon disappear?

Erwin Schrödinger, one of the founders of quantum mechanics, designed a thought experiment (famously known as "Schrodinger's cat") to understand the effect of the observer on reality. Please note that Schrödinger experiment was theoretical in nature, and no real cat was harmed.

In this experiment, a virtual cat was placed in a box. Inside was some radioactive uranium, a Geiger counter designed to measure radioactivity, and a vial of poison. The reason radioactive uranium is used in the experiment is because radioactive decay is a

---

[6] A Zeilinger, 'Probing the limits of the quantum world', Physics World, March 2005

The Science of Consciousness

probabilistic quantum event, meaning there is no way to know if an atom will decay or not. It has 50% chance to decaying and a 50% chance of not decaying during a given time period.

If an atom of uranium decayed, it would set off the Geiger counter, which would then release the poison and silently kill the cat. Before you open the box and look, however, you can't actually know whether the cat is dead or alive. It has 50% chance of being alive and 50% chance of being dead. According to quantum mechanics, the cat is neither dead nor alive, or is both alive and dead at the same time. This is a nonsensical, absurd, preposterous state. How can something be both dead and alive simultaneously?

Of course, in reality, the cat is either alive or dead; but you simply cannot tell until you open the box. The Schrödinger's cat thought experiment is intended to show that nothing in this universe is certain until someone observes it. But another pioneer of quantum mechanics, Eugene Wigner, believed it could teach us something else about the working of the universe — which is that consciousness controls everything. He believed, based on his observations and research, that consciousness must determine existence, as you need an observer to have physicality.

Image on the left courtesy of "6 Dollar Shirts"

You can view a video about Schrödinger's Cat in the member's area.

If reality is based on an observer and consciousness is at the base of reality, then who is observing a new planet full of gaseous masses with no life anywhere to be seen?

Is the Universe or a Particle Self-Aware?

Someone must be observing us, the gaseous planet, and everything else in the universe; otherwise, there would be no people, no planet to call home, no universe, and nothing else for that matter. All that would exist would be the implicate, unmanifested sea of potential.

Schrödinger's cat, the cup on your desk, the bed you sleep in at night, the salad you have just eaten, the tree in the forest, and yourself are all parts of the same reality and universe. If we look deeper, the only conclusion is that some kind of Cosmic Consciousness that is ethereal and envelops the entire universe is observing us, and that even a subatomic particle is a consciousness that is observing, creating, and experiencing reality.

If everything is permeated by consciousness, then everything is conscious, alive, able to think and respond at one level or another. As Hermeticism says: *"As above, so below; as below, so above."* The principles and universal laws that apply to the very large have to apply to the very small as well, and vice versa. This is the basis of the concept of the holographic and fractal nature of reality that we will expand on later in this book.

IS THERE MORE PROOF THAT EVEN A SUB-ATOMIC PARTICLE IS AWARE?

A computer operates through electrical signals that respond via either zeros or ones, meaning something is either true or false. The mind inside a human body operates through electrical signals that respond through either expansion or contraction, growth or fear. Everything in nature is a mirror of the same mechanics. So if the entire universe seems to be based on the same laws of consciousness, then why would we believe that the entire universe cannot think?

Today, researchers from all over the world are endeavoring to create a quantum computer that can have multiple states: True, False, and not True, not False, or True and False simultaneously. Or, if we use quantum vocabulary, a state of superpositioning.

The Science of Consciousness

Seth Lloyd, a professor of mechanical engineering and physics at the Massachusetts Institute of Technology (M.I.T.), has proven that quantum computing is possible, and will one day make current computers completely obsolete. This is because while a computer has to compute a limited amount of processes and information at one time, a quantum computer can in theory process unlimited information.

In quantum mechanics, a physical system, like an atom or an electron, can be in a superposition, which means that it can exist in several states at once. A famous but caricature-like example is Schrödinger's cat, which would be dead and alive at the same time, as we just saw.

Quantum computers exploit this superposition, because a quantum bit, or qubit for short, can be a 1 and a 0 simultaneously. In Lloyd's words: *"A classical computer can typically only follow one instruction at a time, but a quantum computer can do many things simultaneously."*

In 2006, he published his book *Programming the Universe*, (AMAZON link: https://amzn.to/2RP1bmZ Book Depository link: https://tinyurl.com/vm8bkpp) in which he considers the laws of nature and the entire universe as a giant quantum information processing system — a cosmic consciousness.

His twenty-plus years of research has shown beyond any possible doubt that atoms and subatomic particles can think. Every atom and every elementary particle processes and stores bits of information. Quantum computing is still in its infancy, but its working and computation proves that subatomic particles can think, and that the Universe, which is entirely built from such particles, must also be a quantum computer.

"Every physical system registers information, and just by evolving in time, by doing its thing, it changes that information, transforms that information, or, if you like, processes that information." ~ Seth Lloyd

Is the Universe or a Particle Self-Aware?

If the entire universe at the subatomic level is processing information, then it must be thinking and it must be alive; therefore, the universe could be the ultimate intelligent organism.

This consciousness at the base of all things is what humanity has called God, and tried to understand since the dawn of time. This, then, means that this Divine Consciousness is truly omniscient, omnipotent, and omnipresent, as mystics of old have told us for millennia. If consciousness is all that exists in different forms of densities and states, how can we then explain and connect this somewhat spiritual concept with the scientific creations of the Big Bang theory and the history of creation in different religious traditions?

This question will be answered in the next chapter.

The Science of Consciousness

CHAPTER 10:
The Quantum Field and Consciousness

"Consciousness cannot be accounted for in physical terms. For consciousness is absolutely fundamental, it cannot be accounted for in terms of anything else."
~ Erwin Schrödinger

Everything that we call a miracle is just science waiting to be unveiled. Our divine inheritance is available for all; we just have to lift the veil of illusion and separation.

But there are a lot of unanswered questions that the logical brain is trying to figure out. After all, if consciousness is at the base of everything, it makes "The Secret," or the Law of Attraction, look like an extension of the properties of this Source Field rather than the main constituent.

The Law of Attraction will be explained in this book in detail, but like everything in life, we need to create context; otherwise, it will be lost in the realm of understood phenomena. So to understand the association between science, spirituality, and religion, we need to go a bit deeper.

ENTER THE WORLD OF QUANTUM MECHANICS, CLASSICAL FLUID DYNAMICS, AND THE SCIENCE OF ONENESS

In this chapter, some of the pieces of the puzzle laid out in the previous chapters will come together in an incredible tapestry of understanding.

One of the main points in the Science of Consciousness, is knowing where we come from — our true heritage, lineage, and point of creation. We will discuss some scientific facts, and I'll ask you to stay with me, even if some of the concepts might go over your

The Science of Consciousness

head, as I believe in the end it will all make sense. Like in the story of Alice in Wonderland, we will now fall a bit deeper into the rabbit-hole, into the world of subatomic particles. To do this, we need to know a few things about the universe we live in. We will examine each one of these points in detail in this chapter.

1. Based on the Big Bang Theory, the universe originated from one point, "Point Zero."

2. The Universe is holographic in nature, meaning all parts, even the smallest, contains everything as information and potential.

3. The Universe is fractal in nature, meaning all nature follows the same mathematical rules of expansion and contraction, like a program in a computer.

4. The Universe and Life is a frequency-based simulation.

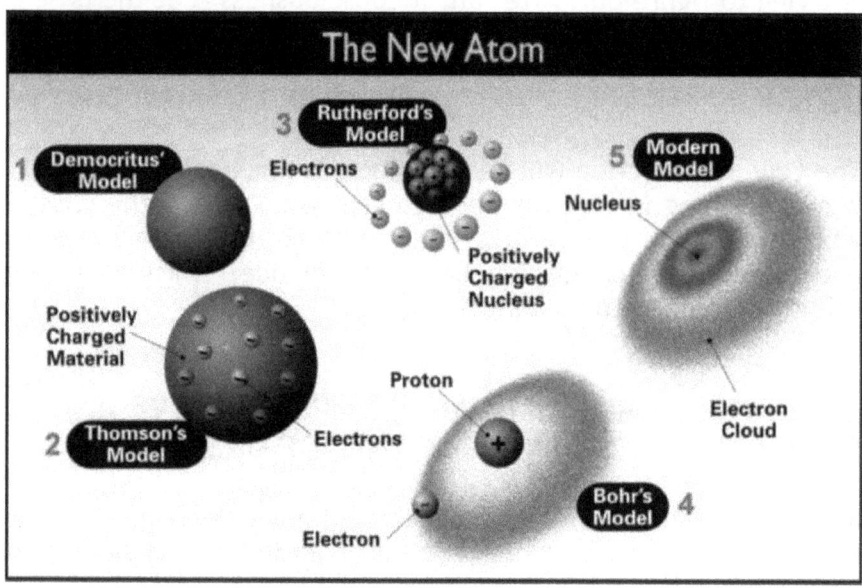

As we learn about the basis of reality, we have come to learn also that an atom is not a series of "physical" particles, but rather a cloud of potential, as shown in the above image.

The Quantum Field and Consciousness

Over time, we've gone from the Newtonian model of the atom to the quantum interpretation, as seen below.

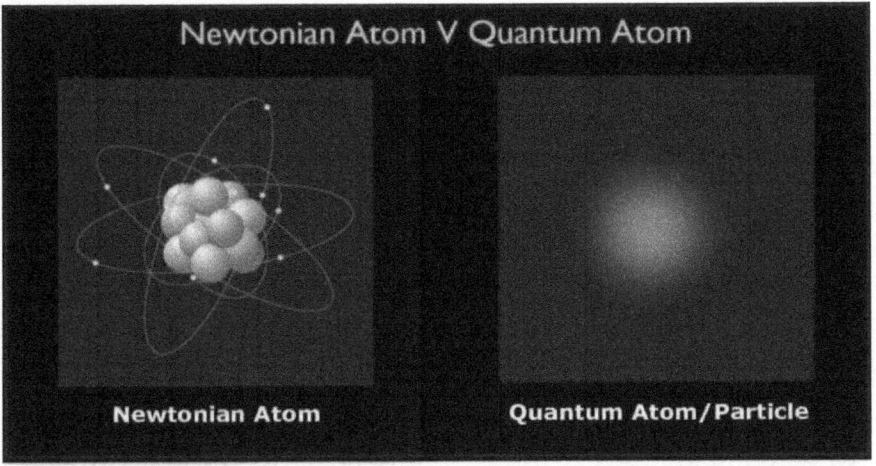

If we go deeper, we can see that everything can be broken down to smaller and smaller particles, until we reach a point of potentiality. Quantum mechanics/physics is, in fact, the study of the very little.

If we look at a sand castle, we can go deeper and see under a microscope that the castle is made of little sand crystals; if we go further, these crystals are made of molecules of different compounds like silica. If we go deeper, we can see atoms, quarks, electrons, etc., as we saw with the story of the ice and vapor at the start of the book.

What is incredible about the discovery of quantum mechanics is that the observer has an effect on the observed matter. This makes more sense if we understand that all frequency-based matter is light in different forms and, if we take this a bit further, is consciousness in light form.

QUANTUM THEORIES HAVE EVOLVED TOO

For a while, there seemed to be two kinds of physicists: one that believed that "consciousness" is the foundation of all things and beings, and the other with "matter" as that foundation, from which consciousness is an emergent phenomenon.

When matter is set as the foundation of being, quantum physics becomes full of contradictions.

David Bohm, Amit Goswami, Lothar Schäfer, and Erwin Schrödinger are among those who came to the conclusion that consciousness must be the at the basis of existence, and for them, the contradictions dissipated like fog in the morning sun.

For the rest, there are those that still perceive reality as based on physicality and matter, and those that ignored the facts, using the famous phrase "Shut Up and Calculate" to avoid facing the implications of consciousness in quantum physics.

When consciousness is set as the foundation, the *prima materia* of all things, there are no contradictions if you are willing to look at the evidence with an open mind.

Matter is a byproduct of consciousness, not the other way around.

Just as our understanding of the atom has evolved, and new understanding has ushered us forward, the same has happened to quantum theory. I will summarize just a few points about this evolutionary path to give you some context before we progress further.

THE COPENHAGEN INTERPRETATION

The link and creative influence between reality and the observer has been called the "Copenhagen Interpretation" of quantum mechanics because it was proposed by Niels Bohr, Werner Heisenberg, and other physicists working in that city. It states that a quantum particle doesn't exist in one state or another, but in all of its possible states at once, as a wave. This superpositioning (being potentially everywhere at once) happens until the particle is observed; then it is forced to choose one probability, and that is the state that we observe. Since it may be forced into a

The Quantum Field and Consciousness

different observable state each time, it can appear that the quantum particle behaves erratically.

This state of existing in all possible states at once is called an object's *coherent superposition*. The total of all possible states in which an object can exist makes up the object's *wave function*. When we observe the wave, the wave function collapses and the object is forced into a state of physicality as a particle.

The problem with this interpretation is that it does not answer 'Who' or 'What' is behind the original observer. It appears that there is some kind of intelligent consciousness at the base of reality. This translates for the Copenhagen Interpretation to the pragmatic research ideology of "Shut Up and Calculate." Don't bother trying to understand the weirdness of the quantum field, or the depth of its functioning or creation.

The quantum world and the Copenhagen Interpretation have a few more disturbing, unsettling aspects like: the uncertainty principle or randomness, as well as measurement issues, which relate to the idea of superpositioning. You can either know the probable location of a photon as a particle or its velocity, but not both. Researchers following the Copenhagen Interpretation have to ignore these uncertainties.

How can we have a state of randomness in a universe regulated by consciousness, intent and coherence?

With De Broglie and Bohm Theory, which has become known as Bohmian Mechanics (Pilot-Wave theory) there is no randomness in the universe, and no superpositioning, as has been postulated. It only looks random because we do not know all the forces involved, as we will see later in the Genesis of Consciousness, which shows how the Source Field (the Void) can be a sea of untamed potential, seemingly random, waiting for an intent to coagulate into different states of density and form.

In this view, the superpositioning rule of quantum physics, which states that an unobserved photon (in a state of wave dynamics) exists in all possible states simultaneously, but, when observed or measured, exhibits only one state, is not completely correct.

The superposition is incorrect because it is not a singular, specific wave that chooses to change when observed, but rather the infinite sea of wave potential expressing itself into what appears to be a state of singularity.

Although this singularity is perceived as such, it is still one with the infinite sea of potential. The separation, the identification and distinction of being 'separate from' is just a limited way of perceiving reality. In the same way that vapor, a drop of water and ice might be perceived as different, in reality they are all made out of the same atoms (H_2O) or light displayed in different states of density and frequency.

In simple terms, the infinite sea of potential does not collapse or coagulate itself into a singular particle or matter, but rather, it expresses itself in infinite ways or forms.

It is the observer's intent that drives the infinite sea of potential into a state of coagulated energy or matter. It is the intent that provides the blueprint, a purpose and a direction.

This also means that life and creation are not a result of randomness but a well-designed system which voids the Copenhagen Interpretation even further.

All this will become clearer later on when the illusion of TIME and SPACE are discussed.

THE MANY WORLDS INTERPRETATION (MWI)

Another renowned quantum point of view is the 'Many Worlds Interpretation', or MWI. This hypothesis tells us that at any given moment, all choices, all potentialities could happen — and do happen. This is a kind of superpositioning on steroids, on a larger scale. Each variance creates a new universe.

With the MWI, you virtually exist in an infinite version of reality. In some branches of reality, you are reading this book; in others you are purchasing your next Lamborghini; in another you are homeless begging on the side of the road; in another you are the prime minister or president of your country; in another you are a psychotic killer; and in yet another, you are a priest or a nun.

Everything that can potentially happen *will* happen that creates a new reality. Any possible scenario has been manifested. The universe becomes a multiverse as a random generating potentiality, where there is NO CHOICE. NO COHERENT INTENT. NO ORDER. NO INTELIGENCE. All possibilities are manifested. This removes free will, the main tenet of conscious creation and manifestation.

Most scientific materialists love this interpretation because it removes the idea of consciousness, the need for an intelligent observer, and ultimately the idea of the existence of God.

"What many take to be a conflict between religion and science is really something else. It is a conflict between religion and materialism. Materialism regards itself as scientific, and indeed is often called "scientific materialism," even by its opponents, but it has no legitimate claim to be part of science. It is, rather, a school of philosophy, (a religion) one defined by the belief that nothing exists except matter, or, as Democritus put it, "atoms and the void." ~ Stephen Barr

The double-slit experiment, among many other experiments, proves the effect of an intelligent observer on this sea of potentiality.

One of the main ideas is that from the implicate order, or sea of unbound, unrestricted potential, a wave can be collapsed into a particle. This idea is called the collapse of the waveform, which means that with no observer, there is no collapsing of the wave; no observer, no physical matter.

"Consciousness is the agency that collapses the wave form of a quantum object." ~ Amit Goswami, quantum physicist

This leaves the MWI with a few massive flaws that cannot be overcome if the observer is included in the equation.

The Science of Consciousness

This would equal to an infinite amount of new universes and potentials being created. This removes the need for an observer choosing a reality; it is random, as all options become expressed, no matter how improbable. There is no intelligent consciousness choosing an outcome, just chaos.

The only small strength in this hypothesis, is that this interpretation allows for the Goldilocks universe. This is a term used to express a world or universe where the ideal conditions are present to form life. For example, the planet lies the perfect distance from the sun, so that it is not too hot and not too cold. The gravitational pull is just right, etc. If there are infinite probabilities, all having been expressed, then having a Goldilocks universe is bound to exist as one of the potentials.

Cosmologists, for example, are facing this exact paradox. It turns out that the fundamental parameters of the universe appear to be perfectly "fine-tuned" for life. For example, if the strong nuclear force were any stronger, the sun would have burned out and died off billions of years ago; if it were any weaker, the sun wouldn't have ignited to begin with. If we move to gravity, we find the same concept. If it were any stronger, the Universe would have most likely collapsed in on itself already; and if it were any weaker, everything would have frozen over. Both the strong nuclear force and the gravitational force are just right.

One of the problems with the MWI theory is that if we believe that there is an intelligence running this reality and experience, as we will see later, with defined laws that govern all aspects of life, then the theory becomes ridiculous and obsolete. Nothing in the universe seems to give validity to the idea of wasting energy, or having been random, or throwing the dice, as Einstein once said.

"God does not play dice with the universe." Albert Einstein

"Einstein of course believed in mathematical laws of nature, so his idea of a God was at best someone who formulated the laws and then left the universe alone to evolve according to these laws." ~ Vasant Natarajan, physicist

The Quantum Field and Consciousness

Randomness is not part of the equation (especially when we review past lives regression and other phenomena), as everything in life is set with laws so precise that otherwise, life would be impossible anywhere. Scientific evidence (quantum computers, the double-slit experiment, etc.) suggests on all counts that there *is* an intelligent source of creation. A greater observer.

Another major issue with the MWI is the question of causation, or cause and effect. The MWI is completely nihilistic in nature, as it proposes a reality that is, at its core, meaningless. Nothing you think, say, or do matters, as all possibilities, no matter how insignificant or unlikely, are expressed somewhere.

Freewill in the MWI context becomes irrelevant, an intelligent observer becomes useless, a coherent intent a nuisance.

This interpretation does not accept that an action results in a reaction; there is no correlation seen between intention and outcome, or cause and effect (Karma). There is no causality, no self-determination, intent, or conscious action. You are not a conscious being living, expressing, and creating reality on a moment-by-moment basis, but a conglomeration of accidental random possibilities.

What a sad reality to live in! I feel sorry for the scientific materialists who have chosen this bleak, purposeless, meaningless reality as their home.

REFUSING TO ACKNOWLEDGE AN INTELLIGENT UNIVERSE

The reason why there is much resistance, defiance, animosity, discord, clashing, disagreement with, and indifference about the idea of consciousness as the source of all things is because this would imply that there really is a God, an intelligent and loving force.

Many scientists do not like the idea of a "God" as it is not something that can be easily measured, packaged, identified or quantified.

The Science of Consciousness

Science and Spirituality always had a difficult relationship.

However, as technical and scientific advances take us further, we are slowly discovering that this separation and conflict is another box, barrier and prison we have imposed on ourselves. It never actually existed.

But if there is a loving God, why is this planet and society self-destructing, apparently run by psychopaths and sociopaths? Why does one child struggle for food from Day One, while another bathes in a golden tub? Where is the justice in that? Why so much destruction, hate, violence, and injustice?

If we have to believe in an intelligent, loving being as the source of all things, then this would not make much sense based on the current reality we live in. But if we believe that CONSCIOUSNESS is at the base of all things, then all the sufferings, adversities, difficulties, hardships, distresses, loneliness, hurts, misfortunes and diseases we are presently experiencing would have to be a direct result of our own thoughts, emotions, words, intents, and actions in this life.

To clarify this point, I will add part of the Near Death Experience I had with the being of light during my motorbike accident.

ALL EVIL IN THIS WORLD IS A RESULT OF DUALITY AND HUMAN IGNORANCE

"If this is a consciousness-based simulation where everything is God, why is there so much evil, anger, war, and conflict in the world?", I asked.

"This reality is based on duality, which started when the primary consciousness decided to express itself; (more on this topic coming up) *and from one point of light, it becomes many. By creating space and time, you also create light and darkness as a duality, meaning you need darkness to see the light, feel sadness to understand joy, alienation to understand inclusion, and activity to understand stillness.*

The Quantum Field and Consciousness

All the beautiful, lofty, inspiring music you enjoy with your Walkman today (smartphones and mp4s did not exist at the time) is only possible because of the silence between the notes. Without the silence, there is no music.

One opposite needs the other in order for it to express itself. Dual aspects of nature are not evil, or wrong; they just are expressions of life. Most of the painful and traumatic experiences you ever had were milestones that helped you grow and evolve. Most of them were decided before your reincarnation on Earth. You, and the villains in your life have come to an agreement to help each other in this lifetime to learn lessons."

"Does this mean that there is no freewill, and everything is pre-determined", I interrupted.

The light being continued, "As you have the power to choose how to define your reality, life and destiny, you have the power to create and the power to destroy. Therefore, we could say that there are aspects of your life that have been pre-determined and agreed upon through the law of cause and effect, soul contracts and some that are left to chance, or the act of creative intention.

In reality there are no victims, villains, or heroes, just participants in the play of consciousness. Your energy field creates a magnetic resonance that attracts the people, places, things, times, and events that match your mental and emotional creation on a second-by-second basis.

This, of course, is very hard to see while you are in the dark valley of the soul, which is when you feel a sense of loss, sorrow, pain, anger and resentment.

Also, if you could read this field of resonance, you could potentially read the most probable future of any individual. It could look like pre-determination for a moment. This is due to the person's subconscious beliefs and how they interact with the environment. The roles they play deviate very little. If you think, feel and behave a certain way, your life will become predictable.

SAME BELIEFS = SAME LIFE

The Science of Consciousness

It is only when you exit the boundaries of the known that your life changes.

The three main characters we play in life are the Hero, the Victim and the Villain.

As love is the key to everything, most individuals look for love from the perspective of one of these three roles, which one adopts to gain attention and love.

Let me repeat this: "All there is, is LOVE and LIGHT!"

A person adopting the Hero stance will look for something to fix, like someone in distress, as this is how they gain the attention, recognition and validation that they need. The reward is a feeling good sensation or on a bio-chemical level a dopamine fix. They can take the form of the Savior, the Healer and the Carer.

A Victim, on the other hand, is a person who feels trapped, helpless or hurt by a Villain or a situation. They tend to put a blame on anything or anyone but themselves, and like having a Hero to come to their rescue. The Victim gets its fix through sympathy, as he or she is not interested in fixing the problem as the problem is necessary to gain attention, love and support from others. Their reward is also a dopamine fix.

The Villain needs a victim to channel the pain, discontentment or suffering they have endured in life. In most cases, the Villain believes they are the Victim and that is how they rationalize their actions. They get their fix from inflicting pain onto others as it makes them feel powerful, in control and validated. Often, the pain that the Villain has endured stemmed from an experience that made them feel weak and powerless, hence, they like to assert their power and authority over others. This exertion of power also increases the dopamine level in the body.

In the end, when each three personas are examined individually, you will see that what the Victim, the Hero and the Villain really needs is love. They will play the same characters over and over again irrespective of the movie's story line, until they tire of

The Quantum Field and Consciousness

playing the same role, and decides to take on a new character to play.

In fact, many of us have played the Victim, the Hero and the Villain at some point in our life or even play all characters simultaneously in one day e.g. You could be the victim in your relationship, a hero to your children, and a villain to your staff or work colleagues.

Having said all this, not all victims enjoy receiving the attention and sympathy from others. Some of them truly want to overcome their pain and struggles and are seeking ways to help themselves. In the same way that some heroes genuinely care for others and do not seek validation or recognition for their altruism. Comparably, a Villain, may unintentionally inflict pain onto others as a result of a knee-jerk reaction to fear and pain, which is often followed by guilt, resentment and regret.

The Hero's biggest fear is to become a Villain. Why because they will lose the love of the victim. Subconsciously, the Victim knows this and manipulates the Hero by making him (or her) believe that if the sympathy, attention and empathy are not supplied, then he/she has failed and will be labeled a Villain, and their love reduced or stopped!

All root fears are related to the fear of not being worthy of love.

Most of the evils of this world are related to unaware souls focusing on FEAR management. This is part of their evolution, where they only see and care about themselves, because their lives are governed by the limited mind (ego), greed and fear.

Fear of not having enough brings the desire for wealth and security.

Fear of being powerless brings the desire for power.

Fear of not mattering, not being good enough, brings the desire for influence, fame, and recognition.

All root fears are related to the fear of not being worthy of love.

The Science of Consciousness

Most people follow unethical commands from their leaders or superiors because they fear losing their acquired position, wealth, power and influence.

Do you want a good follower? Find someone who has a lot to lose. Do you want a society of hypnotized followers? Entertain them, or let them focus on fear. By doing this, they will focus on survival rather than sovereignty. By creating struggle, they will focus on trivial issues rather than the bigger picture, all while being trapped in a prison of their own making.

Only a few are willing to see the true meaning and purpose behind the charade of illusions. By far, the majority of individuals remain trapped and deceived in this illusion of lights, shades, and darkness, rather than further exploring the hidden mysteries of life. Because of all these struggles and limitations, this consciousness-based matrix often seems to be negative in nature; and as some may call it, evil.

Freeing oneself from the chains of dogmas and superstitions; from the pressures, constraints of the thoughts, opinions, rules, beliefs and bonds of other selves, is a necessary part of the awakening of the adept.

In the past, individuals that dared to speak out about this social dream and limited perception have been ridiculed, violently opposed, and even killed. These freed individuals were seen by those who were not free as rebels, different and ignorant as they opposed the status quo.

This is human nature, to fight anything that is not understood, unknown or feared.

Young souls do not yet understand that what you do to another you do to yourself. We are all one. There is nothing that is not God. Young souls do not yet understand that we are beings of light, living a physical experience, and that each thought, emotion, word, and action add to or diminish our light.

The Quantum Field and Consciousness

These fears and limited mind states need to be overcome for the soul to learn, evolve and expand," responded the light being.

You see, your body is just a flesh-coating, a garment, that you are wearing in this life. Furthermore, your body is a physical extension of your mind. These points will become self-evident once we cover Placebo, Nocebo, Multiple Personality Disorder, Past Lives and Reincarnation.

AN UNFORTUNATE SERIES OF EVENTS

Why refuse the concept of divine intelligence or consciousness as the base of reality?

Most of the scientific materialists I have met seem to have lost their spark, the zest for true life-potential and expression. They are so hurt by their own life experiences, or so burned by religious narrow mindedness and dogma, that they have pushed away (with a vengeance) any possibility of a higher source. Unfortunately, this has made them bury their heads in the sand, unwilling to even contemplate the possibility that life could be much more beautiful, purposeful and meaningful than they have given it credit for.

Many religions have been built upon politics, manipulation, the desire for power, wealth and influence. Only a few have kept the true and original teachings, unencumbered by greed and fear, or self-interest.

Hopefully, by now, you are getting accustomed to the idea that there is nothing that is not consciousness, nothing that is not God, a divine force or intelligence, expressed throughout all of entire creation. It is the expression of light and love, through different levels of densities.

All religions and philosophies are based on interpretation. When you remove all the chatter, opinions and beliefs, all is left is consciousness.

"Jesus answered them, "Is it not written in your Law, 'I have said you are Gods'?" ~ John 10:34

The Science of Consciousness

"I said, 'You are gods; you are all sons of the Most High.'" ~ Psalm 82:6

From this perspective, God is not an old wise man sitting on a cloud (we tend to create in our own image things we do not understand), but rather is the consciousness that exist in every expression of life, every speck of sand, every leaf, every bacterium, insect, animal or bird. Even a photon is a light particle of life. There is nothing that is not God. All is one, all is light, all is love — all is God.

It is very sad how much destruction, atrocity, annihilation and human slaughter has been justified on the limited idea of God. In the name of religion, fanatics have tortured, crucified, and killed more people (including defenseless infants, children and women) than most wars and epidemics in known history.

Although many religions have given hope and guidance to many individuals that were once lost, unfortunately, history is also full of examples where religion has failed humanity, destroying entire cultures through the false idea that "my rainbow color" (the analogy used at the start of the book), my perception of God is more valid than yours.

There is a reason for everything, and religion is one of the stepping stones that has helped us to reach higher levels.

I have many friends that are part of religious groups and you can see how their thought, words and actions are inspired by a higher source.

It would be great if one day all religions and philosophies live in harmony instead of competing with each other, and hope that leaders will realize that we are here to build bridges, not walls – and most religious teachings came from the desire to connect to the original source (God).

Bias, bigotry, discrimination, fanaticism, extremism, injustice, racism, sexism, unfairness, dogmatism, and narrow-mindedness is what has pushed analytical people like materialists to refuse

The Quantum Field and Consciousness

anything and everything that has anything to do with God, consciousness, and spirituality. It is not their fault, it is ours as a society.

So, it is no surprise that many of them have become atheists or materialists following the Copernican principle, stating that there really isn't anything special about humans, our existence, or our place in the universe. In the Copernican view, we are insignificant, inconsequential, irrelevant, meaningless, pointless, and purposeless life forms. Matter and physicality are real; all else are pointless speculation.

This is in drastic contrast with the idea that all creation is an extension of the divine intelligence and purpose. Everyone and everything have a place and a purpose in this magnificent tapestry of creation.

While there are quite a few theories that focus on a scientific materialistic point of view, there are others who have not been afraid to include consciousness as the universe's primary source and force.

ANOTHER, MORE INCLUSIVE THEORY

One theory that embraces consciousness, thought, and intent, has been attributed to three imminent physicists that have made incredible contributions to quantum physics. These are John von Neumann, winner of the Enrico Fermi Award, Bôcher Memorial Prize, Medal for Merit, and Medal of Freedom; John Archibald Wheeler, winner of the Enrico Fermi Award, Franklin Medal, Albert Einstein Prize, National Medal of Science; Neils Bohr, International Gold Medal; and Eugene Wigner, winner of a Nobel Prize in Physics, the Max Planck Medal, the Enrico Fermi Award, the Albert Einstein Prize, and the National Medal of Science for Physical Science. Their shared interpretation is known, therefore, as the Neumann-Wheeler-Wigner Interpretation, or NWWI.

The main idea beyond this interpretation is that consciousness is the precursor to and the fundamental causative principle of the universe and physicality — making them sound more like Tibetan mystics and Greek philosophers than scientists.

"If quantum mechanics hasn't profoundly shocked you, you haven't understood it yet." ~ Niels Bohr, quantum physicist

"It was not possible to formulate the laws (of quantum theory) in a fully consistent way without reference to consciousness." ~ Eugene Wigner in Scholosshaeur et al., "Foundation Attitudes."

"Observership" is a prerequisite for any useful version of "reality." ~ John Archibald Wheeler - Davies, *Other Worlds*

This theory is at the basis of all reality, and is what, so far, we are coming to realize more and more in this book.

A FEW POINTS OF CONTENTION

By now, there should be no doubt that consciousness is truly at the base of the reality we live in. But many scientific materialists in the field of physics have criticized and questioned this theory for:

1) Not explaining how this could be the case for the earlier universe, before consciousness had evolved or emerged.

2) Not explaining which organisms have sufficient consciousness to collapse the wave function.

Therefore, we will debunk these prickly points.

The first critique is the result of perceiving only humans and perhaps some animals as self-aware. That, for me, is a matter of not being able to see the bigger picture, and may even illustrate human arrogance. This happens often when we look only at one aspect of reality, and thereby miss the entire picture.

Let's use an analogy...

The Quantum Field and Consciousness

INTERPRETING "REALITY", A LIMITED VIEW

There is a very old story taught in schools all over India about six blind men (the cartoon on the next page shows only four), touching different parts of an elephant. They were asked not to move and experience only one part of this majestic animal. The four blind men, of course, had a different experience of what an elephant is, based on the part they were touching.

John Godfrey Saxe wrote a poem about this story, and the ending unveiled a nice summary of why people argue about their perspective.

*"And so these men of Indostan disputed loud and long,
Each in his own opinion, exceeding stiff and strong,
Though each was partly in the right, and all were in the wrong!*

MORAL,

So, oft in theologic wars. The disputants, I ween, rail on in utter ignorance. Of what each other mean; And prate about an Elephant Not one of them has seen!"

This also happens to most religions. Each great being who has had a great insight and reached a level of enlightenment will try to express their experience in words, using the level of understanding of their own audience.

"Religion is belief in someone else's experience. Spirituality is having your own experience." ~ Deepak Chopra

This is the same attitude that saw us believing that Earth is at the center of the universe and that humans are the only intelligent species in our universe, when there are at least 200 billion galaxies, each potentially containing quadrillions of planets like ours in this universe alone!

FIRST ITEM OF CONTENTION:

The first item of contention is not explaining how this could be the case for the earlier universe, before consciousness had evolved or emerged.

We saw earlier that without an intelligent observer, there is no matter, no physicality, no explicate order. This means that there must be consciousness embedded in all things from the start.

But what most scientific materialists do not take into consideration (as they have removed consciousness from the equation) is that there is nothing that is *not* consciousness, as we saw in the ice, water, vapor story. *Consciousness* is the observer, and there is nothing that is not consciousness, moving from one point of creative expression (the Big Bang) to the diversity we experience in the universe.

Just because a crystal or a mineral does not move or talk, it does not mean that it is not condensed consciousness expressing itself in the form of a crystalline physical object. In this case, consciousness is just more fixated, more still, less self-aware, than a human being.

"The stones are alive. It has not been so understood by the [people] of your culture."- Ra - Elkins, Ruechert, and McCarty, *The Law of One*, Session 2, question 4.

Even a small particle of light seems to be sentient, so there is nothing that is not consciousness or an expression of God.

"The simplest manifest being is light — or what you have called a photon." ~ Ra - Elkins, Ruechert, and McCarty, *The Law of One*, Session 41, question 9.

"Consciousness sleeps in minerals, dreams in plants, wakes up in animals, becomes self-aware in humans." ~ Rumi.

Even a subatomic particle can think and compute calculations, as shown with quantum computers.

The cells in your body are individualized entities with lives of their own. They have the capability for communication, digestion, duplication, and complex behaviors and human-like emotions such as fear and desire.

If everything is holographic in nature, and if one cubic centimeter (0.3937 cubic inch) of vacuum mass-energy can exceed the total mass of the observable universe by 39 orders of magnitude (as we will soon discover), then it is not difficult to envisage the idea of the Big Bang as an explosion of creative power through consciousness.

So, you don't need a human to be responsible for the earlier stages of the universe's development, as there is a higher intelligence, an observer who is not only aware of its creation, but also *is* the creation.

SECOND ITEM OF CONTENTION:

The second item of contention is not explaining which organisms have sufficient consciousness to collapse the wave function.

The Science of Consciousness

This (collapsing of the wave function) is based on the amount of coherence, energy, and direct intent involved. This intent could also be translated as a harmonious thought in line with the desired outcome. To explain this in detail, I will need to cover it in Part III, which I will do shortly. For now, I will leave this topic open.

So, if everything is truly conscious, and light is the simplest form of being, are there examples, case studies, and scientific evidence to prove it?

Yes, there are!

They will be the topic of the next chapter.

CHAPTER 11:
Light as the Basis of Consciousness Expression

"Every time you are tempted to react in the same old way, ask if you want to be a prisoner of the past or a pioneer of the future." ~ Deepak Chopra

CONSCIOUSNESS, LIGHT AND HEALTH

Whatever you see, whatever you touch, smell, feel, or taste, is a coagulation of frequencies. Matter, physicality, is just an interpretation of your brain decoding frequencies, as we saw in the last few chapters.

"If you want to find the secrets of the universe, think in terms of energy, frequency, and vibration." ~ Nikola Tesla

When Dr. Fritz-Albert Popp broke open a DNA molecule using ethidium bromide, he discovered that thousands of light particles — photons — rushed out. This suggests DNA is nothing more than a light-based hard drive, storing and moving light particles in the same way as a fiber optic cable would.[7]

So how much information could we store through this light in a DNA molecule?

In an article in *Science* Magazine by Robert F. Service, dated March 2, 2017, we find that: *"Harvard University geneticists George Church, Sri Kosuri, and colleagues encoded a 52,000-word book in*

---

[7] P.P. Gariev, M. J. Friedman, and E.A. Leonova-Garieva, "Crisis in Life Sciences: The Wave Genetics Response," *Emergent Mind* 2007: 44

thousands of snippets of DNA, using strands of DNA's four-letter alphabet of A, G, T, and C to encode the 0s and 1s of the digitized file. ...Researchers report that they've come up with a new way to encode digital data in DNA to create the highest-density large-scale data storage scheme ever invented. Capable of storing 215 petabytes (215 million gigabytes) in a single gram of DNA, the system could, in principle, store every bit of data ever recorded by humans in a container about the size and weight of a couple of pickup trucks."[8]

A projector uses light to send information, which we perceive as a movie; fiber-optic cable can transfer information through light too, as do microtubules and DNA.

Another aspect of Popp's discovery was that the amount of light contained in the DNA was directly related to the health of the organism. In areas of the body where low light was present, the tissue of the body had become weak or diseased. Another astounding discovery was that whenever we experience negative and destructive emotions like anger, envy, jealousy, and hate, our overall state of being, such as depression and stress, the DNA releases more light to compensate for the lower frequency vibrations of the thoughts and emotions experienced.

Stress, in fact, damages the light quotient and the body. Based on Dr. Popp's and Dr. Peter Gariev's research, healing occurs as a result of light being released by the DNA, which is then directed to the areas of the body that have been depleted.

In a scientific paper published in Ostomy/Wound Management by K.A. Wientjes, entitled 'Mind-body techniques in wound healing' (2002; 48 (1): 62-7) researchers at the Center for Advanced Wound Care in Reading, Pennsylvania discovered that negative emotions such as guilt, anger and lack of self-worth, slowed down the healing of wounds.

---

[8] https://www.sciencemag.org/news/2017/03/dna-could-store-all-worlds-data-one-room

Light as the Basis of Consciousness Expression

The same can occur in destructive and negative relationships, which was proven in a more recent study conducted by J. K. Keicolt-Glaser at the Ohio State University College of Medicine[9].

In this study, the researchers gathered 42 married couples to test the effect of healing on a wound in a conflict-free environment. To do this, they first created a small wound with a puncture on one partner of each pair, and then monitored how long it would take to heal. Then, at a later stage, the same 42 couples were subjected to the same wound puncture, but this time, they were instructed to discuss inflammatory topics like in-laws, money and more.

After examining the data, the results showed that it took an extra full day for the second puncture to heal, than the previous wound. In addition, a chemical called interleukin-6 (IL-6), a cytokine and key molecule in the immune system, also increased during the couple's argument. This meant that the conflict also negatively affected the immune system.

The relationship between conflict, stress and negative states can also be seen in the Chinese medicinal relationships between emotions, energy in organs and meridians.

EMOTIONS & ORGANS IN CHINESE MEDICINE

According to Chinese medicine, each organ emits a specific field of energy and a frequency resonance, which spreads around the body through the line of meridians.

As the physical body is a coagulation of mind, and mind is a coagulation of spirit, your thoughts and emotions play an important role in your overall health and wellbeing. Every organ has a certain frequency signature that corresponds to that of a

---

[9] 'Hostile marital interaction, pro-inflammatory cytokine production, and would healing', published in Archives of General Psychiatry, 2005; 62 (12): 1377-84).

certain emotion. Often, a physical disorder can be linked to a certain organ imbalance and the associated emotion. The reverse can also be true: an imbalanced organ can heighten the specific emotion experienced by an individual. It can become a vicious cycle.

For example, grief is the emotion of the lungs and the large intestine. On a physiological level, this can manifest and trigger a cold, a feeling of being energetically drained, and cause difficult bowel movement or constipation as a primal way of not letting go. In Chinese medicine, lung Qi deficiency can manifest as a result of unresolved chronic grief, which develops into depression. This could eventually interfere with the lung function and oxygen circulation.

Fear is the emotion of the kidneys and the bladder. Kidney issues often arise when we are dealing with fear, like a change in life direction, divorce, loss of a job and financial security, etc. When this happens, our kidneys struggle to hold qi, which in extreme cases can result in you literally peeing your pants. This is one reason why small children urinate in their beds; the fear of peeing and failing produces more of the unwanted behavior.

Anger is the emotion of the liver and the gall bladder. Emotions like resentment, rage, frustration, and irritability can damage your liver; chronic, headaches and dizziness can also become common.

Joy is the emotion of the heart and the small intestine. A lack of happiness and joy can also create problems in your life, as it means that you are not fulfilling your life's purpose and soul's yearning. When you experience this, the heart suffers and can develop palpitations. You can also feel stuck, mentally troubled and have difficulty sleeping. True joy and happiness nourish the energy of your heart and small intestine, which brings about the feeling of peace, calm, and restfulness.

Worry is the emotion of the spleen and the stomach. Most digestive problems that are unrelated to the chemicals or pesticides sprayed in our food, and are destroying the gut flora are the result of worrying and insecurity.

Light as the Basis of Consciousness Expression

The main reason why I raised the discussion on Chinese medicine and its interrelation between organs and emotions is to emphasize that thought and emotions are also responsible for the movement of light in the body. Let me expand on this topic.

Each time you feel a negative, limiting or destructive emotion, your body contracts that causes an imbalance within your system. The imbalance comes from the release of light resources from one organ to another. When the shedding of light from one organ persists over a period of time, its DNA photons becomes depleted, which increases its propensity for diseases or illnesses.

This is yet another confirmation that we are beings of light. This topic will be discussed in more detail in one of the Awakening series called, *You Are Light*.

LACTOSE INTOLLERANCE, A PERSONAL STORY

I will now digress for a moment, as this is an important point. Most individuals are not really gluten, wheat, or fructose intolerant; they are pesticide or chemical intolerant. How do I know this? I have friends who are allergic to nearly everything, but when they travel to other less-developed countries that do not use or have the same level of toxins and pesticides in their food, they are able to eat the "forbidden foods" without any ill effects.

Most artificial, human-made products create a disruption in a person's light field coherence, therefore, when ingested, it affects the organs associated with digestion and excretion.

I will share a personal story with you.

At one point in my life, I became lactose intolerant; being Italian, this was a travesty! I knew that I must have eaten food that contained so many toxins, heavy metals, and pesticides that they destroyed, disturbed, or impaired the intestinal bacteria responsible for digesting lactose. So, I got myself a variety of probiotics, drank Kefir milk, and yogurt. I have a Kefir culture that I have kept growing for the last 10 years now. After two weeks of taking it, I could eat small amounts of lactose products; then after two months, I tried the ultimate lactose intolerance test, which was to have ricotta, creamy pasta, ice cream, and a foamy cappuccino all in one day. Interestingly, I didn't suffer any ill effects.

My diet has changed a lot since, to more plant based, but I am only sharing this with you to showcase the importance of working with nature instead of against it.

If possible, grow your own food organically or buy them from an organic farmer's market. Not only do pesticides, heavy metals and chemicals destroy your gut flora, they also destroy the microbial flora of the soil, the oceans and rivers of our planet. This is also one of the major reasons why most soils have lost over 90% of their capability to retain water and provide nutrients in fruits and vegetables.

The more the soil is destroyed, the less vitamins, minerals and nutrients our food will provide.

The more the soil degrades, and becomes barren of water and essential nutrients, the more the multinational companies add pesticides and chemical fertilizers to jump start a new cycle. This method only adds more toxicity to our food. Although the pesticides do help prevent certain bugs from eating or killing the plant, their toxins are also being absorbed by the plant, including fruits and vegetables, and are affecting the birds, bees and other insects that help pollinate the plants. As they die off, their remnants end up back in the soil, our water system, and the air that we breath.

Now think for a minute... if we add chemical poisons to our fields, what would happen if the same compounds found its way to the rivers and oceans? Could it kill the algae and corals, reduce the oxygen in the water, increase the level of acidity and temperatures of the entire ecosystem? I will let you ponder on that for a moment.

Light as the Basis of Consciousness Expression

BULDING YOUR LIGHT PHYSICAL QUOTIENT THROUGH INTENT

Dr. Glen Rein, a biochemist in the UK, found that we can directly influence the amount of light stored in our body DNA, cells, and organs. In one experiment, he collected tissue samples from human placentas and had individuals project positive and negative emotions towards it. When an individual only focused on *feeling* any of those emotions, the DNA in the placental tissue did not change; its light quotient remained constant. However, when the sender intentionally projected emotions towards the DNA with the intent of projecting positive emotions, it changed.[10]

His research suggests that when elevated emotions such as love, compassion, kindness, and nurturing thoughts are applied with coherent intent, it increases the number of photons in the DNA, which causes a healing effect. At the other end of the scale, when non-elevating emotions such anger, frustration, resentment, anxiety, and fear were directed with coherent intent, these emotions extracted light out of the DNA molecule.

This incredible research demonstrates that when we direct certain thoughts or emotions on a certain person or event with coherent intent, we are effectively creating a bridge between us and the intended target. This, then, influences the target's light levels. Essentially, this is the real secret behind white magic and black magic; or light force and dark force in Star Wars terms. Not only is the level of Light the only building block of all that exists, but it is also the primordial point of consciousness.

"The simplest manifest being is light — or what you have called a photon." ~ Elkins, Ruechert, and McCarty, *The Law of One*, Session 41, Question 9.

In this context, light is alive, conscious, and sentient, and photons are the most basic forms of life.

---

[10] Glen Rein, "Effects of Conscious Intention on Human DNA," in *Proceeds of the International Forum of New Science* (Denver 1996).

The Science of Consciousness

This is also the reason why the first command of God in the Old Testament of the Christian Bible is: *"Let there be light"* Genesis 1:3 KJV

In light of all that we have discovered so far (pun intended), photons which are the base of all things, can store an incredible array of information, and are dependent on conscious intent to coagulate matter and relay information. Are there any other scientific evidence to prove the above points?

Yes — quite a bit, in fact. Authors have filled books with it, including Michael Talbot, Lynne McTaggart, David Wilcock, Gregg Bradden, J.Z. Knight, and Dawson Church, just to mention a few.

In this series, I have only included the case studies that I resonate with the most. So let's have a look at a few these.

HEALING AND BIO-PHOTOS

One of the experimenters of the effects of consciousness and intent, as a way to heal, activate and grow light photons in a body, is Bill Bengston, Ph.D., a professor of sociology at St. Joseph's College, New York. Although he started as a skeptic, wanting to prove that healing using intent and consciousness should be left to science fiction and New Age groups, he ended up becoming a believer — so much so that he also wrote a book on *Energy Cure: Unraveling the Mystery of Hands-On Healing.*

With the collaboration of another faculty member, Dave Krinsley, he designed an objective experiment to measure the effect of human energy on healing (Bengston & Krinsley, 2000).

Please note: lab animals are the unsung heroes of human evolution; to them goes my complete gratitude. I don't condone animal testing, but this research has helped unfold one of the most significant findings of our era, so I have included the research in this book.

The experiment was simple: some mice were injected with mammary cancer (adenocarcinoma), a procedure used in many

Light as the Basis of Consciousness Expression

other cancer studies. The longest any mice survived without intervention was 27 days (Lerner & Dzelzkalns, 1966). The experiment was designed to determine if they could extend the lives of the mice or have any other noticeable effects using the healing hands technique.

The group of mice in Krinsley and Bengston's experiment was randomly divided into two groups in order to provide for a control base. To avoid any contamination or healing influence, the control group was maintained in another building.

Bengston then held the cage of the injected mice in his hands and tried to project an intent for healing for an hour per day.

Two weeks into the experiment, all the mice developed visible tumors. Bengston was highly disappointed, and wanted to end the experiment; however, when Krinsley observed that the mice in Bill's care looked much healthier — moving around, eating, and showing no signs of behavioral change — he advised his colleague to continue. Bengston's mice looked and behaved very differently than the control group of sluggish, inactive mice, two of which had already died.

Krinsley recommended they continue the experiment, saying: *"Perhaps the treatment is slowing down the cancer, even if it can't prevent it. There's no record of a single mouse living past Day 27. Get one to live 28 days, and we'll have a world record. Experiments rarely turn out the way they're supposed to. That's why they're called experiments."*

Around the seventeenth day, something remarkable happened to the test group: their tumors started to visibly change. First they become ulcerated, with scabs replacing the hair on their skin; and by day 28, the ulcerations started to clear up, and their fur began to regenerate.

After another week, Bengston and Krinsley got a biologist to run some further tests, to check the condition of the mice and the cancer, resulting in an astounding diagnosis: the mice in the test group were all cancer-free.

The Science of Consciousness

After this success, Bengston selected a group of student volunteers with skeptical biases, who did not believe in the power of healing, and asked them to perform the same procedure in directing a healing intent on a new group of injected mice. This was to see whether their belief in healing had any effect on the results, or whether conscious intent alone could convey the same results. As it turned out, all mice in the injected group were also healed. Not only that, the mice also developed an immunity to adenocarcinoma. This means that if they were to be injected again, they no longer developed cancer.

So, why would healing still work with skeptics? Let's expand on this topic.

Bengston asked his students to write a journal of their experience and their personal thoughts. When he examined these, he learned that most of the skeptical students participating in the experiment thought that this experiment wasn't about healing the mice, but about testing *them*, the students. They believed that they were the subject of an experimentation testing how gullible, naïve, and unscientific they were.

The mice were without bias; they did not have an opinion on the entire process. They were passive victims of scientific exploitation and exploration, so they could not have influenced the outcome of the experimentation.

The belief that healing would not work did not stop the mice from getting better, indicating that it is the *intent*, above all, that is paramount. The intent had overcome the limited beliefs and biases of the skeptic audience.

Interestingly, the intention to heal also had physiological effects on the participants. The reported feeling their hands getting warmer, and feeling some kind of energy emanating from their bodies.

After these incredible results, Bengston tried something that was more outside of the box of conventional science. He projected healing intention into a bottle of distilled water, and then administered this water to a new batch of sick mice, believing that if intention was the main factor, then this could potentially program the structure of the water for healing as well. This method also worked. All the sick mice recovered and were fully healed.

After this, Bengston focused on healing intent from a distance — and even then, the mice were healed. Many experiments subsequently conducted that involved distant healing proved that separation between the healer and the patient posed no limitations to the process.

He then moved to human trials, with people who were sick with a range of different diseases, with great success.

"Energy healing does not appear to be confined by the usual barriers of time and space." Oshman, 2015. *Energy Medicine: The Scientific Basis.* London Elsevier Health Sciences.

In one of her books, *The Intention Experiment*, medical journalist Lynne McTaggart showcased six different studies using EEG and MRI to show the healing effects on brains scans at a distance. She concluded: *"The receiver's brain reacts as though he or she is seeing the same image at the same time."* (McTaggart, 2007)

"Skull and skin are not limiting boundaries of energy and information." UCLA Psychiatrist Dan Siegel, author of the book *Mind 2017.*

Dr. Daniel Benor has analyzed 191 different controlled scientific studies on spiritual healing, including healing on bacteria, algae, plants, insects, and humans. Sixty-four percent of these studies showed unquestionable, significant improvements on the subject treated.

The power of coherent healing and group healing will be shown in the next book in this series.

DOES THE HEALER HEAL OR DOES HE/SHE BECOME A COHERENT LIGHT CHANNEL THROUGH INTENT?

So, if a skeptic can heal, even at a distance, how is healing possible?

The answer will be quite revealing, once we see it in the context of light as a balancing coherence energy. If we are light beings living a physical existence, then by harmonizing the distorted or depleted light, we can heal a person. In this context, the healer is just a conduit, a medium, a channel creating coherence to allow the sea of consciousness to realign the sick organism, plant, animal, or person into balanced, ordered light.

Consciousness is light, light is alive, and light is also the creative expression of God, which will become more evident in the coming "Genesis of Life and Consciousness" chapter shortly. We and the source of light are one.

"Jesus said, If they say to you, 'Where did you come from', say to them, 'We came from the light, the place where the light came into being on its own accord and established itself and became manifest through their image.' If they say to you, 'Is it you?', say, 'We are its children, we are the elect of the living father.'" Gospel of Thomas: 50

We all come from the same father, as the Gnostics (the original Christians) taught; we all come from the source of Divine light.

"While you have the Light, believe in the Light, so that you may become sons of light." ~ John 12:36

A healer coherently channels the light-based, loving intelligence that is found everywhere. This is why in the Christian Bible and other spiritual texts, we find the concept of, *"It is not I who does these miracles, but the father who abides within me."*

"Believest thou not that I am in the Father (light), and the Father (light) in me? The words that I speak unto you I speak not of myself: but the Father (light) that dwelleth in me, he doeth the works." John 14:10 KJV

Light as the Basis of Consciousness Expression

This concept is further clarified in this channel material by Ra in the *Law of One*:

"The healer does not heal. The crystallized healer is a channel for intelligent energy which offers an opportunity to an entity that it might heal itself. In no case is there another description of healing. Therefore, there is no difference as long as the healer never approaches one whose request for aid has not come to it previously. This is also true of the more conventional healers of your culture; and if these healers could but fully realize that they are responsible only for offering the opportunity of healing, and not for the healing, many of these entities would feel an enormous load of misconceived responsibility fall from them." ~ Elkins, Ruechert, and McCarty, *The Law of One*, Session 66, question 10.

However, when you channel light but are discordant inside, then this powerful energy can have a detrimental effect in your body. Many healers, in fact, become coherent with the disease, rather than coherent with universal light. This can develop into illness or even death. Many empaths (people sensitive to others' energy fields and emotional states) can relate to the above statement.

"The point being that there are those who, without proper training, shall we say, nevertheless heal. It is a further item of interest that those whose life does not equal their work may find some difficulty in absorbing the energy of intelligent infinity and thus become quite distorted (sick) in such a way as to cause disharmony in themselves and others and perhaps even find it necessary to cease the healing activity." Elkins, Ruechert, and McCarty, *The Law of One*, Session 4, question 14.

My grandmother died of many diseases as she was healing people in the name of Jesus. She had the desire to help, but she empathized so much with the patient that she ended up absorbing the disease rather than allowing pure, Divine light as an intelligent force to move through her. Because of this lack of knowledge, she ended up damaging her body.

There is no real healer; it is the light doing the healing. We just function as a channel for this light to be moved through us by our intent. The intent creates the bridge.

QUANTUM HEALING: MELTING A TUMOR USING QI GONG

The transcript below comes from Gregg Braden's Science of Healing Workshop. He is a pioneer in the field of consciousness and healing.

"When we have a feeling in our hearts, we are creating electric and magnetic waves that extend beyond our bodies into the world around us. And what's interesting is the research that show those waves extend not just one or two meters beyond where our hearts reside, but many kilometers away from where our physical hearts are.

"So right now you are having an effect on the outside world many, many kilometers away. When many people come together with one feeling, it can literally change the world.

"It's only a miracle until we understand the science; then it becomes a powerful inner technology.

"This film below (the video clip is available in the member's area) was created in a medicineless hospital in Beijing, China. It shows a woman who has been diagnosed with a cancerous three-inch diameter tumor in her bladder. Western doctors said they cannot do anything, so she went to a clinic in China where they think differently and apply ancient wisdom to modern healing.

"There are three practitioners trained to feel just the precise feeling in their hearts — they create the feeling as if the woman is already healed. We get to look inside her body through a sonogram and watch her cancer disappear in three minutes in the presence of the emotional language that heals.

"What you will see is the woman is awake and conscious without anesthetic, and she believes in what's happening. On the computer screen we will see two images; one image is a picture *of the tumor and the other is a real time image while the healing is happening.*

"You will hear the practitioner chant a word. I want you to know there is no magic in the word (they are chanting "all is healed"); it could be any word. It is the word that they have chosen that tells them this is the feeling that heals."

Within three minutes, we see in real time how an inoperable tumor disappears. This is the power of intent and bringing light coherence where chaos, darkness, and unbalance was once present.

There are thousands upon thousands of cases of "spontaneous remissions," where incurable diseases, including cancers and tumors, disappear, and miracle healings are achieved through one's faith (on any religion) and the active intent of a group of people.

Prayer is a form of coherent intent; this is why many can testify the effects of it in their lives.

Although we say that believing is not the main ingredient for healing, belief can also bring healing in one's life. This has been proven in millions of cases through the power of Placebo and Nocebo, as we will see in the *Biology of Self* book of this Awakening series.

So, if everything is self-aware and there is a greater mind behind all life, then how does our intention directly interact with the field of consciousnesses? How do we manifest what we desire in our lives e.g. wealth, abundance, relationships, and health?

As this is one of the topics that is often asked in my live events, I feel it is fitting to address it here, in the next chapter.

The Science of Consciousness

CHAPTER 12:
The Art of Manifestation, from Wave Potentiality to Physical Matter

"You are what you want to become. Why search anymore? You are a wonderful manifestation. The whole universe has come together to make your existence possible. There is nothing that is not you. The kingdom of God, the Pure Land, nirvana, happiness, and liberation are all you."
~ Thich Nhat Hanh

We have just discussed how everything is connected through a grid of consciousness and light, and how the natural laws of the universe are so precise that even an infinitesimal change would prevent life as we know it from unfolding.

If we go back to the discussion about the origin of the universe, we can now see even more how the idea of the Many Worlds Interpretation loses its validity when one of the main laws of this intelligent universe is not taken into account: the Principle of Causality, a.k.a. "The Law of Cause and Effect." As a scientific materialist, you cannot just ignore this law and bury your head in the sand. It does not change the outcome; it is still there.

Manifestation can be summarized with the Tesla quote below:

"If you want to find the secrets of the universe, think in terms of energy, frequency, and vibration." ~ Nikola Tesla

This means the art of manifestation is nothing more than a series of laws that anyone can apply, as we will see shortly. The continuation of my NDE will further elucidate, clarify, and unify science and mysticism.

The Science of Consciousness

I will resume narrating my NDE experience in a moment, as the next part is extremely fitting at this stage of our progress. But I have to mention that this process of remembering became an interesting one while writing it. Let me explain.

While I was trying to recollect the experience to add it to this book, new concepts and references become available and visible to me. When I questioned this, I had an inner knowledge that this was because the light being can only use what is accessible (as reference) within the spectrum of my experience and knowledge.

Let's use an analogy. If I was asked to describe the flavor of sobolo, a Ghanaian drink made out of Rosella leaves, I would be at a loss for words, as I have never tried it. Even if I could taste this flavor in my mouth (during the accident), I could not fully recognize it or describe it.

As my paradigm of understanding has grown in the last 30 years, as well as my awareness, the message that came through can now be expanded. The way I would describe my experience a few days after the event and how I can describe it today is completely different. It is the same experience, just seen through a better, wider perspective and understanding.

Another interesting thing happened as well. As we saw earlier, this light being — identified as my higher self — has communicated with me off and on since the accident. I was responsible for this, as my focus oftentimes shifted into denser goals. The truth is, although it changed the course of my life, I did not fully review most of this conversation until the passing of my friend Joshua Crook. As I have become more unified, conscious, and awakened in the last few years, this light-based higher self and my personality have become more integrated, and information has started to come more directly.

"I love to think of nature as an unlimited broadcasting station, through which God speaks to us every hour, if only we will tune in." ~ George Washington Carver

Therefore, in writing this next part, I found myself downloading some information that was not part of what I knew during the NDE, but also comprised new insights that I could only have understood today, with the awareness and knowledge I have gained in the last three decades.

So stay with me, as you are in for an incredible ride!

ICE, WATER, VAPOR

Let's resume the NDE experience we explored earlier. To make it flow, I have added the last few paragraphs from the story present in Chapter Five.

And thus answered the light being: *"As ice and water are one, just at a different stage of density, and as water is one with the two gases, hydrogen and oxygen, just at a different stage of density, so are spirit and matter one, just in various stages of frequency and density.*

"All there is... is consciousness in different vibrational states.

"The different phases and manifestations in the molecules of the Divine body — that is, all the levels of density, expression, and physical reality, as you call it — are caused by intent, a dream of being. A desire, if you wish, to keep what the Divine intelligence desires in form. This form is the Divine intent expressed through thoughts and emotions clothed with matter.

"The Divine source's love is what you call the nuclear force, and partly gravity, and is what holds reality together; without this love and intent, Creation would fall apart. Each creative form, be it a child, a man, a flower, a rock, or an insect, has the power of intent. Intent is the creative force moving into motion the laws of creation."

Now the young man felt bold, and asked: *"Is my blood, then, identical with thy blood in composition and Divine essence?"*

And the light being replied, *"Yes, thou art one with God. All is one. Any form of duality or separation is an illusion. You are living in a consciousness-based simulation where your thoughts,* emotions, and intent create the nature of your reality. What you think and feel you become. All of this that you see before you, and all that you cannot see or perceive, has been made for you — to learn, experience, grow, and become perfected."

"So, is this the purpose of life?" asked the young Paolo.

"It is one of many, as it is through the expansion and expression of God in all its creation that it can experience itself!"

The young man understood, and said: "Now my eyes are opened, and I perceive that when I walk, I walk in God; when I eat, I partake of the body of the Divine; when I drink, I drink God's rivers of life; and when I breathe, I breathe God's spirit, as all that exists is within God's being."

And thus the light being responded: "You are grasping the unity of all things, and in doing so, the secrets of creation, as well as the formation of what you perceive as matter in your reality."

CREATIVE POWER & THE REMOVAL OF THE SACRED FEMININE

The young man asked next: "If there is no such thing as matter, and as consciousness and intent are at the base of creation, does this mean I could create and manifest everything I could want in the physical plane?"

"Yes, you could," responded the light being. "Furthermore, the creative powers endowed by the father/mother principle of creative expression are the same power within yourself. That is what is really meant by being created in the image of God, not a physical appearance. How could God be something, and not something else? A rock is made in the image of God; the same for a fish, a tree, and everything else, as there is nothing that is not God. You can't have one and exclude another. This was very well known by what you have called 'primitive' people, like the Native Americans, the ancient Celts, and other Shamanistic traditions."

The Art of Manifestation

"You mentioned Father and Mother principles as God. I understand it conceptually, but we are also told in Christianity that there is the Father, the Holy Spirit, and the Son," responded the young Paolo

"That was a decision made by Church leaders hundreds of years after Jesus. The idea was to remove the sacred feminine. But how can you have a father and a son without the concept of a mother?

"The sacred feminine become the Holy Spirit, but because many rejected the complete elimination of the sacred mother (especially those ones of the original Greek and Christian Gnostic Schools), Mother Mary become the sacred, holy, pure representation of the transmuted Sophia, the Sacred Feminine and Divine Mother. This was a compromise.

"The Divine mind has two aspects. If you wish to see it from a perspective of gender specificity, one is the sender, the other the receiver. The sender is the male principle, while the female is the receiving principle. This is seen as in all aspects of creation. The sperm is the male energy coming from the father; the ovum, the receptive egg, represents the female energy of the mother.

"The sun is the male energy giving light, and the earth is the female energy (the egg or ovum), transforming that light into life and physicality. The Father, or male principle and energy, thus could be seen as the positive aspect of electromagnetic energy, with its active, creative, and radiant properties.

"The Mother, on the other hand, corresponds to the female or negative aspect of this electromagnetic energy. Its nature is receptive, welcoming, and nourishing, like the Earth. This was well known by the people of Khem (Egypt), and this knowledge was summarized in the form of the 22 sacred archetypes, known by you as the Major Arcana of the Tarot.

"This, however, is a greater conversation that we can cover later."

ABOUT MANIFESTATION

"I see. If I may go back to my original question, why can't I manifest what I desire in life? It does not seem to be working. What am I missing?" asked the young Paolo.

"Because your intent is not clear, your beliefs are in conflict — your thoughts and emotions are incoherent, and all over the place," said the light being. "Incoherent intent will always create an incoherent life. Your life is a mirror image of your inner self. On top of all of this, you can't keep your creation in focus and hold it for long enough to coagulate that potentiality from the infinite sea of potential (wave state) to your current reality.

"Until you are identified with matter, with the physical world, you will be subjected to its law of separation, duality, time and space, and space and time. This is one reason there is a time delay between your desires and their actual manifestation. If your intent were uncluttered, and you were in a state of unity — or what your society calls enlightenment — you could manifest anything in matter of milliseconds... or no time at all, as time and space would become irrelevant.

"The moment that you operate from a level of understanding where there is no you and the world, you and the other person, but you and you as all that exists, and that matter is spirit, then manifestations will happen in an instant. Time and space, space and time will then become pointless. You become the "Nothing" and the "Everything".

"Think of reality as a television screen full of tiny pixels that project what your mind believes and accepts to be true: your simulation, interacting and interfacing with other people's simulations. The quality of the image/simulation, the resolution of the image, is related to the level of coherence and the strength of your signal or intent.

"These very tiny pixels have been call by some "Planck particles". They are considered to be tiny black holes — correctly, because in their original state each is like a black dot, a pixel on your television screen, waiting for information and intent to tell it what color to take. They are empty of purpose, undifferentiated, like your body's T-cells or stem cells; neutral blank points of creation, waiting for an intent to give them purpose and a direction for creative expression.

"This tiny Planck Particle/Pixel might not be aware that it is forming part of a leaf, or of a hair on a horse's back, or a particle of gold in a gold bar. All it knows is that is part of a greater picture... In the same way, a drop of water is not fully aware of the larger, magnificent, glittering, imposing ocean if it stays identified with the membrane of its limited drop identity.

AUTHOR'S NOTE: The Planck scale is the smallest length unit by which space can be defined. This means that at its smallest level, the entire universe is made up of data pockets or pixels at the Planck length, with a resolution of the size of $1.616229(38) \times 10^{-35}$ meters. That is 10^{-20} the size of a proton.

"If every Plank Particle is a container for information, then this means that everything we know of is digital in nature, and therefore computable and can be simulated, like the simulated world inside a computer. (Or like the simulated reality in the movie *The Matrix*). *If this is the case, as many studies on consciousness have proven when conducted by your scientists* (and as we will review from different angles in this book), *then the entire universe is made up entirely of information only. This means that the entire creation, the entire universe, is an insubstantial place; all the physicality and materiality is a direct result of a conscious being interpreting the apparent effects of that information/data. We are all one, all part of the one consciousness, the one mind.*

(As Rumi puts it, "the world's existence is not in the world.")

"Nothing is actually moving, or even happening; all that exists is consciousness, mind. All is information creating an appearance of life, spacial movement, interaction, time and space. The simulation, the reality you believe you are experiencing, is just information present in the greater MIND of God, the Infinite Intelligence.

The Science of Consciousness

"In a very real sense, information as data/intent and light forms the substratum of what we call matter, and love (gravity and weak force) becomes the glue that holds that light and pockets of information together.

"This is the secret of manifestation and unity," responded the beautiful being of light, shimmering like a bright luminous opal in the night.

Perceiving that what it just said was not fully understood, it continued.

"Let's expand and focus on manifestation, using an analogy you have learned in your esoterical studies. Visualize your hands, both your right and your left hand. Position your hands at the same distance as your shoulders." (FIG.1)

"Okay, done," responded the young man.

"As you can see, there is space between your two hands. If you were to clap these hands it would take time, as both hands have to travel a certain distance to come together. In this case, space creates the illusion of time. You are defining time as the temporal medium through which to cover the distance between the two hands. (Between point A and point B.) This, then, is Time-Space, time defined as the distance needed to travel between two points. If you were defining space as a medium through which time travels, you would have Space-Time.

"The clapping, in this case, represents the manifestation of your wishes or the intent coming to fruition. Let's say you want to manifest wealth, abundance, and prosperity in your life, but you only spend a few seconds thinking about how good and easier your life will be if your financial situation would change for the better. Once that fleeting moment has passed, you spend minutes, if not hours, if not days focusing on how you will pay your bills, how you will find the money to pay for gasoline, and how much you struggle in your life, etc. Which one do you think has the greater probability to manifest?" asked the light being.

The Art of Manifestation

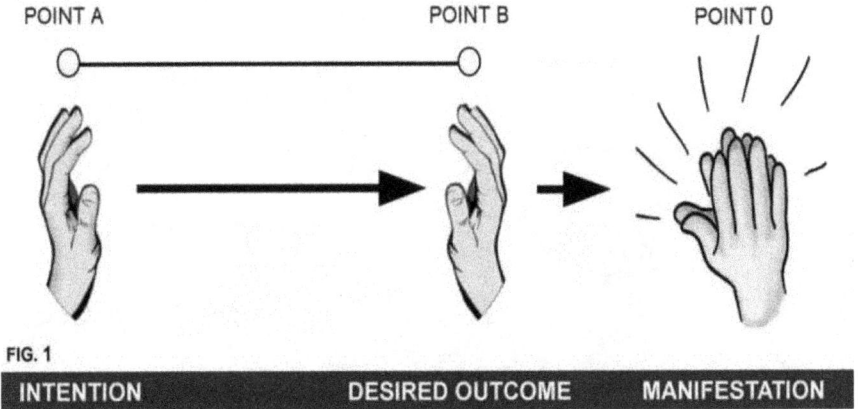

FIG. 1

"The one that I focus on the longest and express though my thoughts, emotions, words, and actions," said the young Paolo.

"Exactly! Your true desire becomes fragmented and lost in the chatter of all the things you do not desire. (FIG. 2)

"Every time you have a thought and emotion that is not coherent with your focus, your manifestation gets delayed, interrupted, hindered, suspended, or becomes irregular. At times, you can even go backwards.

"I am wealth and abundance (moving forward). I am stressing out about the next electricity bill (moving backwards). I feel powerless (moving backwards). I desire change (desire creates more desire; moving sideways or in a chaotic pattern). I am grateful for all the blessings I have (moving forward).

"The worst thought frequency you could have, since the manifestation has not come into your life yet, is that this Law does not work, or that for some reason has not worked for you. When you send out this thought as an energy ripple, you are nullifying your creation, making your new creative command, "It will not happen, it does not work," manifest in your reality.

"This will then become your new self-fulfilling prophecy.

The Science of Consciousness

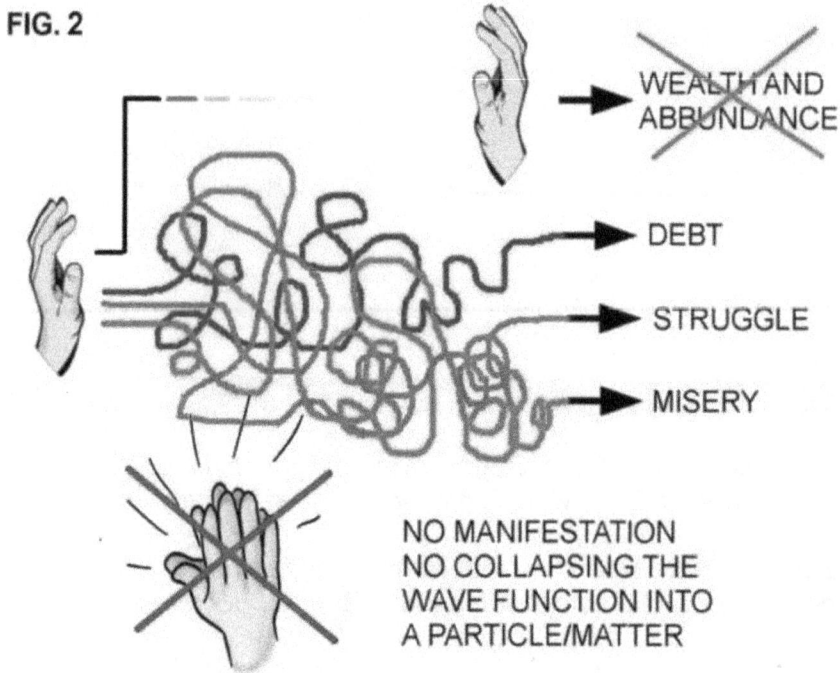

FIG. 2

WEALTH AND ABUNDANCE (crossed out)

DEBT

STRUGGLE

MISERY

NO MANIFESTATION
NO COLLAPSING THE
WAVE FUNCTION INTO
A PARTICLE/MATTER

"If something you have set in motion is not in your life yet, keep nurturing it anyway. Feel gratitude, joy; for if you truly understand the Law of Consciousness and the power of this Divine Intelligence, there would be no doubt," said the light being.

"Can you explain in more detail the art of manifestation? Are there any steps that one must take? Is there a limit to what this Source Field can give?" asked the young Paolo.

"Let me see if I can use a simpler analogy... Just scanning your mind for something you can relate to... Great. I will use cooking pasta as an example. You have chosen to be born as an Italian, so of course it had to be food! Let's continue.

"At the start you need to have a clear intent: "I want to eat spaghetti tonight," you say or think. That is your declaration, in the same way God declared "Let there be Light." Same principle, just at a different scale of creation and importance.

The Art of Manifestation

"Your thoughts bring up some of the memories of the color, texture, and taste of the pasta and the source you are going to use. This is seeding the sea of potential (the quantum foam, Source Field, unbounded consciousness) with an outcome. Without you even knowing it, you hear a train of thoughts, an inner voice, that tells you what you need to do, and even offers insights or ideas that were more deeply buried within your subconscious mind. Like: "I need boiling water to cook pasta. Let's put a pot of water on the fire, and I think I remember having some cream and some mushrooms in the fridge! Ah, I can use those! Great!" The entire dish has been actualized and prepared in your mind even before you have lifted a single finger.

"All this is happening on autopilot, so it's a default behavior for you. You don't fully realize how much of this is your subconscious mind trying to find the quickest and best way to fulfill your desired manifestation. Because this process of the subconscious mind finding potentiality is so subtle, you think it is coming fully from you. It does not compute, and therefore you give it no importance. Do you focus on your breathing or your heart beating? No; it is a default autopilot function. Because your subconscious mind has always been there trying to guide you, giving you "gut feelings", "heart alignments" or making you feel at ease when potentialities are in line with your soul and uncomfortable when they are not, you have learned to perceive it as background noise — when in fact is the most important guidance you could ever get.

"The problem is that most individuals have never taken time to learn what consciousness is and how it operates. Yet this is at the base of your life, your destiny, your body, and the entire universe. Let's continue.... Your next step after "Declaring" what you desire is "Taking Action" in the direction of what you want to manifest. You can feel and think like wealth, abundance, and prosperity are in your life, but you have to BECOME IT, even if it is not yet there.

"This will create a vortex of energy, an electromagnetic force (thoughts = electric, emotions = magnetic) that creates a request, a ripple effect in the Source Field.

The Science of Consciousness

"Practically, with our example of the pasta, this would equate to getting the pot out, adding water from your tap, putting it on the stove, and waiting for the water to boil. As this happens, you organize and prepare all the other ingredients. In the end you will be able to enjoy the spaghetti with butter, cream, and mushrooms, with some beautiful parmesan cheese on top. This would conclude your manifestation.

"Now, this might seem like a straightforward process. However, what happens in life is quite different, as humans are scattered, disorganized, chaotic, incongruent, incoherent, and most of the time they don't know what they truly want.

"The spaghetti analogy could be changed to getting a new car, a better job, a new romance, or more wealth and abundance flowing in your bank account. It does not matter what it is; the same principles and laws apply. This is true for the very small and the very large alike. It takes the same laws, principles, and energy to manifest one dollar that it takes to manifest one million dollars.

"The limit on what you can or cannot manifest intentionally is only limited by what you believe is possible. Most initiates start with smaller things that don't have much resistance, bias, and negative association for them, like a crystal or a flower, or maybe, if we use modern analogies, a car parking space. The more you believe something is possible, the easier it is going to be for you to manifest it into your physical reality.

"As to your last question... There is no scarcity in the universe. There is an infinite sea of potential; this is unbounded, unlimited consciousness, always ready to respond to creative and coherent intent. "Not enough" is an illusion. There is no limit to the amount of desires, wishes, and creative manifestations we can have. Therefore, fear and doubt should never be part of the creative equation.

"Failures in manifestation are not related to a fault of the law, but are the results of our own fears, doubts, and personal limitations. We need to learn how to become intentional, instead

of delegating to others our creative power, outcomes, experience, and destiny.

"Life is not a curse, or something that is happening TO you, but is an experience that is happening FOR you as a mirror of who you are. It's not an event, it's a process. It's not a destination, it's a journey. It's the accumulation of small creative acts. Everything therefore becomes a mirror of you. Money, for example, is a magnifier. Are you generous and kind, even if you have very little? If you win the lottery you will become even more caring and giving. Are you stingy with your money and jealous of other's wealth, if you win the lottery, you'll end up broke again in a few years, because what you are, you manifest.

"Wealth does not create immunity to pain and suffering, because these are caused by our attachment to impermanence, to duality and the sense of separation. All states are an act of being and therefore an act of creation.

"You have come here, into this plane of existence, to be, explore, create. All tools, resources, and the field of potentiality are waiting for you to call it forward and actualize it. This field is the mythical and mystical genie-in-the-bottle story, always answering, "Your Wish is My Command!" But unlike the genie in the bottle who can only grant you three wishes, the Source Field, the Divine, grants them all. As how could it not do this if free will were not in place?

"The genie in the bottle is an analogy. Each wish is a mirror of your being — your light, your darkness, your greatness, and your shortfalls, and also a combination of all your understandings and all your misconceptions and overall perceived reality. It is a story originally taught to initiates, a parable on human nature and the power of creation that we all are endowed with.

"We have been made in the likeness of God, the Source Field. Divine intelligence is just that; we have not learned how to use these powers intentionally yet. The power to choose, the gift of free will, is at the basis of all creative processes. "I am not strong enough", "I don't have enough time", "It's great, I would love to experience it, but it is not for me...", "It will never happen for me", "I'm not lucky enough" etc... are all self-imposed limitations and creative commands that the Source Field responds to.

"To those, too, the answer is always YES: Your Wish Is My Command.

"Don't wish to get out of debt, as you will get more debt. Don't wish to get out of a bad relationship, as you will get more bad relationships. Wishing and wanting only creates more wishing and more wanting. What it translates to on a frequency resonance level is: "I don't have it." As such, you attract more of the same.

"Let's say you want wealth and abundance. So you feel it with all your senses, and you become it, even if in your mind alone. At the start of the new desire, manifestation might seem like a lie, as it is not yet present; yet this is how all manifestations start, as thoughts followed by an intent and emotion. Let's use an analogy: The thought is the direction, while the emotion is the energy, the fuel to get you there. The overall intent is the coherent energy of thought (electrical) and emotion (magnetic), creating an electromagnetic field of attraction. Intention is a mental and emotional state that represents a commitment to carrying out an action or actions in the future.

"The pasta was an easy example. Now let's use a more emotionally charged analogy for the next one: love. You set the intention that you want to find a kind, loving, honest partner to spend your life with. You have declared it, and now the entire universe is moving to give you what you have set and declared as your intention.

"The universe does not speak English, Spanish, or Chinese, but frequency, vibration and energy. This means that the universe does not respond to what you want, but to who you are. It is a mirror of what and who you are.

"The idea of being with another person is very general. But you don't know how consciousness and the Law of Attraction works yet, so you declare that you want to meet a kind, loving, honest partner. You write it on a piece of paper as a list. Soon, after maybe three weeks, you meet a girl like that; but you discover

The Art of Manifestation

that she too is overwhelmed by debts, has not taken care of her personal image, she is overweight, scruffy, and has two children and a nasty, over-controlling ex-partner. You think the universe has failed you — after all, you are too young to be an instant father — but what happened was that you failed to be frequency-specific about what you want. You were not clear with your intention.

"Your mind is like a radio, constantly sending out information and receiving information. You can't turn a radio to a country music station and expect to hear classical music; it simply won't happen. You can't look for a vegetarian partner in a butcher shop. You need to have your intention matching the exact frequency, or very close to it.

"So you change your list to kind, loving, honest partner, caring, compassionate, physically attractive, wealthy, with no children. You love children, but this is not the right time for you to have them. As you read your list every night before going to bed, you start to visualize that this person is already in your life. Soon, out of the blue, a friend invites you at a party unexpectedly.

"There are no coincidences; you and your intention have created a ripple effect that created the synchronicities to make this happen, but because you do not yet understand the laws of consciousness, you believe it is just a random event, meaningless on its own. At the party, you meet a beautiful young woman who matches all the elements on your list. You are ecstatic, over the moon; you go outside and silently you start screaming yes, yes, yes! It works, and you do a little victory dance. As you come back and learn more about her, you find out that she is a bit antisocial, and depressed, and if that were not enough, she lives in another country, with no plan to come back to Italy.

Back to Square One! You don't like long-distance relationships, or antisocial behaviours, so you start your list again... This time you keep the previous characteristics, but also add other things you had not previously thought about, like: positive attitude, compassionate, successful, social, physically active as well as adding an age range (between 18 and 24), living in the same city.

The Science of Consciousness

Now the universe once again starts moving mountains, people, places, times, and events to conjure and coagulate this new potentiality in your life, and bring the best synchronicities to deliver this new person to you. There are multiple people who could match this description who become closer to your field of experience, but you are unaware of them.

"You go to a self-development event, and there she is! Spotless — every aspect in your list is there! However, although her frequency matches your desired outcome, you are still living in a "lack" mentality, struggling to pay bills, and focusing on when the next paycheck will come in. She might have matched what you desired, but you have not thought of what kind of man you must become to be a frequency-specific match for her. She is happy to be with you, even if you are not of the same status or financial standing; but because you are not in alignment with her frequencies, you start feeling unsure and anxious.

"The universe will always find your best match. So you ended up finding a girl who had one of her soul lessons relating to learning that she can't change another, and that she has to love herself fully before she can expect another to do that for her. From your angle, not being at the same level translates to insecurities like: she is too beautiful for me, I am not good enough for her, why would she want to be with such a loser, etc. Both your lessons are to learn that you are enough, and that you don't need someone to make you feel appreciated, accepted. That is your job. As the frequencies are discordant, jarring, and antagonistic, this specific relationship probably will not eventuate and either of you will end up sabotaging it.

"You need to become a frequency match for the other person.

"Wealth follows a wealth mindset. What you are becomes your experience. You can't get wealth, love, or anything in your life if you are not a match mentally and emotionally to that frequency.

"Now, I can see that you are confused. Let me expand on this... You can be poor and struggling, and still attract a successful woman. In the same way, you can be poor and struggling, and attract great wealth and abundance. The condition is irrelevant;

the state of mind and being are everything. Most of the wealthiest, happiest people have very little. Many of the most anxious, unhappy, lonely people are among the richest ones. Mind creates matter. Thoughts and emotions create realities."

AUTHOR'S NOTE: As I learned to manifest more and more as a result of this information, other resources, and personal experiences, many of my students have asked to create an expanded guide to manifestation (like how to create a list) that is easier to understand and apply. After much deliberation I decided to add it to the Member's area as an extra resource, and therefore it will be completely FREE for this book's members.

In this guide, I cover: visualization, mind-set, gratitude, quantum linguistics, how to deal with fears and doubts, how to tune into and trust, how to see emotions as your barometer and compass, how you can use them to greatly speed up the manifestation process, a list of powerful health, wealth, and relationship affirmations, how to change your limiting mind-set that might sabotage you, and much more.

The light being continued, *"On a temporal level, the future is created by your state of being in the now, not by the physical conditions where you live, or the balance you have in your bank account. What you focus on grows; what you resist, persists.*

"Humans spend so much time looking for someone else to love them, appreciate them, filling their void and sense of separation, without realizing that this is and has always been their own job. THEIR RENSPONSABILITY. How can you expect someone to love you and appreciate you if you don't do that with yourself? Like follows like. Life is a mirror.

"The more coherent you are with your intent — the more you become one with what you want to create by thinking of it, feeling the experience of it, being in it — the more you will attract that experience. Then you can interact with the God Source, or the quantum field of potential if you want to call it that, and make the waves collapse into a particle, or spirit collapse into matter, or energy collapse into physicality.

The Science of Consciousness

"Masters are the ones who are no longer concerned about time-space and space-time, separation, duality, and therefore they can bring forward whatever they desire. There is no conflict with what they wish to manifest. Their intention is clear, and their minds and hearts uncluttered.

"If we go back to the hand example, we could say that the distance between the left and right hand (creating time through space) is so close that the clapping (the manifestation of the desire into physicality) happens instantaneously," responded the light being (FIG.3).

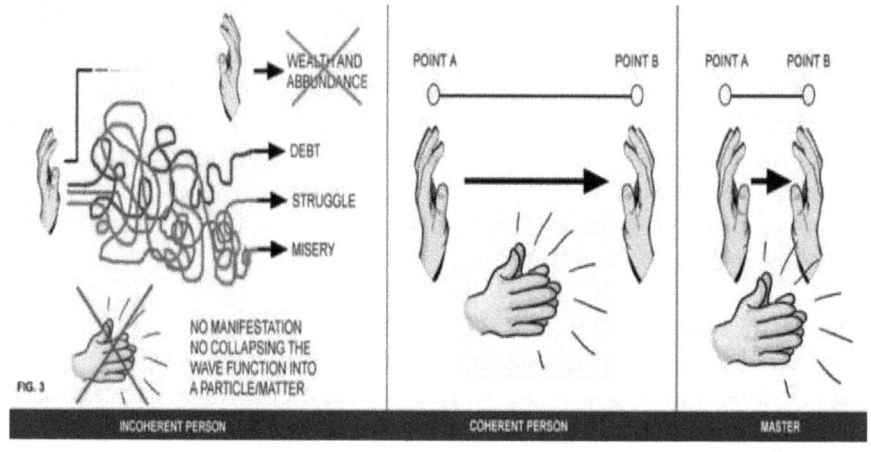

| INCOHERENT PERSON | COHERENT PERSON | MASTER |

"So would I be correct to state that the more coherent, the more aligned I am to what I desire, and the more I can hold my focus, the less time it will take to manifest a reality?" asked the young man.

"Yes, that is correct. There are universal laws in play; these laws do not have opinions, biases, judgments, or favorites. It's the law, and it applies to all in the same way as gravity does. An apple falls the same way as a knife. A good person would fall from a cliff in the same way as a murderer, following the same gravitation laws. Similarly, the laws of manifestation and attraction follow the same universal principles."

The Art of Manifestation

"What are these principles?" asked the curious young man.

"All is one; therefore, the response to all of your creative commands must be fulfilled by the law, as you are both the one declaring and the field of creation," said the light being.

"I don't understand," the young man replied.

"When you become one with all, the universe is yours to command — because the universe is not somewhere where you live, but part of who you are. It is part of your spiritual body. Whatever you ask of this Source Field, of yourself, the answer is always: YES. This will become clearer as you understand the holographic nature of the universe, its fractal properties, and how this Source Field (or morphogenic field of resonance) works. However, I can only communicate with you based on what you know, what you believe and perceive to be true, and what you allow yourself to accept.

"I am sharing this information so that you can research it after you remember this conversation. After you awake in hospital, it will take weeks, if not months, for you to remember everything. This is because the information has been integrated within your different energetic bodies. For now, I can tell you that, holographically, every infinitesimal part of creation contains all the information about everything that has ever existed. The way the universe is built is through light, and fractal mathematics. This will make little sense now, but will become much clearer later. Everything is made in the image of its creator. If we go back to manifestation, we could say that wherever your focus is, energy and creation will follow. What you think about the most, you bring about the most," answered the light being lovingly.

"Based on what I have learned, could I then assume that the amount of time it takes to manifest a new reality, especially when it is in full contradiction of what I am experiencing right now, depends on how much I can be coherent, in line with what I wish to manifest?" asked the young man.

"Yes," replied the light being.

The Science of Consciousness

"Even if it is not there yet, and my current reality is in complete contradiction with what I want to create — like desiring wealth and prosperity when I am poor and struggling? Or wanting health and vitality when I am sick or diseased? Is this correct?" asked the young man.

"Yes it is. However, every word has its own frequency signature that brings forward an outcome. So if your declaration says: "I want more money," what you'll manifest is more wanting, not more money. All declarations have to be made in present tense, because for God, time is irrelevant; the eternal Now is all that exist. If you focus on a future outcome, your desired manifestation will be always projected in the future and never in the now. Time is just a tool to express duality in this physical realm.

"Some workable statements or declarations could then be:

1. I am grateful for this day.
2. I am wealth, abundance, and prosperity
3. I am grateful for my healing and vitality.
4. I am worthy of receiving all life blessings.
5. My mind is full of brilliant ideas.

"Let me expand on that. If your beverage is too cold, you can add hot water. Hot water offsets the cold water, and makes it more neutral in temperature. If a friend is down, and you try to lift him up, you are using the opposite energy to neutralize its polarity. If someone is angry with you and you yell back, you are just adding fire to the fire.

"In the same way, if you are struggling, you need to focus on the opposite vibrational frequency — freedom, abundance, gratitude, joy — to neutralize it. Then, if you continue to focus on these positive intentions, they will not only neutralize the negative, but after a while they will take over your reality and transform your life, bringing light where once was only despair and darkness.

"Reality is made up of a sea of unbounded, loving potential. This potential is made of one base principle: consciousness or God, expressing Itself in the form of light and love. Light forms matter *on a denser level, while love is what keeps objects, matter, creation in a state of cohesiveness. Without light, there would not be matter. Without love, there would be no gravity or cohesiveness between particles and matter.*

"Consciousness, Light, and Love are the sacred triad or trinity, what in many cultures have been defined as the Spirit as an androgynous entity (consciousness), the Father principle (the light), and the Mother principle (the love).

"If your intention is uncluttered by dissonant thoughts and emotions, and you have a clarity of intent, can hold your focus and creative power for long enough to imprint this sea of potential, and can feel it like it has realized already; then the manifestation will unfold naturally and effortlessly.

The reason why individuals do not manifest their desires is because they do not understand the science of consciousness, the laws of creation, and how their focus, energy and intent seed the body of God," said the light being.

"I wish I could share this knowledge with everyone, as so many could benefit from it!" said the young Paolo.

"One day you will, Paolo. Most individuals have it all wrong. Instead of focusing on what they want, they focus on what they fear, dread, and what makes them feel despair, discouragement, and sorrow. What you focus on grows. Where your attention goes, destiny follows.

Instead, they should focus on the reality they want to manifest in their lives. If you plant weeds in the garden of God, the Divine principle will respect your FREE WILL and allow you to experience all the results and consequences of your creation. Every thought, emotion, word, and action is a seed of potentiality you are cultivating and growing.

This is a vibrational, consciousness-based universe. Everything in your life is directly or indirectly, consciously or unconsciously, the result of your thoughts, emotions and beliefs. Each one of these creates an energy field that magnetically attracts the corresponding energy and outcome," said the light being.

"What about infants that are born with certain diseases?" the young Paolo asked.

"As long as you see life as a one-time span from birth to death, as "get it right or you are damned," you will be unable to fully understand how every thought, word, and action creates a ripple effect that influences not only your present life, but also future lives," replied the light being.

"You are describing the Law of Karma, or Cause and Effect?" asked the young man.

"I am, but there is no animosity with the Law of Cause and Effect; it is just a law of magnetism. There is no judgment, no bitterness, no antagonism, no malevolence, no resentment, no favoritism; it's just a universal law that states that every action will form a reaction; every seed in the form of thought, word, or action will bear fruit.

"The reason why it is hard for individuals to accept this is because there is a time delay for most people between their thoughts, words, and actions, and the resulting outcomes. This makes life look like a series of random events, when in reality there is no randomness, no uncertainty, no capriciousness, no inconsistency, and no unpredictability.

"This is actually how you learn. Some of the results of your deeds take many lives to unfold and come to fruition; nevertheless, all is your creation. I know this can be a hard pill to swallow. Maybe one day, especially if you explore reincarnation, life after life, and life between lives, you'll see the beauty and perfection of the Law of Cause and Effect in action.

"The Father and Mother principles are wise beyond your comprehension; after all, how could you have imperfection from a perfect creator? All the perceived errors, suffering, and sorrow are the result of human ignorance in their path of self-discovery. This dualistic reality, full of contradictions, and the power of

The Art of Manifestation

CREATION and FREE WILL are the engines of evolution and are by design.

"You can't know light without darkness, sadness without joy, powerlessness without confidence, trust without betrayal, surrender without control. All are colors in the pallet of duality designed to help you grow and reawaken to your true nature.

"All the perceived chaos and randomness of life is a result of not knowing how we have created an outcome. All this misunderstanding is because most of us live without conscious awareness and intent. We live blind, unconsciously.

If you don't empower yourself by choosing consciously, someone else will do it for you. Giving your power away does not mean that you did not possess the power; it only means you have delegated it someone or something else. By not creating consciously, you allow others to do this for you.

"Most people blame others, and God, for not getting what they desire, when all they can focus on are adversities, difficulties, drama, misery, hardship, suffering, distress, sorrow, and misfortunes. Yet it is all their own doing. If you visualize what you want, if you truly focus upon a reality, you will manifest it. Energy always flows where attention and intent goes.

"To simplify it, we could say that there are four currencies in creation: Energy, Focus or Attention, Vibration, and Coherence. Think of your "Energy" as the emotional charge (Emotion = Energy in Motion) that helps you taking action.

"Focus" is the thoughts that you entertain, and the direction you need to take to manifest your desired outcome.

"Vibration" is the quality of your signal, as intent is transmitted to the Source Field.

"Coherence" is the capability of being congruent in thought, emotion, words, and action with the desired outcome.

If you are exerting any of these four things, but you are doing so in the wrong direction — e.g., focusing on debt and adversity while wanting wealth — you will not get the desired outcome. You will instead get more debt, suffering, wanting, adversity, and lack. What you resist persists, as there is where your focus lies."

"Can I ask more questions? Do I have enough time?" asked the young man.

"Time is relevant to the observer. Using your words; this experience can be slowed down or sped up. We could spend subjective years in this plane of existence, and only a few seconds might pass in your physical experience. Just as you can collapse the wave function into a particle, you can collapse time and space as well.

"For example: "Teleportation," as has been reported in your history, is the disappearance of the physical body from one place, and its materialization at another. This is caused by collapsing space between the two points.

"Bilocation" is being "physical" in two places at once. Before you start sharing this knowledge to a larger audience, you too would have to experience this directly, as well as collapsing time and accomplishing many more fascination phenomena, which the unaware call miracles. "Collapsing time" is being able to make time move faster or slower. Everyone does this unconsciously, every day. "Collapsing space" is similar, but affects mainly gravity. Levitation is something that many mystics in all traditions have mastered.

"Miracle healings" is what your science calls "spontaneous remissions," as they cannot explain them empirically or logically. The body is energy, frequency in a state of condensation. Change your mind, change your body. Lower fields of density always follow higher fields of density. Lower coherence always follows higher coherence. The mind will always respond to the heart. The body will always respond to the body's instructions. The more ingrained the illness, the more you identify with a disease, the harder it will be to change its state.

The Art of Manifestation

"The more you can see everything as consciousness and yourself as the creator of your own reality, the more the physical body, even if broken, can be healed and fully cured. Spontaneous remissions, placebos and nocebos, as well as individuals with multiple personality disorder, are an example of this.

"INCURABLE means CURABLE from WITHIN. IMPOSSIBLE means I AM POSSIBLE if I create the miracles, starting from a point of creation within myself.

"Impossibility is not a law or a fact, it is just an opinion. What was impossible one hundred years ago has become normal today.

"Many of your Christian Saints, Greek Initiates, Hindu Gurus and Sadhus, Sufi Masters, Zen Roshis, Taoist Sages, Tibetan Rinpoches, and Shamans knew these secrets and have performed these miracles in the past."

"I am so grateful, and honored, that such a beautiful entity would share so much of its knowledge with me. I am deeply, deeply grateful for this gift from the Divine," the young man said.

"There is no need to feel honored," replied the light being, "as I am you, your higher self, who just responded to a soul appointment that was decided much earlier than this physical life. I am always here, ready to answer, even after you go back to your physical body. In fact, the subtle voice that you been hearing, which you call the subconscious mind, is just me whispering in your mind. You are me in a denser state, and I am you in a higher state."

"But if I have such wisdom and knowledge as you possess now, and if I am you, why would I need a terrestrial life?" asked the young Paolo.

"Because as a singularity made out of consciousness, we need to experience reality directly in all its shapes and forms, to gain the true wisdom of the ages. You cannot just conceptualize about joy; you need to experience it to truly understand it. The higher self, myself, in this body of light, knows much of God's creation, but I have not experienced some of it directly to the extent that you *are doing now. I am also the sum of all the wisdom you have attained in all your previous lives. It is through personal interaction that we, as a consciousness singularity, yet present in many states of densities, can learn and expand. This is the same thing consciousness has done when creating light, spacetime, and the known universe. As above, so below; as below, so above. All of creation follows the same laws and principles. For this purpose, the higher self sends a part of yourself, what you call the soul, into a physical body to experience lessons, realities, and certain challenges so that true wisdom can be obtained.*

"Through unconditional love and the power of free will, you are given the authority to become the author of whatever story you wish to create. You write the script, you decide the location of the story, the actors, and the adventures and struggles you will face so that certain lessons can be learned. The part of your life that seems to be pre-determined is in actuality just decisions, soul contracts that you have made through the power of free will before this incarnation. In the end, the actors are irrelevant; your brother could have been your enemy or even your partner in a past life. Your former grandmother could be your daughter... It is not the role, but rather the lesson that counts. The main purposes of life are to grow, evolve, discover, explore and create, as has been done by the primary consciousness from the dawn of time," said the lovely light being (or should I say, my higher self?)

"How do I know if I am on the right path?" asked young Paolo.

"Follow what feels right; follow what makes you warm inside. Everyone has an inner compass that tells us when we are leading away from the path we have designed. Follow your joy, love, freedom, gratitude, and bliss. If you do so, your life will start to become magical, your light contagious."

"Do you have any practical examples?" young Paolo asked.

"You might have experiences in your travels to India and the Americas, of a master giving you a 'mantra.' This is a group of words or a sentence that has a special vibrational coherence. It has the power to unify. What most people do not realize when they read a spiritual or self-development book is that unique

The Art of Manifestation

mantras, specific to them at that time in their life, abound. Let me explain.

"When you read a book, for example, there are certain sentences that will resonate with you so much that you will feel elevated, you will feel like you are buzzing, your heart will feel different, and you might even sweat, your thoughts will stop for a moment, and you'll feel like that sentence is incredibly important. This is I, your higher self, highlighting that those words are a bridge between your conscious mind and your infinite mind. These can serve you as a mantra that connects you, elevates you, inspires you.

"Mantras, as frequency bridges, change all the time based on your understanding; so you will find that some 'mantra' sentences that resonate with you at one point might not have the same resonance and effect later on. This is because you are constantly in a state of flux, of change — evolution.

"It would be extremely wise to read a book or re-read it, and have a journal where you write down all those sentences as quotations that had an impact on you. As a form of mindfulness, you can use them as a tool for contemplation or as a mantra. These are all consciousness portals.

"Let us say you have been using, for example: "All is one, all is love, all is light, all is God," or "We are all connected, we are all one," and "I am a Divine being living a physical experience to express, create and evolve. I am Divine light, I am Divine love, I matter, I am worthy, I am the son of the Divine intelligence." These are all great ones.

"Each person will have their own mantra, based on their level of understanding and evolutionary level of progression.

"You are awakening. Until now, life seemed like a futile endeavor, a waste of time, and a perpetual fight in order to survive and acquire things of little importance that don't really matter. But as you start seeing life in its beauty, in its purpose to provide a mirror and a path for you to grow, evolve and become unified, all this reality will start to make sense.

The Science of Consciousness

"Paolo, you are unbounded, perfect, pure, unequivocal, Divine, glorified, holy light, and potential. You were born to create, to express this inner joy, light, love, and potential. All you have to do is to remember," the light being said gently.

"The more I understand, the more I feel at peace, comforted by the thought that not only is all God, but that there is a beautiful, perfect creation between the struggles and challenges of life; and that I am the author of my story, the creator of my reality, the director of this play. This is so beautiful. Thank You, thank you, thank you."

PART III: THE GENESIS OF CONSCIOUSNESS

The Science of Consciousness

CHAPTER 13:
We Are All Connected: Quantum Entanglement

"Life is a field of cosmic consciousness, expressing itself in a million ways in space-time through quantum entanglement." ~ Amit Roy

We have covered so much ground already; by now, many realizations should have lighted up your mind, soul, and spirit like fireworks on New Year's Eve, especially if you've read with an open heart and mind. But there are still many answered questions — enough, in fact, to fill over one hundred books!

One of the major questions I will address now, however, will clarify the genesis of life: where we came from and who we are. Only then can some sense of belonging and true peace be established. But before I cover the genesis of creation from a new perspective, I need to discuss the topic of quantum entanglement. This will be paramount to understanding our connection and unity with all that exists.

QUANTUM ENTANGLEMENT

This does not have to be a complex topic; in fact, you use quantum entanglement virtually every day. Have you ever thought about someone you care about, and all of a sudden they call, or show up again in your life unexpectedly? Have you ever come back home at an odd time, only to find your dog or cat waiting for you at the door? How did they know you were coming? Have you ever loved someone, and felt that something was wrong even if you did not see them or speak with them?

The Science of Consciousness

These three things are examples of a basic level of quantum entanglement.

When two fields of electromagnetic energy are so connected by thought, emotions, and intent that they start resonating with each other, they become in tune or in coherence with one another. When this happens, you have a partial form of quantum entanglement. The more coherent you are with the other person's energy, the more you can feel what they are experiencing. You are "in sync."

To have entanglement, you need two participatory, interacting systems; in the case of human interaction, this is a sender and a receiver. The strongest alignment, resonance, coherence, and quantum entanglement in human experience is the relationship between mother and child. The stronger the emotional connection, the stronger the entanglement.

This also happens when one particle is separated into two units, as shown in the picture in the next page — like monozygotic (identical) twins that have developed from one zygote, which splits and forms two embryos. If we move to subatomic particles, we can see how the same principles apply. Entanglement occurs when a pair of particles are either divided in two, interact, or share spatial proximity in ways such that the quantum state of each particle cannot be described independently from the state of the other, even when the particles are separated by a great distance. When these two systems, particles, or people are quantum entangled, they form a resonance between the two fields.

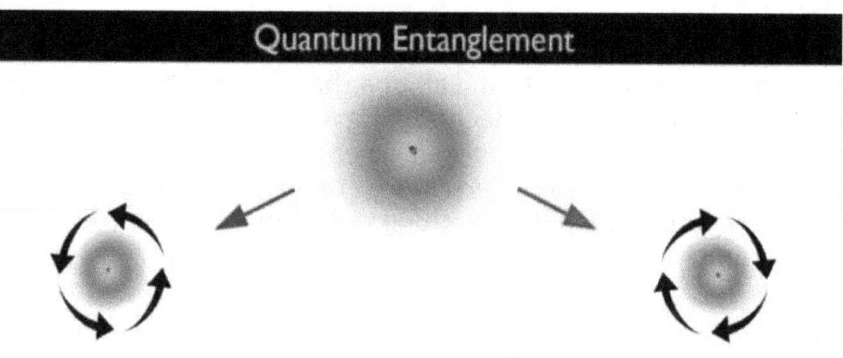

We Are All Connected: Quantum Entanglement

Consider two photons. Coherence results in a sort of frequency melding, a marriage of energies between the two particles. These now-connected photons can be separated by a large distance, hundreds of miles or even more, and still feel each and react when the other particle changes. If one of the photons is affected, no matter where the other photon is in the universe, the other particle changes too, without any delay. This influence and change happens beyond the limitations of space and time, like two radios that can now tune into the same station, even if one radio is in Italy and the other is in Australia.

But the story gets much more interesting. When this entanglement occurs, the two particles take opposite spins (dualistic polarities). So if one particle spins in an upward direction, the other will spin in the downward direction, as seen in the previous image. They become complimentary to each other. This again shows the dualistic nature of reality. In modern times, this has been achieved and observed using a Hadron Electron Ring Accelerator.

This quantum entanglement between light particles helps them remain connected, so that actions performed by one affect the other, even when separated by great distances. This phenomenon of instant communication, faster than the speed of light, disturbed Albert Einstein so much that he called it "spooky action at a distance."

"When observed, Photon A takes on an up-spin state. The entangled Photon B, though now far away, takes up a state relative, but opposite to that of Photon A (in this case, a down-spin state). The transfer of state between Photon A and Photon B takes place at a speed of at least 10,000 times the speed of light, possibly even instantaneously, regardless of distance."[11]

(For a visual of quantum entanglement, please see: https://www.livescience.com/28550-how-quantum-entanglement-works-infographic.html).

Modern physicists like Alain Aspect and his colleagues in Paris have demonstrated through rigorous scientific experimentation on

---

[11] Karl Tate, *Live Science* article, 2013

subatomic particles that the speed of light is not an absolute law when it comes to the world of quantum physics.[12]

A VISUAL REPRESENTATION OF QUANTUM ENTANGLEMENT

At the moment, with the small amount of context provided, we still perceive quantum entanglement as an invisible field that somehow influences whatever or whoever is in-tune with the same frequency. This can be confusing, so let's create a simpler analogy.

We can see wine glasses vibrating in unison if a certain note is played, or radios being able to tune in the same station, but that does not help us visualize this invisible force, so we need to use a different analogy. Quantum entanglement, as it was suggested by Puthoff, can be explained visually by two wooden sticks stuck in the seashore's sand.

Imagine a long, golden beach stretching for miles, with two wooden sticks 6 feet tall inserted a foot down into the sand. As you observe these sticks, a large wave washes over the entire beach with great force, knocking down both sticks at the same time. If you could not see the wave, you might think that there was something strange going on, as both sticks fell at once. You might even think it is some kind of spooky magic! But you would know conceptually, intuitively, that because they had fallen at the same time, that there must be some kind of invisible force affecting both.

If you can see the big wave, you know that the only reason why both sticks fell at the same time is because they were both hit and influenced by the same wave. The big wave is akin to a specific frequency in the quantum field. All systems resonating at that frequency will vibrate in resonance and therefore be affected.

This is very relevant to your life right now, so stay with me.

---

[12] Non-locality experiments by Aspect in 1982 in Paris.

We Are All Connected: Quantum Entanglement

In this light, all tuning forks modulating at a certain tone will vibrate in unison when hit with the same resonant frequency, and remain unaffected when other tones, frequencies not specific to them, are played. The quantum field is full of these "waves" interacting, modulating, oscillating with all that exists, and affecting only what vibrates at the same frequency.

Because this source field is not limited by time and space, if one of the sticks was on an Earth beach and the other one on a beach on a planet located in the Andromeda galaxy, which is 2.537 million light years away, the same specific frequency would knock them both down simultaneously — regardless of distance, as quantum entanglement and non-locality experiments have proven over and over again.

This, of course, would seem very weird if we did not understand the analogy of the sea wave knocking down the sticks, and were able to see the sticks fall on Earth and in Andromeda at the same time.

In this context, rather than two systems communicating generically with each other, we have two systems being affected by the same wave specificity with which they are both in tune. It is this specificity that has made the sticks fall, or the tuning fork vibrate. If the big "wave" vibrated at a different rate than the sticks, the wave, no matter how big, would not have affected them in any way. They would still be standing.

How does this apply to your life, you may ask?

Because you are not separate from the universe you live in, because you are part of all that exists, you interact with and influence all that exists. Every thought and emotion that you have has a frequency that compounds and amplifies the same thoughts, emotions, and frequencies, potentially in the entire universe. Time and space pose no limitation.

Each time you have an intent (coherent thought + emotion), for example, you are creating a frequency-specific wave that affects all the energy systems in that frequency octave.

"Frequency octave" is just a fancy term to explain a frequency signature that has two extremes, one high and the other low; for example, if we use emotions, we could say that sadness is in the same frequency octave as joy, just on opposite scales. Other such octaves could be hate and love, acidic and alkaline, sweet and salty, etc. Every time you have positive emotions like love, empathy, compassion, gratitude, hope, awe, and joy, you are compounding and amplifying these "vibrations" in the entire universe, as well as resonating, vibrating, and oscillating them in your field of influence (friends, family, workplace, community), bringing more light and more coherence to this world. Every time you have negative thoughts, and emotions like hate, anger, resentment, judgment, and envy, you are literally compounding and amplifying darkness, limitation, and incoherence in this world, proving once more that we are truly creators in our own right.

On a practical level, this concept has all kinds of applications. For example, every time a group of people watch a movie or the news together, the fields of resonance of all the people involved become in-sync and amplify the effects of the positive or negative emotions. The same happens with video games, particularly those related to violence, competition, or exploration. Remember, life is a field; whatever seed you plant will bear fruit at some stage, and will come back to you.

Someone who is full of life and joy can potentially cheer up anyone who is in a sad state. However, if the coherence of the sad person is stronger, then the joyful one will start to feel down, and eventually will become miserable. He/she will feel like their life source (light) has been sucked out of them. This is because the stronger coherence always wins. Have you ever been around such a positive, uplifting individual who is so full of light that it is virtually impossible to trigger them and get them to be upset? Well, their inner light, their force, and their coherence is so strong that they make everything better, more beautiful, and more coherent.

In life, however, we are normally more affected by negative people, who so love their hell and misery they cannot let it go. Sometimes the belief that one is a victim and that nothing good can happen to them is stronger than the belief in a better future.

We Are All Connected: Quantum Entanglement

As life is our initiation, if you find yourself drained by attempting to raise someone up, it means the other person has taught you that on a coherence level, they are stronger then you are. Their negativity and their desire for misery is stronger than your belief in hope, creation, and light. They do not want your help; they just want someone to confirm why they are right to feel that way.

There is always a payout. All humans try to avoid pain and seek pleasure. But for some, the pain that they know is less fearful than the potential pleasure that they do not know. Often, when pointing a finger and judging everything else outside of themselves, they don't notice that there are three fingers pointing back at them. By delegating their happiness and fulfillment to a power outside of themselves, they can avoid taking responsibility for the present moment, and avoid being accountable for their own life.

But I digress; let us go back to quantum entanglement.

All of the above knowledge tells us something else: every time you focus on or interact with anything (a loved one, a pet, plants) you are creating a frequency resonance: a quantum entanglement that lasts until you achieve the same frequency resonance. When you change frequencies (the inner vibrational tune you are playing), you will no longer be affected by older frequency fields.

Gambling is a frequency field, like jealousy, envy, and even alcoholism. If you overcome gambling or alcoholism and have learned your lesson, you become no longer frequency resonant, no longer entangled with that reality. When that happens, that wave of life and frequency, related to those limited states, can no longer touch you. You could be in a casino and feel no desire to gamble, or be in a winery and feel no need to drink — or be in a relationship that you are over with, and feel no more anger, resentment, or desire to interact with the other person.

EVERYTHING THAT CONNECTS ON A FREQUENCY LEVEL ENTANGLES

Everything that connects on a certain level creates a state of coherence and quantum entanglement. This is not limited to biological systems: even subatomic particles, machines, clocks, and computers have the capability to become quantum entangled. In his paper available in the member's area, Benni Reznik, a quantum physicist, has discovered that when two random probes interact, they form some kind of entanglement, like people do when they stare at each other for a few minutes or meditate together.

"We explore the entanglement of the vacuum of a relativistic field by letting a pair of causally disconnected probes interact with the field. We find that, even when the probes are initially non-entangled, they can wind up to a final entangled state. This shows that entanglement persists between disconnected regions in the vacuum." ~ Benni Reznik

All this suggests is that, potentially, there are three dimensions of coherence of this invisible Source Field. In the first one this field, which is also called the Zero-Point Field and Void, seems to be an ocean of dormant potentiality and energy (like a flat sea's surface, with no wind and currents) waiting for intent to coagulate it into form, as we will see later in this chapter. Second is a field where potentiality has expressed as a coherent form of information, frequency, and physicality. This creates an excitement in the field. And thirdly is a field that is excited but does not possess any coherence; its chaotic energy is waiting for a more orderly coherent force to give it direction, balance and order. This is like when we are incoherent with our manifestations, desiring wealth and abundance, but believe that we do not deserve them.

If everything that exists is bathed in this Void, in this Source Field, interacting and sharing information, then everything on one level or another is entangled, connected with each other, as we will see shortly.

We Are All Connected: Quantum Entanglement

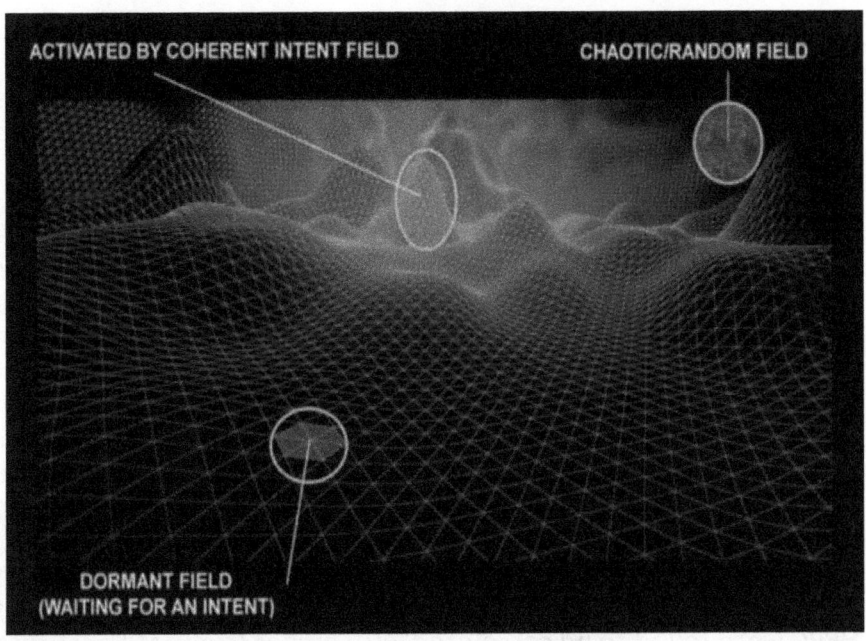

INTERACTING FIELDS

What most people do not realize is that our fields of consciousness are exchanging information all the time.

In 2007, an experiment conducted by Eric Leskowitz, M.D., a psychiatrist from Harvard Medical School's Spaulding Rehabilitation Hospital, proved this connection beyond doubt. He visited the Institute of HeartMath in California, and designed an experiment to see if his heart coherence field could be affected by other people.

At random intervals while Leskowitz was blindfolded, expert meditators behind him entered a state of heart coherence without touching him. When this happened, Leskowitz's heart coherence changed as well, suggesting that his field was interacting and even synchronizing with the people around him constantly.

A similar experiment was also conducted by Steve M. Morris.

The Science of Consciousness

"In 2010 another experiment by Steven M. Morris, Ph.D. examined whether a group of fifteen participants trained in achieving high states of heart rate variability coherence (HRVC) could influence heart coherence in a group of 25 untrained subjects in close proximity.

In a series of 148 10-minute trials using six different experimental protocols, three of the trained participants were placed together with one of 25 additional volunteers to test whether the three could collectively facilitate higher levels of HRVC in the fourth.

A probit analysis revealed a statistical relationship between participants' comfort with each other and trial success. Greater levels of inter-group comfort were seen to be positively linked to increases in HRVC. Evidence of heart rhythm synchronization between group members was revealed through several methods, including correlation analysis, coherence analysis, wavelet coherence analysis, and Granger causality tests. Higher levels of HRVC were found to be correlated with higher levels of heart rate synchronization between participants.

These results suggest that a coherent energy field can be generated and/or enhanced by the intentions of small groups of participants trained to send coherence-facilitating intentions to a target receiver. This field is made more coherent with greater levels of comfort between group members.

The evidence of heart rhythm synchronization across participants supports the possibility of heart-to-heart bio-communications." (Alternative Health Med. 2010;16 (4):62-72).[13]

So if we are truly living in a sea of frequencies — vibrating, oscillating, and waiting for an intent to express — is it possible, then, that at the source of all is also consciousness and intent? How can we justify the notion that at some level, to some degree, we are all quantum entangled to everything and everyone that exists? How did it all start — how, in other words, did the Divine,

---

[13] https://www.heartmath.org/research/research-library/energetics/achieving-collective-coherence-group-effects-on-heart-rate-variability-coherence-hrvc/

We Are All Connected: Quantum Entanglement

God, or whatever we have chosen to call this source of all things create this universe and reality?

These are some of the questions we will answer in the next chapter.

The Science of Consciousness

CHAPTER 14:
The Genesis of Life and Consciousness

"Our greatest human adventure is the evolution of consciousness. We are in this life to enlarge the soul, liberate the spirit, and light up the brain." ~ Tom Robbins

BREAKING THE SEALS

We been talking a lot about consciousness as an expression of God, yet most of us do not understand its origin. We will review this from different angles: religious, spiritual, and scientific, all of which will come together into a kaleidoscopic array of understanding.

The next few chapters are the only ones in this book where I'll go into religion a bit deeper, just to provide a point of reference. There are other books in the Forbidden Knowledge series where religious understanding and Esoteric Gnosis is covered in much more detail.

For those who dislike all religions and have an aversion to texts like the Bible, I ask you to see the references provided as a gleam of light coming through millennia of misunderstandings and dogma, rather than what you might have been used to. For those of my readers who see texts like the Bible as the inerrant word of God, I ask you to keep an open mind too, as most of the more esoterical, true knowledge has been misinterpreted, edited, modified, removed, or destroyed to keep the old narrative going by the ancient leaders of the Church in the first five centuries of the early Christian faith and consequent representatives of Catholicism.

I will also discuss other spiritual traditions, to show the commonality of the message when the literary dust, clutter, and gibberish are removed.

The Science of Consciousness

I am only using references from ancient texts to showcase that this knowledge has different layers of insights, learning, and wisdom. Some of this knowledge has been hidden for a long time, but has come into full view more recently through direct experience, archaeological excavations, and scientific discoveries.

It is time to BREAK THE SEALS that have been keeping the KEYS of true knowledge shut for millennia, in dogma, bias, misleading "facts," superstition, and ignorance. This is one reason why the PDF of this book is being made free for all. This will clarify where we came from; it will explain a lot about ourselves, our true heritage, sovereignty, and the process of evolution and involution, all of which are based on consciousness.

So let's begin!

Now that quantum entanglement has been put into context as an ocean of frequencies affecting resonant systems, we can move on to the creation of consciousness and the genesis of life, and unveil how the current universe and reality we live in began — answering the old dilemma of how everything came from... nothing!

POINT ZERO AND THE CREATION OF REALITY

We could say that God did it, but then we would be left with the questions of HOW did It do it? And WHO is God? Who created God? And also, WHY did It create the universe and our experience in the first place?

In this chapter, I will try to explain what I have personally understood through my direct mystical experiences, meditations, and the knowledge acquired during 30+ years of study and research. It will not be a complete picture, as our limited minds and understanding are still too primitive, inadequate, incapable, and lacking when compared to the greatness and magnificence of Divine expression. But I will try nevertheless.

In most spiritual traditions, Creation begins with a sea of infinite potentiality, described as a void or a dark space, without time, space, or limitations. This blackness is what Nassim Haramein, one

The Genesis of Life and Consciousness

of the greatest minds of our time, views as a sea of infinite potential: the SOURCE FIELD.

One interesting point about this Void comes from an unlikely source — the RA material, which is comprised of five volumes of audio recordings transcribed as text, channeled during the 1980s. This entity is the same blue avian depicted in Egyptian texts, described as the God of the Sun.

If you are interested in the RA Material, you can find a link for Book Depository here: https://tinyurl.com/y7l2bxqt and Amazon here: https://amzn.to/2KJNp1L.

Of course, humans tend to make gods out of everything that they do not understand, or out of beings who can display powers beyond the human comprehension of the time. Having a powerful flashlight lighting up darkness, a music player with loud speakers, or flying in a helicopter or using a shotgun two thousand years ago would have been enough to make any of us into Divine beings.

Individuals reading, for example, the *Book of Enoch* might easily think that they are reading the story of higher entities/alien abduction, which can be seen as angels in non-technologically advanced societies. A copy of this manuscript can be found in the Member's Area.

This "Ra" is just a very advanced entity with blue skin (a common theme among many advanced entities like Krishna, Rama, the Healing Buddha, etc.) who came to assist humanity to grow and evolve, as seen in the next illustration. I am using this non-scientific reference first, because it is one of the best descriptions of the genesis of consciousness and reality I have ever read.

In regards to the origin of the universe, Ra tells us:

"The first known thing in creation is infinity. Then infinity becomes aware... As the Creator decides to experience Itself, it manifests what we would perceive as outer space (the void).

The Science of Consciousness

As the Creator continues to experience Itself, It manifests Free Will and Love. The action of Free Will upon Love creates manyness.

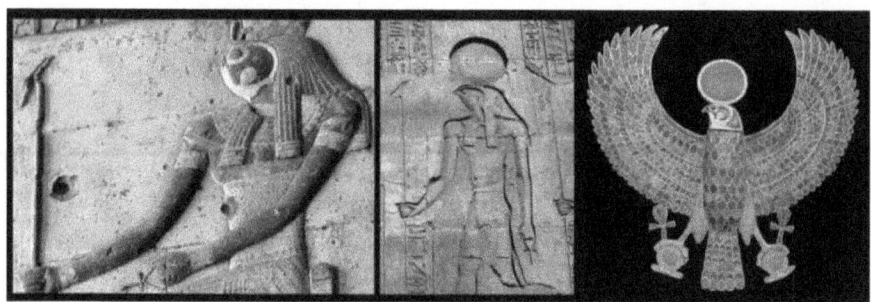

Manyness first starts out as an outpouring of randomized creative force (like a smoke, cloud, or sea of potentiality), *which then creates patterns, time, and space. The patterns of energy begin to regularize their own rhythms and fields* (fractal geometry and mathematics), *thus creating dimensions and universes.*

The galaxy, and all other material things, are the products of individualized portions of intelligent infinity. Each individualized portion of the One would become a Co-Creator and create a universe.

Each universe would evolve with its own set of natural laws. Any portion of any universe, no matter how small, contains, as in a holographic picture, the one Creator which is infinity." ~ The Law of One

Let us break this down further.

This explanation is present in different shapes in many religious and spiritual traditions. One of the most modern ones can be found in the Ramtha school.

At the beginning there was infinity, the VOID; imagine a dark space full of infinite potential — not dark or darkness as in evil or bad, but more like the sacred womb of creation, neither male or

The Genesis of Life and Consciousness

female. This is Divine intelligence, God unexpressed, and the Alpha, the origin of all things.

As it became aware of itself, it desired to be, and became a point of expression. This primordial INTENT was declared and it became so; it emerged from the Void. You could call this the primal point of consciousness, or "Primary Consciousness."

However, wherever this Primary Consciousness would go in the infinite void, there was no point of reference. As the void was infinite, whether this point went left or right, up or down, would not have mattered. It was always at the center of the void, as the void was all there was. No point of reference meant no time and no space.

This is state expressed very well by Nassim Haramein: *"In an infinite fractal (more on this later) of rotation, how do you define the center? Every point is the center. You are the center of the universe observing the universe from your very own center.*

"Wherever you pick a point of observation in the fractal, that point becomes the center from which you're observing the universe.

"That point becomes stillness. Why stillness? Because in that point now, all the spins of the universe cancel out... And that's how singularity occurs. Singularity is the point at the center of your experience of the universe; that is the point of stillness from which you're observing the universe."

This primary point of consciousness decided after a while to manifest a mirror duplicate of itself. This desire to create through Free Will and Love, as the Ra material mentions, creates the many-ness; or the many from the one. One became two, or "Secondary Consciousness"; this is Stage Three in the previous image.

Secondary Consciousness was a mirror image of Primary Consciousness, and in the same way that entangled particles have opposite spins and characteristics, so did the Primary and Secondary consciousnesses. You could say that one was the

The Science of Consciousness

negative of the other: again, not negative as in bad, but a complementary aspect of it, as with two quantum entangled particles.

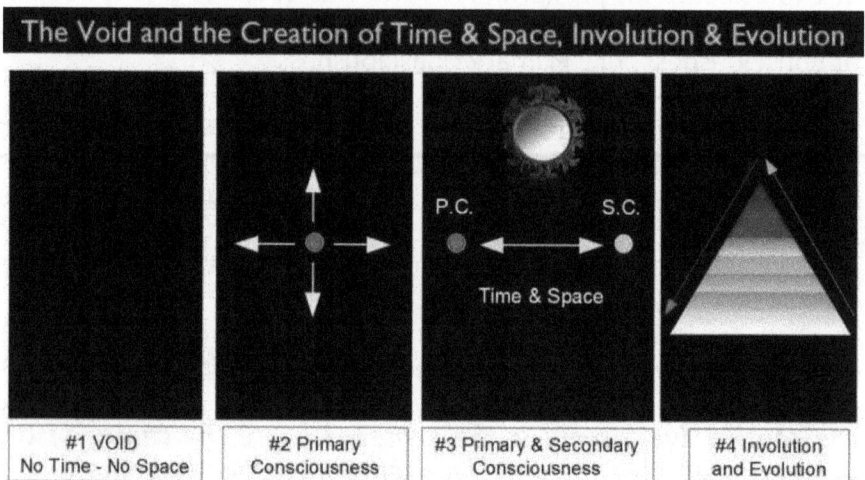

So we have, as shown in the previous image, this sequence:

1) The Void.
2) Primary Consciousness bathed in the Void.
3) Primary Consciousness creates a mirror self: Secondary Consciousness. In doing this it creates space and time, and duality; e.g. male/female, hot/cold, etc... the many-ness.

This is what scientist would call the Big Bang; from one, the many are created. We could also call these Primary and Secondary consciousnesses the Father and Mother aspects of reality. This dynamic and journey can also be shown from a quantum entanglement perspective.

THE OCEAN OF INFINITE POSSIBILITIES

I would think that it would be very hard to perceive, 5,000 years ago, consciousness as an unbounded sea of unlimited potential

The Genesis of Life and Consciousness

and pure energy. The narration, therefore, in ancient texts like the Torah (the Old testament in the Bible) would have to come close to what the recipient of the time could understand and/or accept.

Modern theologians and the Catholic Church have stopped seeing Genesis as a literal, factual story of creation but as an allegoric, symbolic tale, which further enforces the below point.

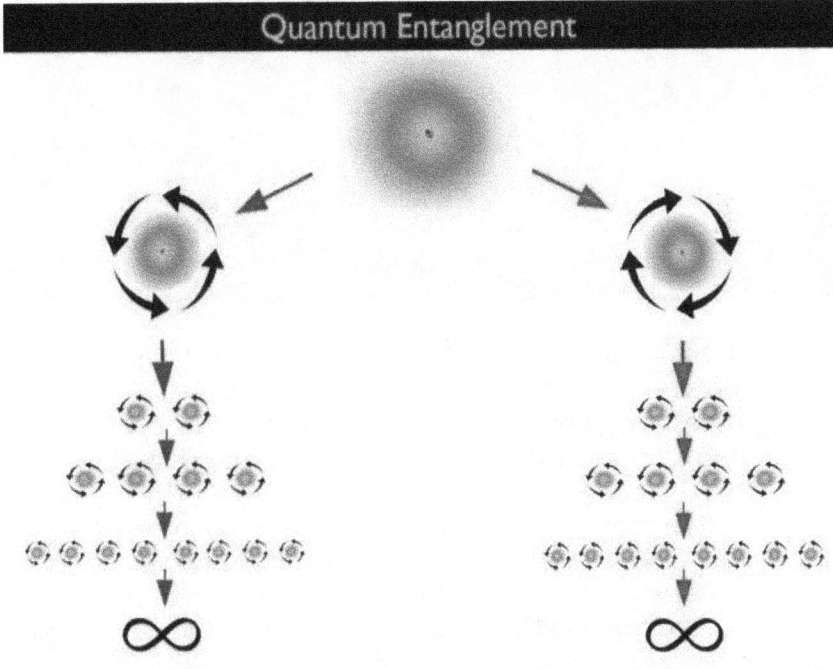

Scientifically, we can compare the Void or field of unlimited potential to the Zero Point Field, and to some extent, it can also be seen as the Higgs Field. In ancient times, the quantum wave fluctuation, the sea of unlimited potentiality, and the Higgs field and Boson particles in the source field could have been perceived as a sea, with waves.

This field of potentiality is also what, in Islamic view and the *Quran*, is described as a cloud of smoke. But for now, let us go back to the Old Testament and Genesis. I will translate, based on the context just provided in the last few pages, the first few passages of the Christian Bible.

1 In the beginning God created the heaven and the Earth. Genesis 1:1 (KJV).

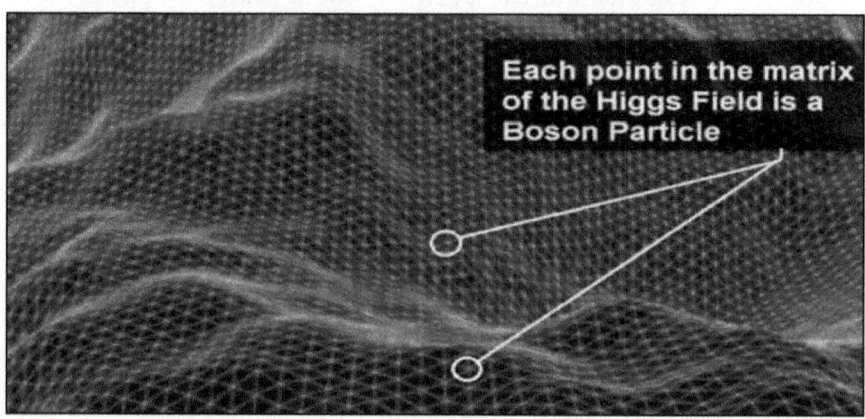

We start the first passage of the Old Testament with the first action of creation: separating from the Void, the ocean of consciousness and potentiality, a singular point of consciousness which in this frame of understanding is referenced as "Earth."

It is a point, a sphere (the Primary Consciousness not yet given full life/light). The heaven represents a dimensional reality (as normally heaven does in Gnostic knowledge), which is the space (the Void) surrounding the Earth/point/Primary Consciousness.

2 And the Earth was without form, and void; and darkness was upon the face of the deep. And the Spirit of God moved upon the face of the waters. (KJV)

This passage clarifies that the Earth is indeed not a physical, astronomical planet, but an energy field that is both empty and formless. The Primary Consciousness is not yet identified; it is a cloud of pure potentiality, a point of expressed consciousness. Therefore, it does not have mass and is void, because mass and fullness would require time and space, which have not been created at this stage.

The Genesis of Life and Consciousness

The darkness is the Void, the Divine womb from which all things are born. This deep darkness is like an infinite ocean, as the Spirit of God, now in Primary Consciousness state, can move upon it. Wherever it goes, there it is. There is no reference, and therefore there is no movement. Wherever it goes, it goes nowhere; it is the center of all, as space is not yet present. These waters are a representation of the WAVE state (sea/waters of potential) of the quantum field, as there is no ocean, no liquid present at that stage of Genesis; just heaven, the pristine Void, and a singularity of consciousness.

So like a boson floating in the Higgs Field, Primary Consciousness floated on the dark Void (see the previous illustration). This is further explained in Genesis 1: 6-7, as we will see shortly.

In Passage 3 of Genesis, we see that after the Earth was created, God seeded this formless space with Light.

3 And God said, Let there be light: and there was light.

We know that this formless point was seeded by light because of the next passage, which describes the seeding of the "Earth" as consciousness from a formless, empty point of awareness to the first point of light coagulating into form.

4 And God saw the light, that it was good: and God divided the light from the darkness.

Now that light has been formed, it distinguishes itself from the dark Void that surrounds it.

6 And God said, Let there be a firmament in the midst of the waters, and let it divide the waters from the waters. 7 And God made the firmament, and divided the waters which were under the firmament from the waters which were above the firmament: and it was so.

Waters, as we saw earlier, are a representation of the quantum wave-like state. This can be translated as the Higgs Field or the sea of potentiality, described in language that could be understood by primitive individuals through the spiritual experience, knowledge, and reference point of the time. Separating waters from waters, in a consciousness based simulation, means creating different level of frequency and density. These are also call "Heavens" in Judaism, Christianity, and Gnosticism, as we mentioned earlier. What we are told here is that a mirror image with quantum entanglement was created with the firmament above the waters and the firmament below the waters. This suggests that there is a scale (as in music) of different octaves of density, or heavens, as well as two polarities, like matter and dark matter.

We have here Primary and Secondary Consciousness, yet still without a fully creative power. It has the power to create by mirroring itself, but not by direct creative effort, as it has not been given this power yet, based on the Old Testament. Separating waters from waters is also the point where the one now becomes the two, and then the many. Like the entangled photons, one becomes the opposite of the other (higher waters and lower waters); the same happened with consciousness, now expressing as light and darkness, consciousness separating one polarity from the other.

Again, this darkness is not bad, destructive, or negative; it is just another form of expression, like matter and dark matter, cold and hot. This is the Secondary Consciousness, expressed as an opposite yet complementary aspect of the light (Primary Consciousness). Think of old-style photographs; you need the positive light and negative image to create a full-color image. This is the same concept. When this happens, time and space is formed, as now you have two points in space, creating TIME-SPACE and SPACE-TIME.

Why time-space and space-time? Because in this dimensional reality, we interpret time in relationship to space. Everything time-related in our physical life is defined as the movement in space, from Point A to Point B.

"I left home (point A), drove to work (point B) and it took me an extra 30 minutes (time)! The traffic was horrendous today!" we say to our colleagues.

The Genesis of Life and Consciousness

In the mirror "reality," this is reversed; there, space is defined in relationship with time. The same is true of all other forces, like gravity. The force that we call gravity, pulling objects together, is, in the other reality/dimension, "levity," pushing objects apart. This conflict between levity and gravity is everywhere, even when it is not visible.

This is a topic we will not explore here, as this might create confusion, and derail us from the topic at hand.

Based on the discussion in this chapter so far, we could say that the entire exercise of creation is for God, consciousness, to express itself through itself. And if you think God is not expressing itself, learning and evolving, but are part of an Abrahamic religion like Judaism, Christianity or Islam, then you should ponder the Old Testament in the Bible, or Torah for the Jews: Genesis, Chapter 1, Verse 4 again: *And God saw the light, <u>that it was good</u>: and God divided the light from the darkness.*

The concept of Elohim seeing that something is "Good" in comparison with something that is "Bad" establishes a concept of exploration through self-expression and manifestation. That is also the principle through which the prodigal son, the Jesus, son of Man, became unified, enlightened, as the son of God, or Christ Consciousness, or Sophia (the female aspect of Christ Consciousness in the Gnostic tradition), went into the denser planes of existence to learn and overcome the sense of separation and duality.

This concept of the primary God expressing itself is well established in all other religions, like Hinduism and Buddhism.

FROM ONE TO THE MANY

Back to the Genesis of Creation. By now, we have one Primary Consciousness that has created the many by splitting itself into complementary parts that we have called Secondary Consciousnesses. When this happens, as just explained, you have time and space.

The Science of Consciousness

Intent offers a frequency resonance, a blueprint that creates and modifies matter, life, and creation. This is why the Ra material mentions:

"Many-ness first starts out as an outpouring of randomized creative force, which then creates patterns, time and space. The patterns of energy begin to regularize their own rhythms and fields (fractal geometry and mathematics) thus creating dimensions and universes." ~ Ra, *The Law of One*

Now, within the Void, you have what scientists call dark matter and light matter, as we saw earlier. This light separates from the void, the sacred womb; and the creation of a second point of consciousness is what scientist have called the Big Bang, or the creation of the known universe.

The second point of consciousness is really the creation of the many-ness, as expressed in the RA dialogues. In fact, the moment that the ONE creates the MANY, you have time and space, and with time and space, as you go down the ladder of consciousness (heavens), you also have greater density, duality and separation.

THE PONTIFICIAL ACADEMY OF SCIENCES & THE BIG BANG

How does the Roman Catholic Church interpret this data in regards to the Big Bang? Well, you might be surprised.

Now, if some of the readers of this book still think that the Big Bang is a belief that goes *against* Genesis in the Bible, we can look at the first person who suggested this theory. In 1603, as scientific evidence was knocking loudly on the door of dogma, a Roman prince, Federico Cesi (1585-1630), who was a botanist and naturalist, created an academy dedicated to science and named Galileo Galilei as its president. This was the Academy of Lynxes.

This research institution dissolved after the death of its founder, but was recreated by Pope Pius IX in 1847 and given the name Accademia Pontificia dei Nuovi Lincei ("Pontifical Academy of the New Lynxes"). It was later refounded in 1936 by Pope Pius XI, and given a new name: The Pontifical Academy of Sciences. This academy aimed, and still aims, to promote the progress of the mathematical, physical, and natural sciences and the study of related epistemological problems.

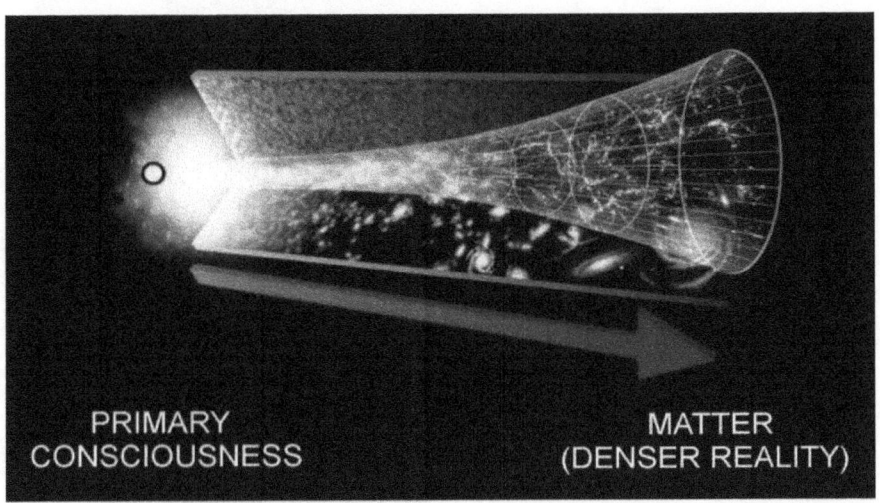

FROM THE ONE -----------> TO THE MANY

Georges Henri Joseph Édouard Lemaître (1894-1966) was a Jesuit-trained Belgian Catholic priest, mathematician, astronomer, and professor of physics at the Catholic University of Louvain. He was the first to identify that the recession of nearby galaxies can be explained by a theory of an expanding universe (the Big Bang theory), which was observationally confirmed soon afterwards by Edwin Hubble.

He was the first to derive what is now known as Hubble's Law, or the Hubble-Lemaître Law. Lemaître also proposed what later became known as the "Big Bang theory" of the origin of the universe, initially calling it the "hypothesis of the primeval atom."

Today the Roman Catholic Church has acknowledged that it no longer sees the Biblical creation in Genesis as a literal, factual explanation, but a figurative, allegorical one. In fact, the entire Bible seems to be allegorical in nature, as we will see in the Path of the Initiate and the God Code books.

Even what we think is literal, like a simple prayer, might in fact be completely different in meaning, as we will see in the next chapter.

AN IMPORTANT REALIZATION...

All of this ties together with the concept of creation. If we go back to the Big Bang, there is a vital, incredibly important realization about this split from the one to the many (from Primary Consciousness to Secondary Consciousness), which is that all creation is quantum entangled with the first point of light, or the first point of GOD'S expression as a singularity.

All that exists, visible and invisible in the explicate, unfolded realm of reality, comes from one single point of light exploding, expanding into the many (what scientists call the Big Bang). This unveils a great important point, which is:

WE ARE ALL ONE; WE ARE ALL CONNECTED. WHAT YOU DO TO ANOTHER YOU ARE DOING TO YOURSELF.

"You are every thing, every being, every emotion, every event, every situation. You are unity. You are infinity. You are love/light, light/love. You are. This is the Law of One." 1.6 Ra, The Law of One.

This will become very clear when the holographic nature of reality and the fractal structure of the universe are covered in much greater detail in the next few chapters.

THE DIVINE VEDIC TRINITY

No matter what ancient tradition you consider, some aspect of all we have discussed here is also present in their philosophies.

On a deeper level, the genesis of consciousness leaves us with three definite aspects. First, an infinite sea of potential without start or end, absent of time and space, or the Void. Secondly, an aspect of light as a creative force. Thirdly, we have an aspect of darkness as a balancing energy that has the potential to create and also destroy.

This action of destruction is visible in black holes, recycling and transmuting light and gravity into pure void potentiality. The same concept is present in light matter being destroyed by dark matter. This destruction is not evil as such, just a representations of cycles ending and new cycles beginning. The Hindus, as well as the Buddhists, believe that there have been many Big Bangs, many cycles, and science seems to coming to the same realizations.

"...the Big Bang represents just one stage in an infinitely repeated cycle of universal expansion and contraction." Neil Turok, Physicist.

What the spirit world calls death in that realm is a rebirth in the physical realm. What we call death in this realm is a rebirth in the spiritual realm. There is no real death, just transmutation of forms.

This knowledge of these three aspects of the Divine is reflected in a few religious and spiritual traditions. One of the closer similarities is with the Hindu Vedas. In the Hindu Vedas, we find that before the creation of the universe, Lord Vishnu (the VOID) is sleeping in the ocean of all causes. We see again the symbolism of the ocean for the Higgs field. His bed is a giant serpent with thousands of cobra-like hoods. (IMAGE 1.)

Vishnu is the personification of the eternal, endless, unlimited sea of potentiality that exists forever, without any beginning or end.

While Vishnu is asleep, a lotus sprouts of his navel (note that the navel is symbolized as a point, like Primary Consciousness is considered the root of creation). Inside this lotus, Brahma (Primary Consciousness) resides. Brahma represents the universe which we all live in, and it is this Brahma who creates life forms and physicality as we know it.

Brahma is the personification of our temporary physical universe that was created in the Big Bang. From one point of light, all is

The Science of Consciousness

formed. When Brahma breathes out universes are formed; when he breathes in, all creation is collapsed within.

IMAGE 1   IMAGE 2

Now, this universe represented by Brahma is not a permanent universe. In the Vedas Brahma lives for 100 GOD years, and then dies, and a new universe (Brahma) is born, through another Big Bang. 1 Brahma year of is 3.1104 trillion human years; to put this into context based on calculation on the age of this universe, we are around the first day of the 51st year of the Brahma.

Within each year there are sub-cycles, what the Hindu call the Yugas.

Many such universes like ours exist in this sea of unlimited potentiality the Hindus call Vishnu. Vedas say that thousands of Brahmas/Universes/Big Bangs have passed away! In other words, this is not the first time the universe has been created.

The opposite of light, or matter, is dark matter. When a particle and its antimatter counterpart meet, they annihilate each other, releasing a burst of energy — a proof of Einstein's famous equation, $E = mc^2$, which revealed that mass can be converted to energy and vice versa. This burst of energy creates new form of expression; what is seen as death from one point of view becomes birth from another.

The Genesis of Life and Consciousness

This destroying effect is called Shiva in Hindu texts, leaving us with a trinity of gods: Vishnu (the foundation of all that exist, and the preserver), Brahma (the creator of physicality and universes), and Shiva (the destroyer). (IMAGE 2)

It may be that we live in an endless universe, both in space and in time. There have been many Big Bangs in the past, and there will be many Big Bangs in the future. The Big Bang is an explosion of creative forces, and in a way, light as information and life. This is one reason why certain cultures still celebrate LIGHT.

THE CEREMONY OF "AARATI" IN HINDU TRADITION

The arti (pronounced 'aarati') is one of the most important and popular ceremonies of the Hindu faith, and is often called the "Ceremony of Light." It is a prayerful ceremony performed as a form of thanksgiving, where devotees are reminded of God's glorious presence, providence, and their direct connection with Brahma, God.

In one of the prayers, which translates as: *"God, you are like my father, and my mother, you are my light, you are my life, I surrender my light (soul) to you,"* this legacy is remembered.

The arti ceremony is said to have descended from the ancient Vedic concept of fire rituals, or homa. In Sanskrit, the word 'aarati' is composed of the prefix 'aa', meaning complete, and 'rati', meaning love. Complete Love. The aarati is thus an expression of one's complete and unflinching love towards God. It is sung and performed with a deep sense of reverence, adoration, and meditative awareness.

As a practice, the ceremony of light involves waving lighted wicks before sacred images to infuse the flames with the Deities' love, energy, and blessings. Sometimes instead of flames from ghee-soaked wicks, the light from camphor is also used, as was done by the Judaic tradition in the Middle East.

Some ceremonies of light also involve honoring the five elements represented in the world — Space (white cloth), Air (wisp), Light (flames), Water, and Earth (flowers) — and symbolize the offering of the whole of creation to the Deity during the arti ceremony.

This is often followed by prayers sung in praise of the Deity while the wicks are waved. After the short prayer, the lighted wicks representing one's soul are given to the mother Ganges (the Ganges River) and surrendered to her flow and currents, representing the trust one should have with their soul, life, and destiny and with Divine intelligence.

The idea of Light and Mother and Father principles seen in Hinduism as differentiated aspects of God is not dissimilar from the early Christian Gnostic schools, and the Essene tradition of Light and the Cosmic Father and Mother.

CREATION IN ISLAMIC TRADITION

In the Quran, we see this act of creation as a cloud of potentiality, a cloud of smoke waiting for an intent — God's intent to coagulate it into different and denser states.

"Then He turned to the heaven when it was smoke..." ~ Quran, 41:11

Out of this homogeneous "smoke" — a quantum ocean of potentiality, which easily could appear as a moving, fluctuating cloud of smoke — God formed and separated each state from each other, like Heaven and Earth. This is also the representation of gaseous galaxies cooling down and becoming denser, or more physical, like steam turning into water and then turning into ice.

We also find this other passage in the Quran: *"Have not those who disbelieved known that the heavens and the Earth were one connected entity, then We separated them?"* ~ 21:30

Same visual, same concept, just expressed in a different way.

Now that we have covered all of this from different angles, we are left with one more item of discussion before we can close this chapter: at what level of intent/coherence does one create?

QUANTUM INTERPRETATION: THE SECOND ITEM OF CONTENTION

We left this topic open last time. Let's close it now. It might feel odd to cover it now, but it will make sense with the information we have just covered.

The second item of contention in our discussion on the quantum mechanics interpretation, in particular the Neumann-Wheeler-Wigner interpretation or NWWI, was not explaining which organism has sufficient consciousness to collapse the wave function — meaning coagulating something from the field of potentiality into physicality.

Based on what we have learned so far, as consciousness descends in density, it disconnects more and more from Primary Consciousness. It becomes more physical, and less self-aware. To further clarify this point, I will go back to the Ice-Water-Vapor story.

1) The denser the state, the more consciousness is in a fixed state; e.g., a brick is denser than water.

2) The more fixed the state, the harder it is to shape or change it into something else; e.g., a brick is harder to change than water.

3) Furthermore, the greater the change, the more energy is required; e.g., a brick requires more energy to change than water.

So we could say that a brick is more solid than an ice cube. An ice cube is more solid than water, which is more solid than steam, etc.

Collapsing the wave function or manifesting a "physical object" or even creating a "biological system" requires a level of coherent intent. So, which things have sufficient consciousness to collapse the wave function?

The one that can have a coherent intent strong enough and long enough to coagulate a possibility into physicality from the sea of unlimited potential some physicist call the Zero Field, others the Quantum Foam, and others the Mind of God. The more fixated a state of energy is as mass and matter, the more energy (intent) and coherence will be required to transform it into something else.

During day-to-day life, this principle applies to us as well. The clearer you are as an observer of what you want to manifest (i.e., collapse from wave to particle) in your life, and the more you can hold the intent in your mind as a blueprint, the easier it will be to unfold what you wish to manifest into your reality. The more coherent and laser-focused you are, and clear about what you desire as the observer, the faster the manifestation.

A bacterium will have a very limited amount of expanded knowledge and awareness to be able to collapse the wave function and manifest the food it needs, because that is not how it believes it can operate.

If everything comes from one point of light, super-condensed, and if everything is consciousness, then this primordial seed was also the highest point of coherent consciousness. So the only way we can answer clearly and see the design behind the creation is by understanding that all these levels, these densities, are hierarchical in nature, meaning the higher level, with the most amount of coherence and unity, has created the level below it, and so on and so on. If we look at it from this perspective, all these different levels, even on a spiritual sense, become self-explanatory.

The question: "Which organism have sufficient consciousness to collapse the wave function?" becomes completely debunked.

CHAPTER 15:
The Genesis of Consciousness: Involution and Evolution

"Those who do not move, do not notice their chains."
~ Rosa Luxemburg

INVOLUTION, EVOLUTION. AND DUALITY

If we go back to the genesis of consciousness, we can see that there is descent (involution) from energy to physicality, from spirit to matter, from wave to particle, from one density to a lower, more condensed one. This is translated in spiritual traditions as "Waters" and "Heavens."

This descent from the one (Primary Consciousness) to the many (Secondary Consciousness) can also be viewed with the story about the Ice, Water, Vapor, and molecules at the start of the book, but in reverse. The lower the frequency, the denser the matter (e.g., Ice); the higher the frequency, the more ethereal the form (i.e., Steam or Ionized Plasma).

This is the plane of matter, physicality and duality, where lessons are learned by reconciling paradoxes and opposites. In the same way that you can't understand light until you have experience darkness, or learn about silence without sound, or feel joy without sadness, you need one side, one polarity, to understand the other.

The creation of Secondary Consciousness was the first level of primordial complementarity. As we go down on the density level, however, this complementarity is seen as duality with a negative, unfavorable, opposing, dreadful, imperfect, deficient, and fallacious light.

This was a misunderstanding of many LIGHT-DARKNESS philosophies like Christianity, Jainism, Arianism, and

The Science of Consciousness

Zoroastrianism, just to mention a few. What you focus on grows. When you fight the mud, you get dirty; the trick is to rise above the mud or quicksand of duality. That was the secret many ancient philosophies did not fully understand or recognize.

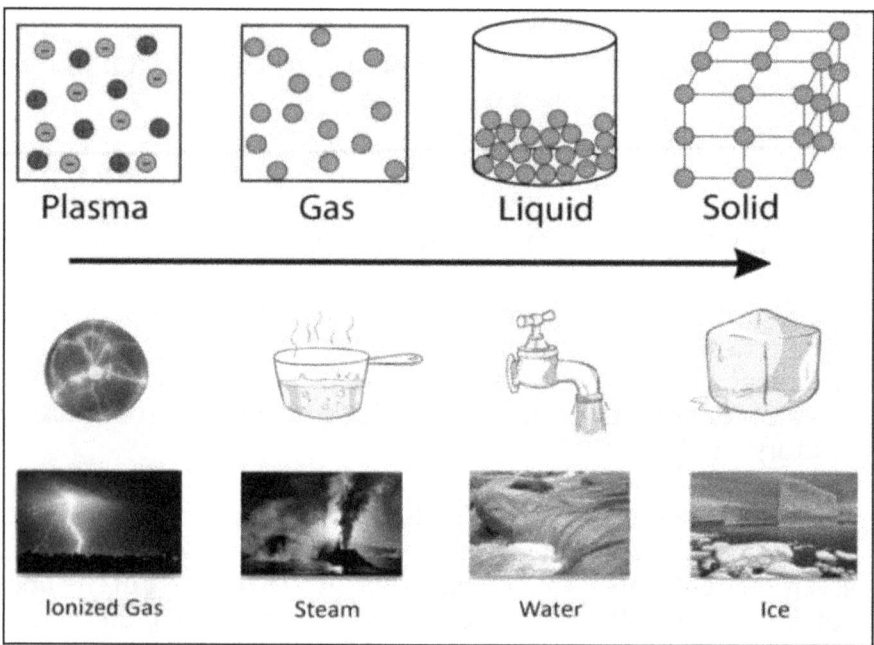

As any practicing Buddhist will tell you: *"You don't engage and fight the mind and thoughts; you just let them pass like clouds in the sky. The more you give them energy, the more all you will see is the clouds rather than the calm, blue sky behind them!"*

Some advanced mystics and masters know that this duality needs to be seen as complementarity, that opposites and paradoxes need to be reconciled. As Hermes Trismegistus said in the Kybalion while talking about the Principle of Polarity: *"Everything is dual; Everything has poles; Everything has its pair of opposites; Like and unlike are the same; Opposites are identical in nature, but different in degree; Extremes meet; All truths, are but half-truths; All paradoxes may be reconciled."*

Oneness, entering the "Kingdom of Heaven," or "Enlightenment" happens when we overcome the illusion of separation of the

The Genesis of Consciousness: Involution and Evolution

opposites and are able to reconcile the paradoxes of life. This is paralogical thinking, a state of being where opposites are fully reconciled, and the great play of consciousness is revealed.

This unification of these opposites has been depicted visually as the colors RED for light, fire, and yang energy, and BLUE for darkness, water, and yin energy. From a Christian perspective, we often see Jesus's tunic in these colors as well, as secret societies connected with the Gnostic knowledge, like the Essene, knew of the secrets of duality.

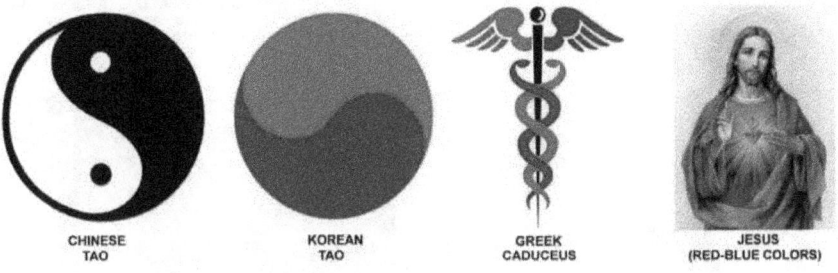

| CHINESE TAO | KOREAN TAO | GREEK CADUCEUS | JESUS (RED-BLUE COLORS) |

The Tao represents the union of opposites, happening at the level of the seventh chakra or energetic seal.

"20 And when he was demanded of the Pharisees, when the kingdom of God should come, he answered them and said, The kingdom of God cometh not with observation: 21 Neither shall they say, Lo here! or, lo there! for, behold, the kingdom of God is within you." Luke 17:20-21 (KJV)

Another representation of this union of opposites is seen by the two wings of the caduceus, which means the reconciled duality (red serpent, blue serpent) allowing the spirit (wings) to soar. This symbology of the wings is the Christian "Holy Spirit," which has also been depicted as the "Dove" descending on Jesus during the Baptism of Divine Fire.

In the east (Indian and Buddhist traditions) it is also seen as the opening of the Crown chakra (Sahasrara) with its thousand petals.

The Science of Consciousness

"All that is real in me is God; all that is real in God is I; The gulf between God and me is thus bridged. Thus by knowing God, we find that the kingdom of heaven is within us." ~ Swami Vivekananda

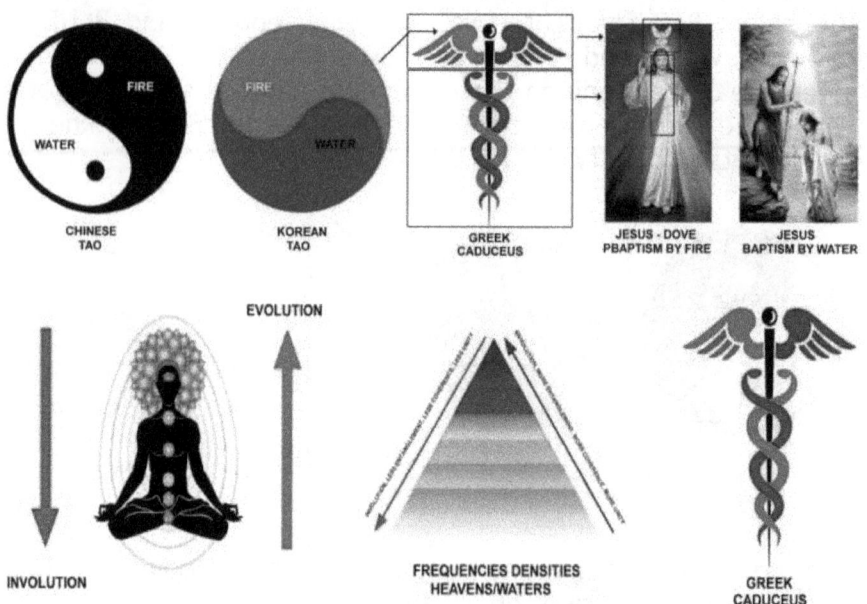

(3) Jesus said, "If those who lead you say to you, 'See, the kingdom is in the sky,' then the birds of the sky will precede you. If they say to you, 'It is in the sea,' then the fish will precede you. Rather, the kingdom is inside of you, and it is outside of you. When you come to know yourselves, then you will become known, and you will realize that it is you who are the sons of the living father. But if you will not know yourselves, you dwell in poverty, and it is you who are that poverty." ~ Gospel of Thomas 3, Nag Hammadi Library

This Gospel of Thomas was rejected by the church because it showed two things: First, that Enlightenment is an inner state anyone can potentially achieve. It is a union of the self when we recognize that the Kingdom of Heaven is inside of us and outside of us, as there is nothing that is not God. And second, that everything and everyone are the sons and daughters of the Divine Father.

The Genesis of Consciousness: Involution and Evolution

A PDF version of the Gospel of Thomas can be found in the member's area, under this chapter.

This is also true if we talk about our soul journey, our path back to the Source: from particle to wave, from a physical being subject to the separation of duality, to a unified, exalted, and perfected human.

THE MISTRANSLATED PRAYER ABOUT CREATION

"When setting out on a journey, do not seek advice from those who have never left home." ~ Rumi

As the above quote so eloquently exposes, many of the spiritual and church leaders who have come after master teachers, saints, and prophets have had no experience of the unity and connection with the Divine. Few have spent hours, days, months, or years in quiet contemplation and meditation to experience this Divine light within.

How do we know this? Because once you have a direct experience of oneness, you are so filled with understanding, compassion, and love that you would not judge, and you would not have the desire to divide and conquer. How could you kill another, for example, when you have realized through the experience of unity that the other is you, and that what you do to another you do to yourself?

Religion, unfortunately, is borrowed belief, not personal experience, and many spiritual seekers are awakening today to this knowledge and reality. By entrusting the "truth" to a middle man, you are trusting someone else's version of the truth, inevitably coloring all of your life choices — and therefore your destiny.

This can have very detrimental effects and greatly limit outcomes. When you experience this inner connection, the walls fall, and the bridges are built; furthermore, the limited identity gets expanded and the wheel of suffering created by the pursuit of duality starts to vanish. Many of the original, beautiful teachings of great masters have been lost in translation, modified to keep the desired narrative going, so that the churches of the time could gain power, wealth, and influence, and become the middle man, the delegate and spokesperson between God and us.

In this section, I will review the original lost secret related to the genesis of creation, in the form of an ancient prayer that literally billions of people are repeating, word by word, every day... incorrectly.

Let's look closer at this.

Jesus, aka Yeshua Ben Joseph, was a native Middle Eastern man born in Palestine who spoke Aramaic, a language related to both ancient Hebrew and classical Arabic. However, when one language is translated into another, many changes can be introduced, based on the knowledge and beliefs of the person translating the material, and the intent of the organization sponsoring the work.

Aramaic, like Hebrew and Arabic, is a multi-dimensional language with multiple meanings, not as black-and-white as Greek, which draws sharp lines between means and ends, or inner and outer. However, most if not all the English translations we have derive from Greek texts.

In Aramaic, for example, "Kingdom of Heaven" referred to a state of unity that can be found inside and outside of us, not somewhere in the sky. For example, *"Blessed be the meek, for they shall inherit the Earth"* in the original Aramaic version can actually mean (rather than what we have been told), *"soften what's rigid inside, and you shall receive physical vigor and strength from the universe."*

Luckily for us, we can go back to the Syriac Aramaic manuscript of the Gospel, also known as the Peshitta Version, from which we can extrapolate the original meaning. Peshitta means true, simple, sincere, and this version might be as old as the 2nd century, positioning it closer to Jesus's time. Dr. George M. Lamsa, the pioneering Aramaic scholar of the 1930s, pointed out in his *New Testament Origin:* "*Not a word of either the Old or New Testament was originally written in Greek or any other European*

The Genesis of Consciousness: Involution and Evolution

language. Almost everything which was written in Germany, England, and America relative to Eastern Christianity was conjectural or biased. Therefore, the whole body of evidence to the Bible theology and the people of the East must be re-examined in the light of the present finding and the Aramaic language" (pages 1, 17-18).

If we look at something that most Christians are familiar with, the Lord's Prayer, we find a huge difference in terms of words and the meaning from what we have been given.

Now that we have under our belt some understanding of Primary and Secondary Consciousness and the void, the Male and Female principle of creation and light, the real translation will be much clearer to understand. Below is what most Christians around the world have been accustomed to repeating as the Lord's Prayer.

"9 After this manner therefore pray ye: Our Father which art in heaven, Hallowed be thy name. 10 Thy kingdom come, Thy will be done in Earth, as it is in heaven. 11 Give us this day our daily bread. 12 And forgive us our debts, as we forgive our debtors. 13 And lead us not into temptation, but deliver us from evil: For thine is the kingdom, and the power, and the glory, for ever. Amen." ~ Matthew 6:9-13 King James Version (KJV)

The Aramaic version is: *"Abwoon bwashmaya. Nethqadash shmakh. Teytey malkuthakh. Nehwey tzevyanach aykanna d'bwashmaya aph b'arha. Hawvlan lachma d'sunqanan yaomana. Washboqlan khaubayn (wakhtahayn). Aykana daph khnan shbwoqan l'khayyabayn. Wela tahlan l'nesyuna Ela patzan min bisha. Metol dilakhie malkutha wahayla wateshbukhta l'ahlam almin. Ameyn."*

For most of us, this is just gibberish. And it translates quite differently from what we been accustomed to believe if we use the original Aramaic version. In fact, it translates as:

"O Birther! Father-Mother of the Cosmos, you create all that moves in light. (Abwoon bwashmaya); (Our Father which art in heaven)

The Science of Consciousness

Focus your light within us — make it useful: as the rays of a beacon show the way. (Nethqadash shmakh); (Hallowed be thy name).

Create your reign of unity now. Through our fiery hearts and willing hands. (Teytey malkuthakh); (Thy kingdom come)

Your one desire then acts with ours, as in all light, so in all form. (Nehwey tzevyanach aykanna d'bwashmaya aph b'arha); (Thy will be done on Earth, as it is in heaven)

Grant what we need each day in bread and insight: subsistence for the call of growing life. (Hawvlan lachma d'sunqanan yaomana); (Give us this day our daily bread)

Loose the cords of mistakes binding us, as we release the strands we hold of other's guilt. (Washboqlan khaubayn (wakhtahayn). Aykana daph khnan shbwoqan l'khayyabayn); (And forgive us our debts, as we forgive our debtors)

Don't let surface things delude us, and enter into forgetfulness. But free us from what hold us back from our purpose. (Wela tahlan l'nesyuna Ela patzan min bisha); (And lead us not into temptation, but deliver us from evil)

From you is born all ruling will, the power and life to do, the song that beautifies all — from age to age it renews. (Metol dilakhie malkutha wahayla wateshbukhta l'ahlam almin.); (For thine is the kingdom, and the power, and the glory, for ever)

Truly — power to these statements — may they be the ground from which all my actions grow!" (Ameyn); (Amen)

~ Translation by Neil Douglas-Klotz from his book *Prayers of the Cosmos*

Let's break it down a bit further before we move on.

The birth of expression of consciousness comes from Primary Consciousness and Secondary Consciousness, from the cosmic

The Genesis of Consciousness: Involution and Evolution

Father and the cosmic Mother creating, birthing, all that exists in light, including ourselves.

Allow this inner light, the Divine seed and our true legacy to guide us and find our path back to unity.

Let this unity, where our eyes and other physical senses can finally be opened and awaken, so that the kingdom of heaven (unity with God) can be fully realized in physicality through our intent, heart, passion and actions.

Let our thoughts, words, and action be in alignment with your will, in light (wave/heaven) as in physicality (matter/Earth).

Grant us physical substance, so that we can sustain this life (bread) as well as knowledge and wisdom (insights). Give us therefore our daily lessons, so that our small identity as sons of man, living in separation and duality, can be expanded; and help us becoming the perfected sons and daughters of the light, the Divine.

Don't let duality, separation (maya), and the surface desires based on impermanence delude us and trick us, and therefore make us forget who we truly are (we are the sons and daughters of the light) and where we are supposed to go (the state of unity).

We can see that Evil is not present in the Aramaic version as in Essene and Gnostic knowledge, SIN is the endorsement of duality and forgetfulness, and SATAN or EVIL is considered anything that is DUALISTIC in nature and SEPARATES us from unity with God.

As a creator, you have all names, as you are all things, visible and invisible, tangible and intangible, both in wave form and in physical form. You, God, are not an individualized being, but all that exists, the substratum, the source of all life and all existence.

This last version, directly translated from the Aramaic original text, is quite different from what we have learned. This is one reason why many of my readers (especially the ones from Christian denominations) and some of my students use this version when connecting to the father/mother principle.

Now that we have seen how a simple translation can leave behind so much truth, knowledge, and understanding, let's move to another teaching that has been lost in the memories of time.

THE HIJACKED MESSAGE OF JESUS

This unified state is what we have called the God-Man, the Perfected Man, the Adam-Kadmon (Kabballah), the Enlightened Being, the One, the Unified Self, the Resurrected Christ, and the Awakened Buddha, among many titles.

(Romans 8:13-17) *"For if you live according to the sinful nature (duality/separation), you will die; but if by the Spirit you put to death the misdeeds of the body, you will live, 14 because those who are led by the Spirit of God are sons of God. 15 For you did not receive a spirit that makes you a slave again to fear, but you received the Spirit of sonship. And by him we cry, "Abba, Father." 16 The Spirit himself testifies with our spirit that we are God's children. 17 Now if we are children, then we are heirs — heirs of God and co-heirs with Christ."*

When we live as physical beings, in duality (the Bible describes this state as sinful nature), as sons of the Earth and man, we suffer and perish, as we are subject to the laws of matter and physicality; but when we live as unified beings (in spirit), our lives will be based on the law of light, and as such we will become the sons and daughter of God.

All references to "Christ" as the ONLY son of God have to be seen from this perspective as an inner state, describing the unification with God.

Christendom is a unified state of being, not a person. This message and the Gospels were edited, changed (as we will see later) to align Jesus the Man with Sol Invictus, the Sun God of the Romans at the time when Christianity was made legal in the Roman Empire. The Holy Spirit descending on the man Jesus is the anointment of the Divine fire (representing unity with the Divine, or enlightenment); this is one reason why Christ which comes from the Greek χριστός, Chrīstós, which means "Anointed One."

The Genesis of Consciousness: Involution and Evolution

It is only when you are anointed, unified, perfected, lifted from the son of man living in duality and separation, that you can have true light, life, and understanding. This is the true meaning of becoming the Christ, or Son of God, and becoming one (unified) with the Father.

In this light, ONLY through overcoming duality, separation, and becoming unified, becoming the Christ (Adam-Kadmon, Buddha, etc.) can one connect with this Void, Primary Consciousness, or God. This is why in John 14:6-21, we find: Jesus answered, *"I am the way and the truth and the life. No one comes to the Father except through me."* Not through Jesus the man but through the "UNIFIED STATE," "CHRIST CONSCIOUSNESS," which can also be called ADAM-KADMON CONSCIOUSNESS or BUDDHA CONSCIOUSNESS.

This is one of the most misunderstood quotes in history, and the cause of wars, persecutions, judgment, and hate for the past 1800 years. We all share the same source, the same Father, no matter our denomination or belief. The titles and labels might change, but the message remains the same.

This is one reason billions of Christians say "OUR father, in heaven..." or more correctly: *"O Birther! Father-Mother of the Cosmos, you create all that moves in light."*

Other remaining quotes in the Bible that retain the original message can be found in the Old and New Testament as:

"Yet, O LORD, you are our Father. We are the clay, you are the potter; we are all the work of your hand." ~ (Isaiah 64:8)

"For you created my inmost being; you knit me together in my mother's womb. 14 I praise you because I am fearfully and wonderfully made; your works are wonderful, I know that full well." ~ (Psalms 139:13-14)

"44 But I tell you: Love your enemies and pray for those who persecute you, 45 that you may be sons of your Father in heaven. He causes his sun to rise on the evil and the good, and sends rain

on the righteous and the unrighteous (FREE WILL)." ~ (Matthew 5:44-45)

"For whoever does the will of my Father in heaven (becoming unified, one with the father light — enlightened) is my brother and sister and mother." ~ (Matthew 12:50)

"There is one body and one Spirit — just as you were called to one hope when you were called — 5 one Lord, one faith, one baptism; 6 one God and Father of all, who is over all and through all and in all." ~ (Ephesians 4:4-6)

"1 How great is the love the Father has lavished on us, that we should be called children of God! And that is what we are! The reason the world does not know us is that it did not know him. 2 Dear friends, now we are children of God, and what we will be has not yet been made known. But we know that when he appears, we shall be like him, for we shall see him as he is. 3 Everyone who has this hope in him purifies himself, just as he is pure." ~ 1 John 3:1-3

If we see the Christ consciousness as the seed of God, the light legacy we all possess, then a great deal can come to light in the Bible. This will be covered in much greater detail in the Forbidden Knowledge books.

INVOLUTION, EVOLUTION, LIGHT, & COEHRENCE

The farther we move from "God," from Primary Consciousness, the farther we are from unity, oneness. The more we fall into a state of physicality, matter, density, and separation, the more we are trapped in the illusory reality of pain and suffering, cause and effect, separation and duality.

Both mystical, direct experience and scientific discovery has once again come to the same conclusions, one through empirical evidence and the other through personal experimentation. All paradoxes can be reunited and pacified by this new perspective.

The Genesis of Consciousness: Involution and Evolution

This involution and evolution as a form of expression, experience, and self-discovery also matches our soul journeys and path in this 3rd density plane of existence, as we will see in the *Many Lives, Many Lessons, One Destination* book in this series, where reincarnation, soul levels, soul lessons, and paths are covered in much greater details.

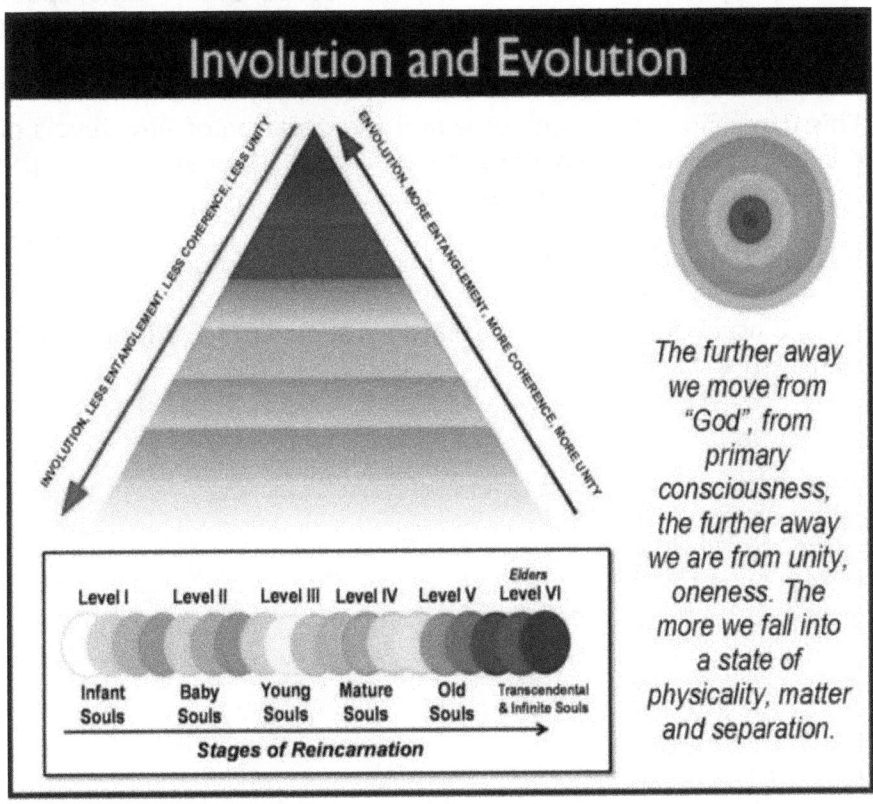

INVOLUTION: Less entanglement, less coherence, less light, less wave, less understanding of the unity of all things, and the less the remembrance of our connection to the Divine. The more the involution, the denser, more physical we become.

EVOLUTION: More entanglement, more coherence, more light, more wave, more understanding of the unity of all things, and the more the remembrance of our connection to the Divine. The more the evolution, the less dense and the more light we become.

The Science of Consciousness

All of these levels are dimensions, Kingdoms of Heaven on different levels of density. The void, the space that we have called empty, is in fact not empty at all, but like a field, an ocean of unlimited energy waiting for an intent to coagulate it into form, as we will show in the next Chapter. New matter, new worlds, as the concept of the expanding universe is showcasing, are continually being formed in this space/time, time/space consciousness-based simulation, as consciousness expressing itself creates.

This expansion of our universe and the creation of new levels of density and matter have one purpose only: the evolution of the self as, by, and through consciousness.

Is there a way to find where we are on a consciousness scale?

Well, a psychiatrist, Dr. David Hawkins seems to have found a way to measure it.

CHAPTER 16:
The Vibrational Scale & the Missing Teachings of Jesus

"Beneath the broad tides of human history there flow the stealthy undercurrents of the secret societies, which frequently determine in the depth the changes that take place upon the surface." ~ A. E. Waite

INVOLUTION AND EVOLUTION IN ONE'S LIFE: THE CONSCIOUSNESS SCALE/MAP

The Map of Consciousness was created by Dr. David Hawkins, a psychiatrist, who experienced several life-altering events throughout his life. Following each event, he noticed a shift in his level of consciousness, with lower-state emotions like anger and fear bringing him down and elevated emotional states like love, compassion, and empathy bringing him up. As a psychiatrist, he looked to find parameters, a way to measure these consciousness shifts within himself and others.

The Map of Consciousness is a numerical scale whereby one can measure different states of awareness and consciousness. Dr. Hawkins believes that every word, every thought, and every intention creates what is called a morphogenetic field of resonance, or a magnetic field, that attracts resonant frequencies or reject opposing ones.

These energy fields, he believes, can be measured by a very simple process, using kinesiology. Kinesiology is defined as the study of muscles and their movements, especially as applied to physical conditioning, where the practitioner can contact directly the subconscious mind of the patient and find through muscle testing answers to often-buried questions.

The Science of Consciousness

Kinesiology first gained scientific attention from the work of Dr. George Goodheart, who discovered that benign physical stimuli such as beneficial vitamin and mineral supplements would increase the strength of certain indicator muscles, whereas hostile stimuli like food creating allergic reactions would cause those muscles to suddenly weaken.

In the late 1970s, Dr. John Diamond refined Goodheart's research into a practice called "Behavioral Kinesiology," where indicator muscles would strengthen or weaken and could be successfully tested in the presence of positive or negative physical, emotional, and intellectual stimuli as well. After this, Dr. Hawkins took the research and applications further, by discovering that this kinesiologic response conveys man's capacity to differentiate not only positive from negative stimuli, but also anabolic from catabolic, and very dramatically, different levels of consciousness.

The Map of Consciousness (next illustration) reflects this knowledge and millions of calibrations using muscle testing of statements, photos, etc. in many areas of human endeavor and philosophical thought. This research, which spanned over 20 years, resulted in a map of consciousness and the related frequency for each emotion in the human experience.

In a nutshell, the more you feel light-based, elevated, expanded emotions (like compassion and love), the higher our frequency becomes, whereas the more you feel dark-based, inferior, contracted emotions (like fear and anger), the lower your frequency. This is what some esoteric circles have called the difference between being the Sons and Daughters of Light and the Sons and Daughters of Darkness.

Your frequency, your light, becomes a barometer of your evolution. There are self-absorbed, selfish, egoistical people who go to church, synagogue, temple, ashram, or mosque ever week, and are still very low on the evolutionary scale. In the end, all your thoughts, emotions, words, and actions are the real mirror of who you are spiritually. No one can hide or manipulate this truth. If we go back to the evolutionary scale, we can see that one can test the frequency of specific texts, and even past leaders and specific

The Vibrational Scale and the Missing Teachings of Jesus

individuals. In this context, which some might agree or disagree with, we could see for example that:

535 is the energy frequency related to celebrating Christmas, probably because of all the gifts given and love felt.

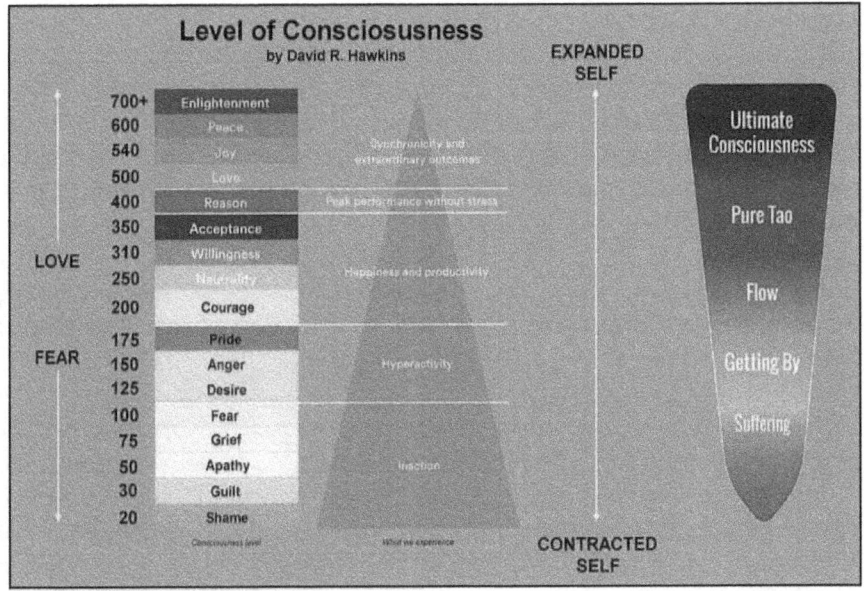

Composite Image courtesy of "thebigwhisper" and "Aaron Doughty"

The overall Old Testament calibrates at only 190. However, Genesis is at 660, Psalms is 650, and Proverbs is 350. The New Testament calibrates higher at 640. However, if Revelations (which calibrates at only 70) were removed, then the New Testament would calibrate at 790.

795 is the teaching of Bodhidharma, the Heart Sutra and the Lotus Sutra.

930 is the calibration for the Bhagavad-Gita as well as the original Gnostic teachings of early Christianity before the second century, which are considered the original teachings of Jesus and the Essenes, before they were completely hijacked by the Roman church in the first 500 years after Jesus.

HOW JESUS' TEACHINGS WERE CHANGED...

Current Christianity is seated at 510 on this consciousness scale, which is still in the love/light area, but reflects a massive drop from the 930 of the original Christianity, which suggests that most of the original meaning and message has been lost, even on a consciousness scale.

At the start, closer to Jesus' time, the teaching was still on an elevated position vibrationally (930 on the scale), where the unity of spirit, compassion, equality, knowledge, light, and love were expressed. But as time passed, a new religion was created, based on old paradigms of understanding dressed in new names and semblance, full of the same falsities, control, authority, domination, and restraint. This will be self-evident with the evidence and documents unveiled in the Forbidden Knowledge Series.

"After my departure, there will arise the ignorant and the crafty, and many things will they ascribe unto Me that I never spake, and many things which I did speak will they withhold, but the day will come when the clouds shall be rolled away, and the Sun of Righteousness shall shine forth with healing in his wings." ~ Jesus, The Essene Gospel of Peace.

What you been told and what was actually originally taught are two very different things, as we will see in this body of work.

There is much that has been lost from the original teachings of Jesus, which contained reincarnation and other concepts that were removed 300+ years after Jesus, in order to give more leverage, influence, and power to the church of the time. There are some aspects that have been completely changed, like Jesus the Man becoming the unified Christ (or anointed in the spirit of God), which all of us can achieve. All of these books and the series I am writing are an attempt to bring some of the original teachings and their great light back to life, and back to everyday life.

By making Jesus the ONLY son of God, the church removed our birthright legacy. We are all sons and daughters of the Void, of the Source Field, of God. In making the Christ state an unattainable

The Vibrational Scale and the Missing Teachings of Jesus

goal for humanity, he was sold as a person rather than as a state that all could achieve, and in making Jesus supernatural, God-like from birth, the church gained the power it needed (through the removal of the original message, coercion, fear, and massive persecutions) to make themselves the ONLY intermediary between men and God — making one of the main tenets and teaching of Jesus nearly lost forever.

These original teachings included: we are all one, we are all sons and daughters of the Divine father, the path to unity is going from the son of man to the son of god, or in simpler terms going from duality to unity, from matter to spirit, as taught in Aramaic in the Lord's Prayer and many other examples of his teachings and the Gnostic knowledge.

Jesus' life and teaching was adapted at the start by the Flavian Emperors to match past history, fit certain aspects and prophecies of the past, and to become a more placid, loving King of the Jews figure. Then, during Constantine's times, he was conflated with another local god, Sol Invictus, whom Romans were accustomed to. Sol Invictus ("Unconquered Sun") was the official sun god of the later Roman Empire and a patron of soldiers, and was an adaptation of the cult of Mithra. This was well known by all initiates of secret societies, including Leonardo da Vinci (Priory of Sion), painting him as the "Sun" in between the 12 disciples (represented as the astrological sign in the zodiac), as demonstrated in the book *You are Light* in this series.

It would have been hard to make Jesus' message acceptable, approachable, and inspiring to the Roman people, who were used to honoring and respecting only the authority of the gods of the time. This was especially true if the masses were told that their own people (the Romans) were the cause of most if not all of the chaos, destruction, atrocities, perversions, and pain faced by Jesus and his people.

Although it was supposedly a Roman authority who kicked Jesus out of Nazareth and tried to kill him, and the Roman authorities and military regime who oppressed Jesus' people, and it was Pontius Pilate — another Roman governor — who convicted him and crucified him (more on this story in the Forbidden Knowledge books), the Romans were otherwise made to seem innocent bystanders. All the blame was placed on a common adversary, the Jews, a foe that everybody was accustomed to hating and upon which all the audience could agree to.

Even the later Apostles' message was adapted after the middle of the first century. After all, the main purpose — to establish and share Jesus' message — was to convert the people in the Roman Empire (the main power of the time, spreading to all the lands in the Mediterranean Sea) and therefore, they had to adjust their message to their audience. This, of course, is Marketing 101, as valid then as it is now.

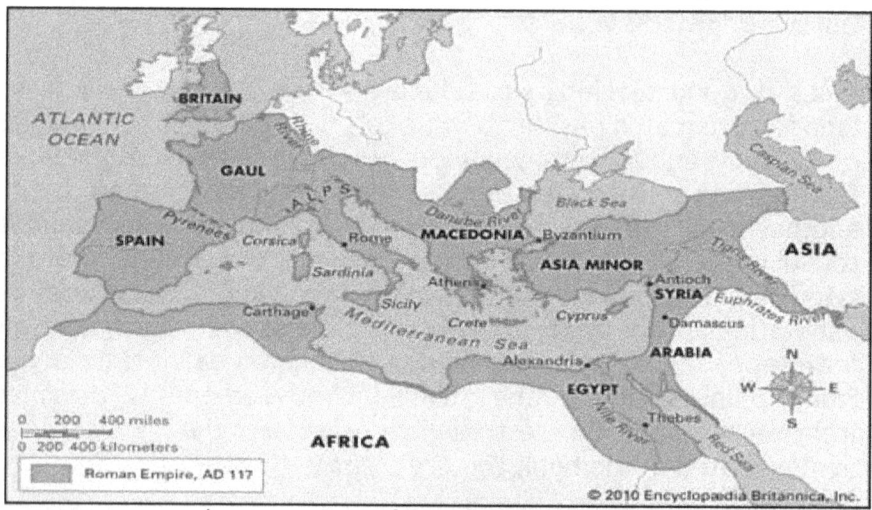
Image courtesy of Encyclopedia Britannica

So to make the message more comfortable and easier to accept, Emperor Constantine adapted most of the characteristics of the Sol Invictus God into Jesus, Yeshua Ben-Joseph, making him the new Sol Invictus — the new Sun god, the new Son of God, and a God in his own right for the Christian faith. All this happened over 300 years after Jesus' message. Sol Invictus was the main creed of Emperor Constantine at the time. He was converted and baptized in his bed while dying, and probably unconscious.

Romans celebrated the birth of the Sun, with the festival of "Natalis Invicti" on 25 December: the same day that was adapted for Jesus' birth at a later stage, as in earliest times there was not a consensus regarding Jesus' birth date.

This date also coincides with the winter solstice in the Northern Hemisphere, the period in the year with the least amount of daylight, and when the "Light of the world," Sol Invictus, has to appear to bring back the sun and restart the cycle of life, or spring.

Please note the halo around his head representing the sun — present in most Christian representations of Jesus — and the symbol of the eagle, used by both the USA and Germany, which is the original symbol of Sol Invictus. The eagle is said to be the only bird or animal that can look at the sun without being blinded.

The inscription reads: the SUN, sanctified and sacred

This lost teaching and forbidden knowledge that included: All is God, the Kingdom of Heaven (unity/enlightenment) is within us; what I, Jesus, can do, you can do; my father is your father; was all swept under the rug, in order to continue the great deception, and continue a false narrative.

SECRET SOCIETIES & ANCIENT BLOODLINES

This construction and misunderstanding of seeing Jesus the man as the only son of God is the reason why secret societies like the Priory of Sion, the Templars, and other more modern secret societies have protected certain bloodlines, like the Merovingians, and manipulated and controlled leaders of state, monarchs and world economies, and policies for centuries. It is sad that many once light-based groups that formed in secrecy to survive, and to protect more esoterical knowledge, have been hijacked by darker forces, even if most of their brotherhood at lower degrees are completely blind and unaware of what the upper echelon of power does.

"The very word "secrecy" is repugnant in a free and open society; and we are as a people inherently and historically opposed to secret societies, to secret oaths and secret proceedings.

"For we are opposed around the world by a monolithic and ruthless conspiracy that relies on covert means for expanding its sphere of influence — on infiltration instead of invasion, on subversion instead of elections, on intimidation instead of free choice, on guerrillas by night instead of armies by day.

"It is a system which has conscripted vast human and material resources into the building of a tightly knit, highly efficient machine that combines military, diplomatic, intelligence, economic, scientific and political operations.

"Its preparations are concealed, not published. Its mistakes are buried, not headlined. Its dissenters are silenced, not praised. No expenditure is questioned, no rumor is printed, no secret is revealed." ~ President John F. Kennedy. Speech at Waldorf-Astoria Hotel on April 27, 1961.

If the members of these secret societies truly understood the content of this book, and the lineage that unites us all, they would leave their secrecy behind, their limited oaths and alliances, and would share the LIGHT-BASED secret knowledge that could benefit humanity — all beings, rather than a few.

We are united in the lineage of light.

THE PATH IS IRRELEVANT, THE MESSENGER IS IRRELEVANT, THE DESTINATION IS ALL THAT MATTERS

In light of all we have learned, the path becomes irrelevant, as we mentioned with the example of the prism at the start of the book. The messenger also becomes irrelevant. The cause of the awakening does not matter, only that there *is* some form of awakening, expansion, and greater understanding.

If we continue on the vibrational scale, we can see that 960 is the calibration for Mahayana Buddhism (greater vehicle), and 970 is the Upanishads, which are Hindu scriptures that constitute the core teachings of Vedanta. Does this mean that everyone should start studying the texts from Mahayana Buddhism or the Upanishads? Well, it would help increasing your frequency; but in a way, it is not as important as what you love, relate to, and connect with naturally.

All paths of light bring us to the Source of all things. We can call this God or something else; the name is irrelevant. We all share the same cosmic Father and Mother. Our lineage is all the same: light, as we will see more and more.

Awakening is a personal experience, unique to each of us. Some like meditation, others contemplation, others devotion, and others still, prayer. Whatever works for you to connect, to expand, is the RIGHT PATH. We need to stop looking at the labels and boxes we have created for ourselves, and start having a direct communion with this higher force; then our souls, hearts, and minds can truly open up to the magnificence and beauty of this creation — beyond dogma, beyond superstitions, and beyond the limitations of the ego.

The Science of Consciousness

All paths are similar, once we remove the clutter and the false ideologies, dogmas, and beliefs thrust upon us by entities that have not experienced this light within, and only use the information for their own personal purposes. We are all on this path together. If we stop looking at the other person as different, as the enemy, the world will be filled with fairness, justice, and a respect and moral conduct unknown for millennia: not because it is what we think gods want, but because we have recognized the "other" as ourselves. In the end, therefore, the message, the destination, and the goal is identical.

We are all, in a way, sons of daughters of Adam, especially when you understand the root and the meaning of the name. "A-Dahm" is the name in Hebrew for MAN, and "Adamah" is the name for LAND. *Men of the land.* We are all men and women of the land.
Christ comes from the Greek χριστός, Chrīstós, which means "Anointed One." The root of the word is derived from the Greek verb χρίω (chrī̄o), meaning "to anoint." In the Greek Septuagint, christos was used to translate the Hebrew מָשִׁיחַ (Mašíaᵃ, messiah), meaning "one who is anointed," or touched by Spirit; or in Christian terms, the Holy Spirit.

Anyone who is therefore touched, anointed by spirit, is in a way a Christian. We are all baptized in the Void, in the waters of the womb, and then we get baptized by the spirit, the light when we become united, unified, and enlightened. This last term (enlightenment) means, after all, becoming full of light, or one with the light.

An apocalypse is a revelation: seeing something which has been hidden. It comes from the Greek word, Apokálypsis, which means "lifting of the veil," or learning something secret. This is exactly what we are doing with this book. We are all experiencing a personal revelation or apocalypse.

Even if we see the meaning of the word "Islam," we find commonalities; the word means "Surrender to God," and "Muslim" means "One who Makes his Peace with God" and a "Follower of God." In this context, anyone who surrenders to God and follows God is both a Muslim and a follower of Islam.

The Vibrational Scale and the Missing Teachings of Jesus

Buddha means "the awakened one" or "the enlightened one"; this is like saying *Christ*, and is the same concept. Anyone who becomes enlightened can be said to have reached the Buddha State.

All major contemporary religious traditions of the Middle East — Jewish, Christian and Islamic — stem from the same source, and the same ancient language. In ancient times, God was in fact called "**EL**" or "**AL**", which means "That Which Is," "The One," or "that One which expresses itself uniquely through all things." From these words roots derive all major names for God, like **EL**at (Old Canaanite), **EL**ohim (Hebrew), **AL**laha (Aramaic), and **AL**lah (Arabic). Yet people still kill each other over the messenger, the meaning, and interpretation (often false and misleading), rather than focusing on the core message that was once clearly given.

Focusing on the message, the destination, has been part of the teachings of all great beings, like Jesus, Krishna, Buddha, Guru Nanak, Rumi, and many others, including saints, prophets, bodhisattvas, and masters of all lineages. Almost all this knowledge has been forgotten. Most of humanity is lost, chasing an impermanent happiness that fades each time a new goal is achieved, forever trapped in the hamster wheel of duality. Based on Hawkins' research, most of humanity (85%) calibrates below the critical level of 200.

When we look at personal consciousness states, Hawkins mentions that 540+ is the domain of saints, advanced spiritual students, and healers.

A capacity for enormous patience and the persistence of a positive attitude in the face of prolonged adversity is characteristic of this level. The hallmark of this state is Compassion. 600+ is associated with transcendence, Self-Realization, and Unity Consciousness. At 1,000, one would be considered an Avatar, like Jesus, Krishna, or Buddha.

By becoming more light-like, more connected, more unified, more coherent, your frequency rises.

The Science of Consciousness

All of this alludes that cycles, scales, are present at all levels; from the very small (human life) to the large (religions); and even on a cosmic level, they move from wave to particle, and from light to matter.

PART IV: INTERACTING WITH THE MATRIX FIELD

The Science of Consciousness

CHAPTER 17:
Empty Space Is Not Empty at All
(the Void and the Field of God)

"Space is not empty. It is full... The universe is not separated from this cosmic sea of energy" ~ David Bohm

Although this chapter seems to go backward rather than forward in our conversation, all the concepts covered so far beg another question, which is: "How could life be created from emptiness? Is the Void really empty?"

Paul Dirac, an English mathematician and one of the architects of quantum field theory, postulated that there is no such thing as emptiness. Even if you removed all matter from the entire universe, you would still observe a field of subatomic activity, vibrating, pulsating, and oscillating while exchanging information. This is also implicit in Heisenberg's uncertainty principle, which states that you cannot know all the details of a subatomic particle, like mass, speed, and position, because they are always fluctuating and its energy is constantly redistributed in the field. These fluctuations seem to be related on many levels on consciousness.

Subatomic particles do not look like little soccer balls or green peas, but more like clouds of potentiality, vibrating like pockets of waves, vibrating, resonating, and exchanging information with everything around them — appearing and disappearing from the Zero Point Field or the void, as we called it earlier. In the same way the ocean is still, flat, and undisturbed if no current or wind is present, the Zero Point Field is also undisturbed until Primary and Secondary Consciousness decide to interact.

The Science of Consciousness

One of the reason why is called "Zero Point" is because even at a temperature close to absolute zero (-459.67 Fahrenheit, -273.15 Celsius) these subatomic fluctuations are still present. Even in this orderly state, where everything is pretty much frozen, you still have a small interaction between subatomic particles, equal to half a photon's worth of energy.

According to Erwin Laszlo, author of *The Interconnected Universe: Conceptual Foundations of Transdisciplinary Unified Theory*, this incredibly small amount of energy at that temperature would still end up producing a nearly inexhaustible amount of energy, closer to 10^{40}, or one followed by 40 zeros, if you included all these small exchanges in the universe.

"There is enough energy in a single cubic meter of space to boil all the oceans in the world." Richard Feynman

The Big Bang created a lot of heat and energy. The more heat you have, the less coherence you have, as all particles are in a state of chaos. Consider the particles in steam versus the stability of a cube of ice.

It is only through chaos that creativity can spring forward. If there were no chaos there would be no learning, no expression. This is seen, for example, as the Void before the interaction of Primary and Secondary Consciousness, or a calm sea; and the activation, via intent through consciousness and movement in the field, also seen as a rough sea.

It is this conscious intent that creates a movement in this field or a "disturbance in the Force," if we use the terms of *Star Wars*, which is in some ways a documentary on quantum physics and mystical traditions.

Is there any scientific evidence that can help fill this "void" (no pun intended) in our perception and the universe? Yes, there is. If we look at the world of quantum physics, with its tiny molecules, particles, and subatomic particles, we can see that there is an incredible amount of empty space in matter.

Empty Space Is Not Empty at All

If we look through the lenses of cosmology and astrophysics with quasars, galaxies, solar systems, stellar objects, and planets, there are also vast expanses of empty space.

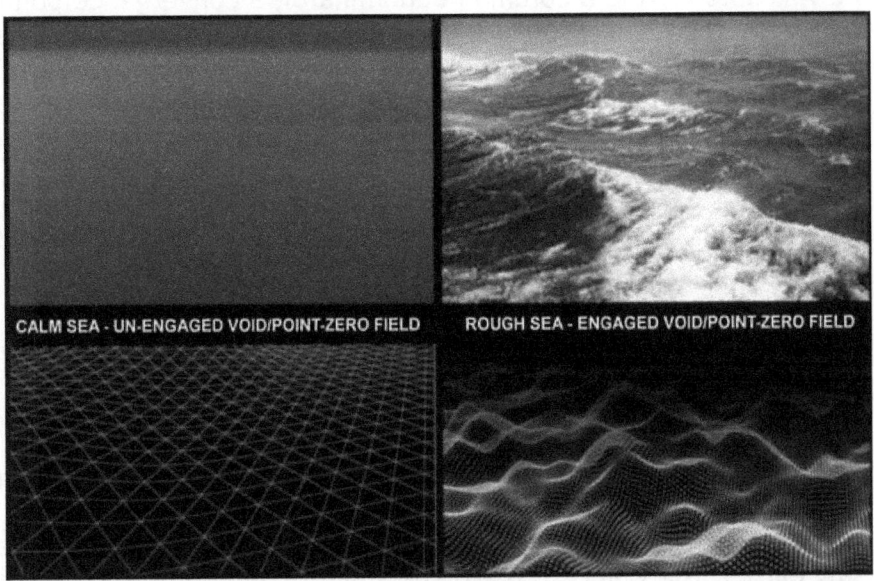

Is there a set of mathematical formulas that could calculate precisely the emptiness of both systems: the very large and the very small? After all, mystics of old, like Hermes Trismegistus, have all mentioned in one of the hermetic laws: As above, so below.

"As above, so below; as below, so above. As within, so without; as without, so within." ~ *Hermes Trismegistus*

This principle embodies the truth that there is always a correspondence between the laws and phenomena of various planes that manifest as being and life.

So in theory, using this knowledge, the laws that apply to the very small should also apply to the very large. However, until recently there was no bridge between Newtonian physics and quantum physics; the two realms seemed as different as vinegar and oil.

Unifying or connecting these two scientific paradigms had troubled a great physicist called Nassim Haramein for most of his life. After over 25 years of research and experimentation, however, he was able to find a common denominator, a convergence point between the two scales of existence. He knew that one commonality was space — emptiness, the void. He concluded that space wasn't actually empty, but quite full. A number of physicists are starting to agreed.

"No point is more central than this, that empty space is not empty. It's the seat of the most violent physics." ~ John Archibald Wheeler

"Physical objects are not in space, but these objects are spatially extended. In this way the concept of empty space loses its meaning." ~ Albert Einstein

So Haramein looked to the smallest system of measurement known, the Planck Scale, to see if it could fit the microcosm (subatomic particle) as well as the macrocosm (planets and galaxies). As we saw earlier, the Planck scale is the smallest length unit at which space can be defined. This means that at its smallest level, the entire universe is made up of data pockets or pixels at the Plank length, with a resolution of the size of $1.616229(38) \times 10^{-35}$ meters. That is 10^{-20} the size of a proton.

What he found was that empty space was full of vacuum energy fluctuations, which translates to a sea of energy waiting to be called into action. But that was not all; a single cubic centimeter can exceed the total mass of the observable universe by 39 orders of magnitude.

To put this in to context, we could say that something about the size of a pea has the dormant, hidden energy potential (in the vacuum/void) to create 39 universes. To put this further into prospective, from a different angle, our universe has about 200 billion galaxies, possibly more. So they could have, based on current data, around 10^{24} planets. This mean 1 followed by 24 zeros, or 1,000,000,000,000,000,000,000,000 planets in our observable universe. If only one in 100 of these planets is in the Goldilocks zone, allowing life to proceed like on Earth, and if that

Empty Space Is Not Empty at All

life was intelligent and had the same technological level as we possess today, using electricity for all their needs, the vacuum energy potential contained in a grain of sand could power all these planets for all eternity.

That is the power of the "Void," or "Quantum Fluctuation."

We have become accustomed to thinking that space has no value or purpose, but now we can start to realize that we are surrounded by a sea of potentiality. Thinking that there is not enough, having a scarcity mentality, loses its power when we realize just how much creative power exists in all of the space around us.

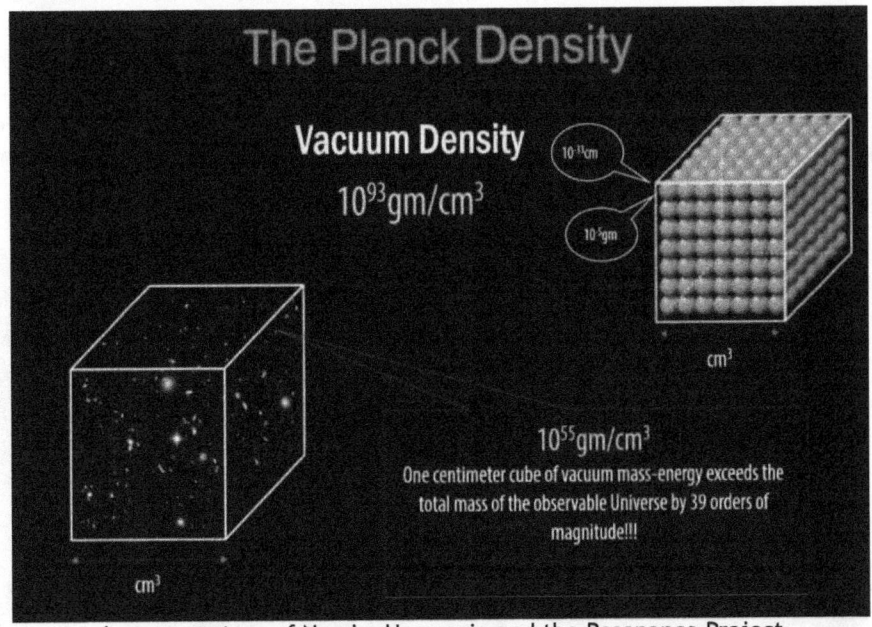

Image courtesy of Nassim Haramein and the Resonance Project

"One of the most surprising predictions of modern quantum theory is that the vacuum of space is not empty. In fact, quantum theory predicts that it teems with virtual particles flitting in and out of existence. Although initially a curiosity, it was quickly realized that these vacuum fluctuations had measurable consequences. This type of renormalization due to vacuum fluctuations is now central to our understanding of nature.

However, these effects provide indirect evidence for the existence of vacuum fluctuations and the creation of real photons." ~ https://www.nature.com/articles/nature10561

Translated into simpler words, this means that LIGHT is created out of the quantum fluctuations from the VOID, as is described in ancient texts. Light is the first particle to come out, as proven by the Dynamical Casimir Effect. This is the same concept of the light issuing forward from the void (Primary Consciousness) as described in the previous chapter.

"When you get down far enough into the quantum world, there may be no distinction between the mental and the physical. There may be only the concept. It might just be consciousness attempting to make sense of a blizzard of information. There might not be two intangible worlds. There might be only one. The field and the ability of matter to organize itself coherently." ~ From *The Field* by Lynne Mc Taggart — pp. 159-160 — Discussion with Robert Jahn and Brenda Dunne, Amsterdam, 19 October 2000, Also R. Jahn, 'Modular Model'.

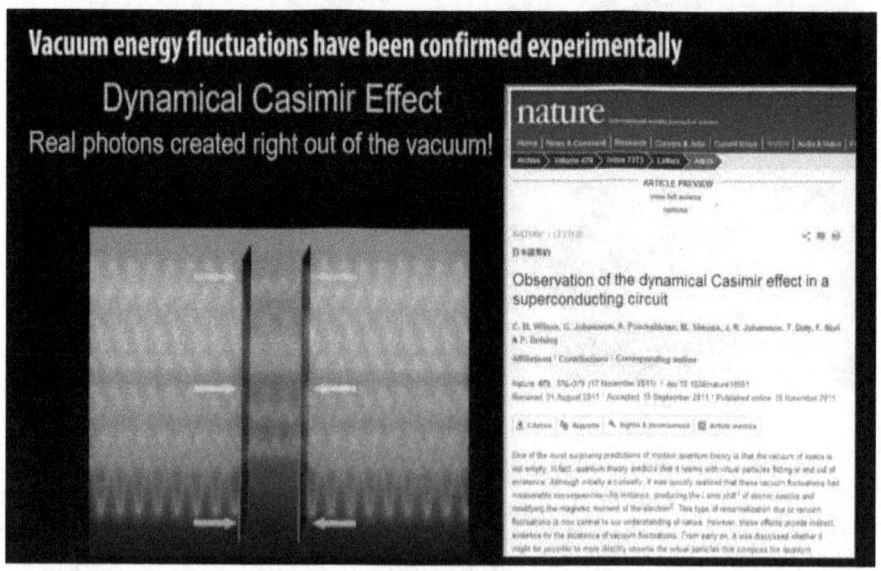

Image courtesy of Nassim Haramein and the Resonance Project

Empty Space Is Not Empty at All

For those of you who like formulas and scientific facts, below are two slides from the YouTube video called: "The Connected Universe | Nassim Haramein | TEDxUCSD", from which some of this chapter's content comes.

At the scale of the very large (an X-ray galaxy source in the constellation Cygnus), using the Planck Scale, we can determine the quantum gravity of an object and its mass. At the scale of the very tiny (a proton), also using the Planck Scale we can determine the quantum gravity of an object and its mass. This is similar to the Primary Consciousness created from the vast primordial void.

Accessing this everlasting, infinite energy source could resolve all or most of our environmental problems if allowed to be used by the masses. However, as our world governments are often funded, controlled, and influenced by multinational corporations, many new technological advances that could move us forward by a thousand years are being kept in lockdown.[14]

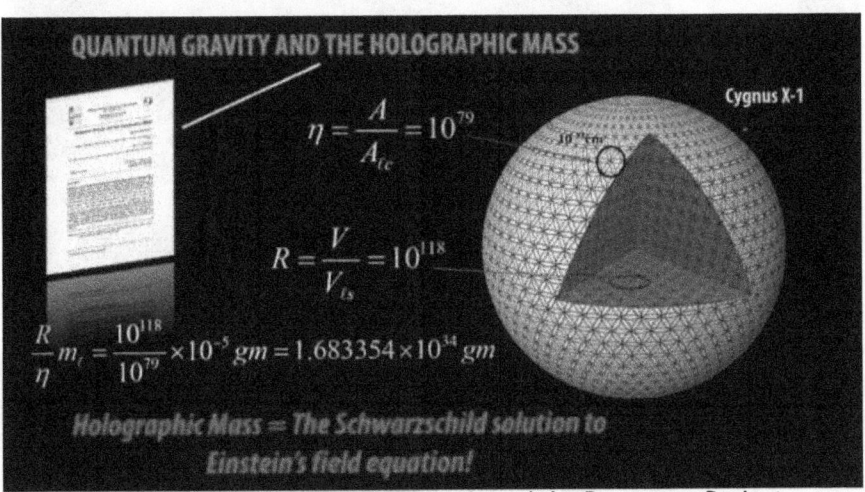

Images courtesy of Nassim Haramein and the Resonance Project

Secrecy orders, for example, allow U.S. defense agencies to control patents, including those that are privately developed. The invention secrecy in the U.S. dates back to at least the 1930s, but

---

[14] https://www.youtube.com/watch?v=xJsl_klqVh0 (18 Minutes)

it became official policy in 1952 with the "Invention Secrecy Act," which allows USPTO to keep patents deemed "detrimental to the national security" on lock-down.

Now, let's make something clear here. "Detrimental to the national security" means any invention that can disrupt or damage the profit of multinational corporations. This is the reason why you don't have free electricity from the vacuum field, or antigravity cars running on everlasting, never-polluting quantum fluctuations, or Internet based on light- and quantum-wave fluctuations, but rather have 4G and 5G with microwave interference that damages your electromagnetic field, your brain, and your overall health.

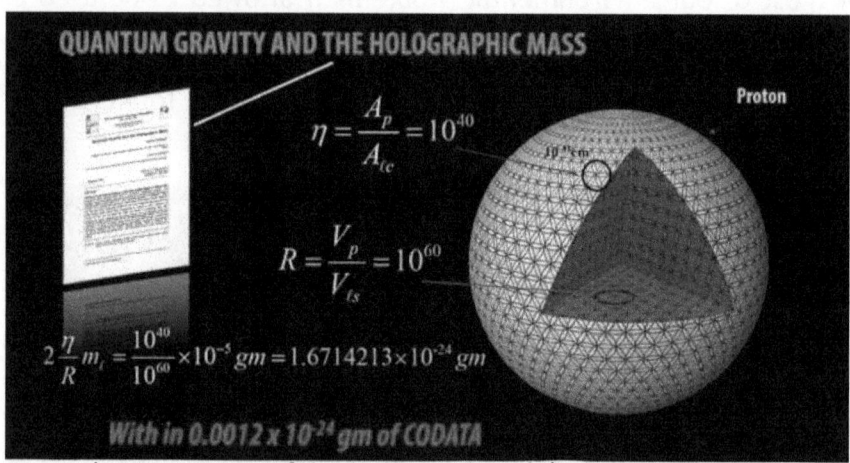
Images courtesy of Nassim Haramein and the Resonance Project

Some inventions, especially for the military and government agencies, have filtered through, but are only available in these closed organizations. Some others have been declassified and are allowed very, very slowly to trickle through the masses.

The knowledge on free energy is not theoretical any longer. This infinite vast vacuum or Zero Point Energy field has been harvested with, for example, the below technology. See Anomalous Thrust Production from an RF Test Device:
https://ntrs.nasa.gov/search.jsp?R=20140006052
The full document in the Member's Area.

"Test results indicate that the RF resonant cavity thruster design, which is unique as an electric propulsion device, is producing a force that is not attributable to any classical electromagnetic phenomenon and therefore is potentially demonstrating an interaction with the quantum vacuum virtual plasma." ~ Brady David (NASA Johnson Space Center, Houston, TX, United States).

Or "Gravity-Superconductors Interactions: Theory and Experiment" by Giovanni Modanese:

https://www.youtube.com/watch?v=sH1p6Cn7ft4

HARVESTING ZERO POINT ENERGY

In 1973, American physicist Harold Puthoff, inspired by the research of Russian nuclear physicist and Nobel Laureate Andrei Sakharov, started to experiment on how to harness this unlimited amount of free energy. He spent over 30 years closely examining the Zero Point Field and discovered that the constant energy fluctuation accounts for the stability of the simplest particle, the hydrogen atom[15], and therefore all matter. Without this Void or field, all of the universe would collapse in itself. We already understand this, as how could you have a field of reality without the Source Field, God, and consciousness?

But there is more...

Puthoff and his team of researchers also suggest that this source field is also responsible for gravity and inertia, two of the main properties of mass.[16]

---

[15] Harold Puthoff, "Ground state of hydrogen as zero-point-fluctuation-determined state," *Physical Review D*, 1987; 35:3266

[16] Bernhard Haisch, Alfonso Rueda, and Harold E. Puthoff, "Inertia as a zero-point-field Lorentz force," *Physical Review A*, 1994, 49 (2): 678-94; 'Physics of the zero-point-field: implications for inertia, gravitational mass', *Speculations in Science and Technology*, 1997 (20): 99-104

Because of his research, Puthoff was employed by Lockheed Martin and a number of American universities to develop this unlimited source of energy from the Zero Point Field, a program that was declassified and disclosed to the public in 2006.

This free energy system has yet to be made available to the public, although many patents are present in the patent office, because of the potential freedom from fossil fuels that could result.

CONCLUSIONS

ONE: Empty space is not empty at all; it is a sea of potentiality (quantum fluctuations) waiting for a coherent intent to form LIGHT. This can now be proven scientifically through the Dynamical Casimir Effect and the emission of light from vacuum energy fluctuations.

TWO: All of nature, from the very small to the very large, follows the same mathematical formulas, in this case the Planck Scale.

THREE: The empty space contained in a grain of sand has enough energy to power entire universes forever, which coincides with the idea of the holographic nature of the universe, as we will see later.

FOUR: The Zero Point Field accounts for the stability in the universe. Without this Source Field, nothing would exist. It is easy to see how mystics of old have called this God, the Void, the Formless, and the Timeless, using the knowledge of the time.

CHAPTER 18:
Can the Void Be Programmed Through Intent?

"Our intentions create our reality."
~ Wayne Dyer

ENTANGLEMENT AND THE FIELD

Until this moment, we did not have the full context to explain, plainly and visually, how quantum entanglement happens.

What we know so far is that if two particles, or even two people, interact and enter a state of coherence, they become in tune. In humans this often results in their brainwaves, heartbeats, and breathing syncing up. In this way, as with twins, or mother and child, what happens to one is felt subconsciously or consciously by the other. Hundreds of experiments have in fact proven, without any possible doubt, that two coherent system create a form of communication that can affect everyone who is participating.

Many of us had a direct experience associated with quantum entanglement and field communication and coherence, even if we did not know that was what was happening. Let me elaborate. Did you ever observe your pet (dog or cat) all of a sudden jumping from its place of rest and running to the door, in excitement and anticipation? They knew that you or another loved one was coming home, even if it was not at the regular time. They sensed your presence in their field, and knew you were closer and wanted to greet you, make you feel special, appreciated, and welcomed.

What about when you've thought about a friend, partner, or child, just to hear the phone ringing, and answered to have that person say, "You just popped out in my mind and I had to call!"

Robert Jahn at Princeton University, who developed the Princeton Anomalies Engineering Research (PEAR) with his colleague Brenda

Dunne, has conducted over 25 years of research, much of it peer reviewed, in the field of Remote Influencing.

In one of the experiments, test subjects were asked to effect a random generating machine displaying the image of Indians or cowboys. Over the course of over two and half million trials, the two researchers proved that human intention can influence electric devices. This same research was then replicated independently by over 68 different investigators all over the world.[17]

William Braud, a psychologist and director of the Mind Science Foundation in San Antonio, Texas, demonstrated how coherent intent can affect the direction in which fish swim, as well as the capability to break down cells in a laboratory.[18] Braud and Schlitz also demonstrated how people's personal fields get activated and the electodermal activity changed by being stared at, meaning we know if someone is looking at us; we feel it because by focusing on us, they are communicating with our field.[19]

In 1980, Dr. Elisabeth Targ proved that distant healers were able to improve AIDS victims' health.[20] I could go on and on.

---

[17] R.G. Jahn et al., 'Correlation of random binary sequences', *Journal of Scientific Exploration* 1997; 11:345-67. 'Evidence for consciousness-related anomalies in random physical systems', *Foundation Physics* 1989, 19 (12): 1499-514.

[18] William G. Braud and Marilyn J. Schlitz, 'Consciousness interaction with remote biological systems: anomalous intentionality effects', *Subtle Energies and Energy Medicine* 1991; 2 (1): 1-27.

[19] Marilyn J. Schlitz and William G. Braud, 'Distant intentionality and healing: assessing the evidence', *Alternative Therapies in Health and Medicine*, 1997; 3 (6):62-73

[20] F. Sicher, E. Targ, 'A randomized double-blind study of the effect of distant healing in a population with advanced AIDS,' *Western Journal of Medicine* 1998, 168 (6): 356-63.

Can the Void Be Programmed Through Intent?

DNA FORMING OUT OF INTENT

So, now that we have created some scientific context, let us have a look at how consciousness as a coherent force field can create life out of nothing. This would clarify and explain how life formed in the first place.

We know from many spiritual holy texts that all life started as a thought of the Divine. This is going to be very hard for scientific materialists to digest and accept, so we need to provide some case studies or scientific data to hope to persuade some of the most hardcore skeptics.

We all know that DNA is essential for any life form to form. We think as DNA as a blueprint for life. However, most of us still believe that life is created from the evolution of a single monocellular organism into more complex life forms. Based on what we have learned so far, however, consciousness is at the base of all things. Is there any scientific evidence proving that consciousness creates life and even DNA, potentially out of thin air or another neutral element, like water?

Yes, there is.

In 2011, Nobel Prize winner Dr. Luc Montagnier did an experiment that, if not hidden under the rag of ignorance and scientific materialism bias, could change our lives forever. So far, this discovery has been completely ignored by mainstream science, and the media has been extremely busy rejecting and discarding anything that has to do with consciousness — calling it pseudoscience even if it comes from a Nobel Prize winner and renown researcher, and even when there is indisputable proof.

In his experiment, Montagnier demonstrated that DNA can be spontaneously formed out of nothing more than water.

Montagnier started his experiment by hermetically sealing a test tube containing pure, sterilized water (H_2O). Close to this sealed container he placed another test tube containing small traces of DNA, floating in sterilized water. Montagnier then electrified both tubes, with the same frequency and low current of seven hertz, creating the same electric fields in both containers. After that, he waited to see if anything would change.

Surprisingly, after 18 hours, small traces of DNA started to appear in the empty container, the one that contained nothing but pure sterilized water.[21]

UNDERSTANDING THIS EXPERIMENT FURTHER

How could DNA, with its complex molecular structure, have formed in simple sterilized water? To answer this question, we need to review what we have learned so far about electricity, magnetism, thoughts, emotions, and intent.

When you have a movement of electrons, you have electricity. The reason why you have an electric current flowing in a specific direction is because as the energy flows through a conduit when you turn the switch on (like an electric copper cable) it has nowhere else to go than to follow the direction of the cable. With this electricity, you can power your mobile phone, a fridge, and even an electric car. It's neutral energy ready for any use. This is common knowledge.

In the same way, a body's stem cell or T-cell is an undifferentiated cell that can be programmed to endorse the energetic blueprint of potentially any cell. The electricity we use every day to power devices is energy without intent or identification, ready to power any object indiscriminately without judgment. Electricity does not say: "I like powering an electric car, but I will not give my energy to a ballistic missile, as that will cause death and destruction!" It does not discriminate.

As we have seen, thoughts have an electric charge. This again is an undifferentiated, unpolarized energy. You could vocalize your thoughts and say: "I love you" or "I hate you" without any emotion, and to the other person it will feel meaningless. It is the magnetic

---

[21] John E. Dunn, "DNA Molecules Can 'Teleport,' Nobel Prize Winner claims," *Techworld.com*. January 13, 2011.

Can the Void Be Programmed Through Intent?

field generated by the emotion that gives meaning and force to the thoughts. You could say "I care for you" but have such an anger and hate that the other person would know instantly that you have lied, and that what you are expressing is the opposite of what you are conveying verbally.

That's why repeating a prayer or mantra without emotion does nothing more than keep the mind occupied and make you lose your voice, and is close to useless. Thoughts, when aligned with what you are feeling, provide a direction the energy of emotion (energy in motion) can follow, like an electric cable or circuit. In this way, the thought functions as the cable, and the emotions as the directed energy.

Intent is the sum of a coherent thought followed by a strong emotion that drives action. Intent, therefore, has a polarity, as it is composed by thoughts that create an electric flow, and emotions that create a magnetic field.

It is the magnetic field that gives energy its specific, differentiated characteristics. When this happens, you have to follow the laws of magnetism, and are no longer free from restraint.

With magnetism, opposite polarities attract, while the same polarities oppose. This is because all forces in nature tend to seek a point of balance and equilibrium. This is not dissimilar from what we discussed earlier about finding equilibrium in the Chinese tao, the Greek caduceus, and the union of the two snakes (energy flows), Ida and Pingala, through the shushumma (center channel) in Indian philosophy. The truth is always the same, just depicted in the knowledge, colors, shades, and semblances of the culture from which it originates.

If we go back to our DNA experiment, we could say that consciousness is information. DNA, the primal serpent, is also information with a biological formation. Just recently, Harvard researchers at the Wyss Institute for Biologically Inspired Engineering used sequencing technology to store 70 billion copies of a yet-unpublished book in DNA binary code. The Harvard researchers stored 5.5 petabits, or 1 million gigabits, per cubic millimeter in the DNA storage medium. The results were published in the peer-reviewed journal *Science*.

"The total of the world's information, which is 1.8 zettabytes, [could be stored] in about four grams of DNA," said Sriram Kosuri, a senior scientist at the Wyss Institute and senior author of the paper.

Information has its own electromagnetic field. This field creates an energetic blueprint. Consciousness is just waiting for an intent (an electromagnetic field of coherence and resonance) to take form. In Motagnier's experiment, the electrical charge activated the coherence field (magnetic field signature) in the DNA test tube.

This field's influence, like a rock thrown into a lake, creates a ripple effect, activating the same resonance or blueprint in virgin, unprogrammed systems close by with receptive, resonant elements (think of a blank piece of paper), in this case the sterilized water. The particles of the water reorganized themselves to match the electromagnetic field and coherence in the DNA, creating the same.

The wave potential (waiting for intent to manifest) can then become a particle or particles and even create the molecules needed out of the Zero Point Field, or the Void if we continue with the same terminology.

This is not teleportation, as has been portrayed in the experiment paper, but rather a resonant coagulation of intent into a virgin, unsullied substance, in this case sterilized water. Water, with its crystalline nature, can store, amplify, and transmit information. This is one reason for quartz watches. The quartz in your watch is a crystal. The field of resonance in the other test tube's DNA therefore was able to program the pure, unsullied, blank, virgin water into a new field of creation: DNA.

The Russian biophysicist and molecular biologist Pjotr Garjajev and his colleagues also explored the vibrational behavior of DNA, and concluded: *"Living chromosomes function just like solitonic-holographic computers, using the endogenous DNA laser radiation."* (A soliton = a solitary wave, a self-reinforcing wave packet that maintains its shape while it propagates at a constant velocity.)

This means that the researchers managed, for example, to modulate certain frequency patterns onto a laser beam; and with it, influenced the DNA frequency and thus the genetic information itself.

You just need one electromagnetic field to function as a programming information wave, and consciousness will coagulate into the coherent form matching the signal, as we will see in the next case studies.

GENETIC CHANGES ARE NOT IN THE DNA, BUT RATHER CAN BE FOUND IN THE ELECTROSTATIC, ENERGY BLUEPRINT

Below is another experiment proving that gene expression and DNA are in reality light-frequency information, related to morphogenic fields (which we will cover later). If this is true, as we are starting to understand more and more that it is, then by changing the electrostatic field (morphogenic field of resonance), we can change one plant or being into another.

Let's review a case study that potentially can be done at home... if you are not concerned about patent infringements and lawsuits. The agricultural division of Syngenta (also known as Ciba-Geigy), a Swiss corporation, discovered in an experiment by Heinz Schurch how to reverse time genetically for seeds, and even fish...

Let me explain. In 1989, the chemical giant Ciba-Geigy registered a patent (Number 0351357) in Europe, that enabled them to revert modern seeds to the original forms of the plants using simple electrostatic fields (stress fields, not direct electric current). The patent, which is simply called "Improved Cultivation Technique," showcases the basic experimental design, rather than mentioning the farther-reaching effects. A copy of this patent can be found on Scribd here:

https://www.scribd.com/document/48607880/THE-CIBA-PATENTED-TECHNOLOGY

The Science of Consciousness

Why is this important?

Well, for starters, most of the seeds used today in agriculture — including corn, wheat, and non-grain vegetables — have been engineered to make money for the big agricultural conglomerates. Some of these changes have been made by gardeners and farmers over thousands of years, no doubt with much toil, and bred away. Some others, used commercially, might have improved drought resistance but are designed to be sterile.

Some seeds, for example, that once produced plants that had viable seeds that could last indefinitely, now have a life span of one or two cultivation cycles, so that you are forced to go back and buy more from the same organizations. The original forms of plants are much, much more resistant than all of today's hybrids. These plants need neither fertilization nor chemical additives, and keep better nutrient retention and may even have increased flavor.

Today, in fact, even organic vegetables have an insipid taste, and only on holidays in third-world countries that cannot afford fertilizers or pesticides and use more natural systems can we still savor the real taste of ripe fruit on our palates. Although some of these plants in their original form may not have the desired color people have become accustomed to recognize them by — or may have a stunning presence, or even have thorns to prevent predators, which through generation of hybridization have been eliminated — they are much more resilient to disease than modern forms.

Consider the tulips in this experiment, which suddenly started growing thorns just like the rose bush. Apparently, a long time ago, tulips also had thorns that gardeners bred away. This would be an interesting experiment for all those people interested in home gardening or strengthening their crops, or large-scale farmers, if the patent was made free to the public.

The experimental design was simple, and could be conducted in less than a day with material from any hardware store. For three days, the seeds of a plant are laid out to germinate between two aluminum plates that are hooked up to a DC power source. Then they are planted in the normal way, or in a greenhouse to continue the germination process.

Just to give you an idea of the effects, within three days in the electrostatic field, the "Wurm" fern, with 36 chromosomes, transmutes to the "Hirschzungen" fern with 41 chromosomes! Why is this phenomenal? Because the Hirschzungen fern went extinct a long time ago, so long ago that it was previously known only in petrified form from old coal deposits. But what is interesting is that in the next few years after the first Hirschzungen fern was brought back to life, it mutated into many possible fern varieties: Wurm ferns, Buchen ferns, South-African Leder ferns, Hirschzungen ferns, and others.

At this point, the researchers asked themselves whether the information for the shape of a living being was actually stored in the genes, or whether was the result of electrostatic charge (morphogenic fields), as the experiment seemed to suggest.

The new/old ferns showed further unbelievable abilities. Normal ferns can only be propagated in a certain way, while the new/old ferns developed a kind of duct network between all the veins in the leaf, allowing any part of a leaf to be used for propagation. Thus, the plant increases manifold its ability to propagate.

The original wheat shows a similarly spectacular ability compared with today's completely overbred varieties, which most people are allergic to due to the increased amount of pesticides used in the growing process; and the co-components are of much higher value, too. The older, primordial, original wheat can be harvested after four to eight weeks, depending on conditions, while the norm today is a minimum of seven months. Stronger wheat, less susceptible to pests, and much, much faster! Just imagine the possibilities for countries suffering from famines.

These experiment suggests that there is an energetic field, a memory that is kept inside every living organism. Theoretically, we would just have to zap and immerse a seed or embryo with extra energy into an electrostatic field, to allow this original blueprint to resurface. This would render obsolete all the efforts toward breeding, hybridization, and engineering from multinational corporations to create a "once and done" seed.

The experiment conducted by Ciba-Geigy was also done with trout roe, and here, too, a much more resistant original form of trout was created.

Another incredible result was the reviving of spores after 200 million years of extinction. The samples were taken at a depth of 140 meters from 200 million year-old strata in salt-works on the Rhine, and revived using the same basic technology. This reinforces the idea that potentially, at any time, nature has the power to use specific electrostatic fields to revive all life. For nature, *extinct for now* does not mean *extinct forever*.

Ciba-Geigy, of course, buried this incredible finding, perhaps because it had too many "disadvantages" for the conglomerate. Are there other example of this frequency of energy field being able to change one creature into another?

TRANSFORMING ENERGIES, TRANSFORMING SPECIES

An Italian scientist called Pier Luigi Ighina (a collaborator of Marconi, the inventor of the radio) spent over 40 years in the field of magnetism, light, and frequency. In his research, he endeavored to classify and index the particle vibrations that had been discovered in each atom found in nature. He discovered that when he changed the vibratory state of a group of particles, the material itself could transform.

In one of his experiments, he used the field oscillator he developed to alter the atomic vibration of an apricot tree, so that it gradually became the same as that of an apple tree. After 16 days of the apricot tree being zapped by this new morphogenic field of resonance, he ascertained that the branches, the leaves, and the fruit had mutated, almost completely, into those of an apple tree.

Curious about the effect on animals, he went "Frankenstein Rogue" and altered the vibrational state of the tail of a rat to change it,

Can the Void Be Programmed Through Intent?

in four days, into the tail of a cat. Unfortunately, after such treatment the rat died (perhaps its body was incapable of enduring such a rapid molecular change). It is believed that a sense of guilt prompted Ighina to use his knowledge for more beneficial purposes. He therefore tried to fix the fractured bones on a rabbit by sending the corresponding vibration of the healthy bones of another rabbit. This is like sending the body a direct blueprint and command to heal the fractured bone using the field of resonance of a healthy bone. This enabled him to excite the atoms within the rabbit's fractured feet until they were healed in record time.

In this way, Ighina understood that sick cells (including cancerous ones) of any individual were curable through a simple, gradual alternation in their vibrational index, if this was correctly calculated, basically bringing coherence, harmony, and light where there was none or very little. However, like many scientists before him who dealt with frequency, consciousness, light, and resonance, and in spite of his results, Ighina was never recognized as an orthodox scientist by the academic community. Rather, he was either ignored or ridiculed for his daring work.

Today, the scientific community is finally starting to look at some of his discoveries. Streets and conferences have been founded in his name; and following his death in 2004, Ighina's body of work has helped to awaken even greater interest in his fascinating research.

There are 10 more peer-reviewed scientific case studies in regards to this that will be discussed in my book *You Are Light*.

The way consciousness creates fields of resonance that can create matter is the reason why your mind becomes your physical experience. What you think and feel, you attract and become. Thoughts and emotions become manifested possibilities. It is intent that gives the energy for the quantum fluctuation of the void to become matter.

This tells us something incredibly important — the secret of all biological life, in fact, which is this: the entire field of potentiality is waiting for a coherent intent (thought + emotion) to create biological life.

Life is created by coherent intent, which creates fields of energy.

LIGHT AS PANSPERMIA, THE SEEDING OF LIFE

British astronomer Sir Fred Hoyle and Dr. Nalin Chandra Wickramasinghe concluded from their research that 99.9 percent of all the cosmic dust floating in the universe and our galaxy is made of bacteria that have been freeze-dried in the vacuum of space.[22]

"Microbiology may be said to have its beginnings in the 1940s. A new world of the most astonishing complexity began to be revealed. I find it remarkable that microbiologists did not at once recognize that the world they had penetrated had of necessity to be of a COSMIC ORDER. I suspect that the cosmic quality of microbiology will seem as obvious to future generation as the sun being the center of our solar system seems obvious to the present generation." ~ David Wilcock - The Synchronicity Key

What most people don't realize is that "empty" space is full of dust (full of life) that emerges from the surface of stars like our sun, and is ejected as solar winds, seeding the planets in the universe. Stars or bright stellar bodies are, in this light, laboratories for interstellar life.

Although the heat might not be conducive to many bacteria, scientists have found that even in nuclear reactors and the most inhospitable areas of this planet, bacterial life still exists. If a comet falls into an ocean or river with some coherent DNA aboard,

---

[22] F. Hoyle, "Is the Universe Fundamentally Biological?" in *New Ideas in Astronomy*, eds. F. Bertola et al. (New York: Cambridge University Press, 1988), pp 5-8; Suburban Emergency Management Project, Interstellar Dust Grains as Freeze-Dried Bacterial Cells: Hoyle and Wickramasinghe's Fantastic Journey, *Biot Report* #455, August 22, 2007
http://web.archive.org/web20091112134144/,
http://www.semp.us/ publications/bio_reader.php?BiotID=455.

Can the Void Be Programmed Through Intent?

this will be enough to transmit this signal and information to the water, creating new life where there was none before.

This is known as panspermia (from Ancient Greek *pan*, meaning "all," and *sperma*, meaning "seed"), which is the hypothesis that life exists throughout the Universe, distributed by space dust, meteoroids, asteroids, comets, and planetoids.

What is interesting, however, in light of this entire chapter, is that you might not even need LIVE bacteria to create life, but only the remnant energetic blueprint, the morphogenic field, the light instructions to initiate life again.

PANSPERMIA & THE ABORIGINAL DREAMTIME

This matches the story of creation of the Dreamtime of the Australian aborigines.

While searching on Google Earth for possible ancient meteorite collisions, Sydney astronomer Duane Hamacher found a bowl-shaped crater in Palm Valley, about 130 kilometers south-west of Alice Springs. Knowing that the aborigines had very detailed stories in regards to creation (Dreamtime), he contacted the local Arrernte people. Mr. Hamacher and Ray Norris, a CSIRO astronomer, believed that the Aborigines were the world's first astronomers. *"It is impossible to survive on a continent like this for 50,000 years and not have an intimate knowledge of the natural world around you, including the night sky,"* he said.

Looking for clues, Hamacher found another Arrernte Dreaming about a large impact crater called Gosse's Bluff, which formed about 142 million years ago, which *"Closely parallels the scientific explanation,"* he said. *"We found evidence of shocked quartz, which is only produced when there is a substantial impact."*

The crater, about 108 miles (175 kilometers) west of Alice Springs, is known as *Tnorala* and considered a sacred place by the Western Arrernte people, as it is said to represents when the Arrernte people were first created. *"Our ancestors tell us we came from

The Science of Consciousness

this collision, of the dancing woman (Milky Way) and the fallen infant (meteorite)," one of the Arrernte elders has mentioned.

INTENT SEEDING WATER

It's there an easier-to-prove, practical experiment that proves how even an intent can seed water?

Yes, there is.

An interesting experiment conducted by the Institute for Static and Dynamic for Aerospace Constructions in Stuttgart, Germany proved how a person's field can program and be absorbed by the particles of water. This set of studies, conducted by Dr. Bernd Helmut Kröplin, involved a group of students filling a hypodermic syringe with water, holding the syringe in their hands, and then releasing a series of droplets onto a microscope slide.

What they discovered was that each person's group of droplets had assumed the geometrical composition of that person's field.

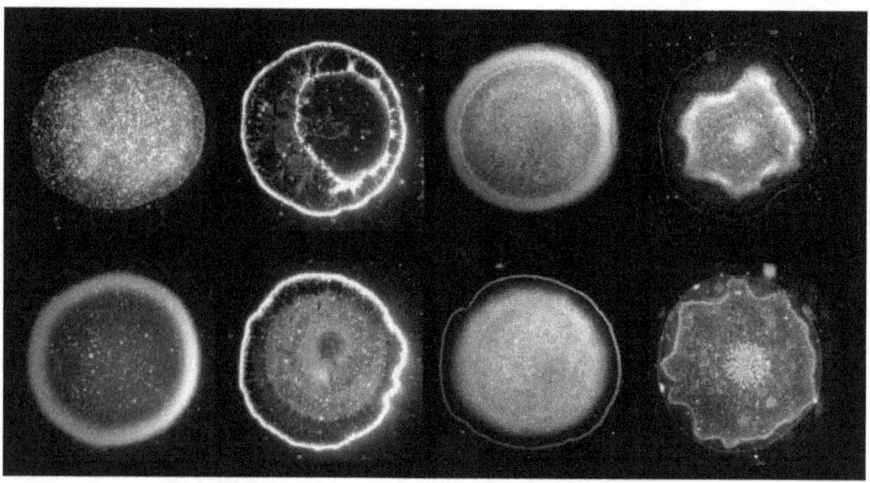

Image courtesy of Dr. Bernd Helmut Kröplin

Can the Void Be Programmed Through Intent?

The droplets produced by the same person, even if 20 droplets were squeezed, where virtually identical to each other, but very different from another person's.

"To our surprise, we could demonstrate that the drop image is changed in the vicinity of the experimenter by the individual energy field around him or here. Each experimenter creates an individual, reproducible set of drop images without any special mind or through activity." ~ Kröplin & Henschel, 2017

In the same way people have a unique fingerprint, so does their energy field have an exclusive signature unique to them.

Kröplin and his associate Regine Henschel have put together a beautiful book called *Water and Its Memory* showcasing the result of this experiment.

The Science of Consciousness

CHAPTER 19:
From Chaos to Coherence

"Love is an element which though physically unseen is as real as air or water. It is an acting, living, moving force...it moves in waves and currents like those of the ocean." ~ Prentie Mulford (1834-1891)

THE METRONOME EXPERIMENT

In 1665, Dutch mathematician Christian Huygens observed how two clocks' pendulums standing in close proximity started to slowly but without fail swing in unison with each other. He called this phenomenon "entrainment," where two oscillating systems fall into synchronicity. Even if the two pendulums were started at opposite sides, after a while they ended up swinging together. This is not dissimilar from two waves peaking and troughing at the same time, and therefore creating some sort of harmony, or synchronization, which scientists call being "in phase."

All nature tries to follow harmony and coherence, and to bring order wherever there is chaos. In music, this phenomenon is easily observed, but it can also be detected in nature. For example, in the Bay of Fundy, which lies between Canada's Nova Scotia and New Brunswick, the time required for a single wave to travel the entirety of the bay and come back is matched by the time of each tide. This is called tidal resonance.

Mental coherence in humans creates stronger electromagnetic fields; and for this reason, it has also been called by some charisma, personal magnetism, mesmerism, and charm. Nature is full of examples of the power of coherence, where the stronger coherence always wins over the less coherent system.

A great video showing how nature always looks for a point of equilibrium and balance can be seen in the metronome video.

The Science of Consciousness

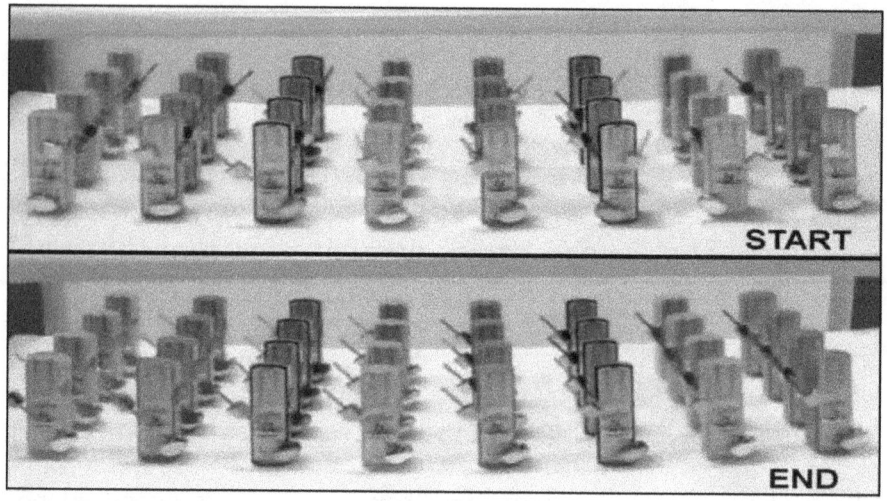

The video shows 32 metronomes out of tune, little by little getting into perfect sync. The 32 Metronomes were started all out of sync of each other; within a few minutes, all of them started to move in sync, demonstrating that chaotic, unruly systems always look for a point of balance and equilibrium. This can be seen in the video in the Members area, or at https://www.youtube.com/watch?v=5v5eBf2KwF8.

LAUGHTER: CHANGING THE COHERENCE IN PEOPLE

There is a beautiful story of three laughing monks told by Osho or Bhagwan Shree Rajneesh, who was a controversial leader and mystic during the 1970s, as he challenged people's beliefs and ideologies. This story, told so beautifully by this spiritual teacher, is very relevant for our coherence conversation, as we will see shortly.

"I have heard about three monks. No name is mentioned, because they never told their names to anybody; they never answered anything. So in China they are only known simply as "the three laughing monks."

From Chaos to Coherence

They did only one thing: they would enter a village, stand in the marketplace, and start laughing. Suddenly people would become aware and they would laugh with their whole being. Then others would also get the infection, and then a crowd would gather, and just looking at them the whole crowd would start laughing. What is happening?

Then the whole town would get involved, and they would move to another town. They were loved very much. That was their only sermon, the only message — that laugh. And they would not teach, they would simply create the situation.

Then it happened they became famous all over the country — the three laughing monks. The whole of China loved them, respected them. Nobody had preached that way — that life must be just a laughter and nothing else. And they were not laughing at anybody in particular, but simply laughing as if they had understood the cosmic joke. They spread so much joy all over China without using a single word. People would ask their names but they would simply laugh, so that became their name, the three laughing monks.

Then they became old, and in one village one of the three monks died.

The whole village was filled with expectations, because now at least when one of them had died, they must weep. This would be something worth seeing, because no one could even conceive of these people weeping.

The whole village gathered. The two surviving monks were standing by the side of the corpse of the third, and laughing such a belly laugh. So the villagers asked, "At least explain this!"

So for the first time they spoke, and they said, "We are laughing because this man has won. We were always wondering who would die first, and this man has defeated us. We are laughing at our defeat, at his victory. He lived with us for many years, and we laughed together and we enjoyed each other's togetherness, our presence. There can be no other way of giving him the last send-off; we can only laugh."

The whole village was sad, but when the dead monk's body was put on the funeral pyre, then the village realized that not only were these two joking — the third who was dead was also laughing... because the third man who was dead had told his companions, "Don't change my dress!"

It was conventional that when a man died, they changed the dress and gave a bath to the body, so he had said, "Don't give me a bath because I have never been unclean. So much laughter has been in my life that no impurity can accumulate near me, can even come to me. I have not gathered any dust, as laughter is always young and fresh. So don't give me a bath and don't change my clothes."

So just to pay him respect they had not changed his clothes. And when the body was put on the fire, suddenly they became aware that he had hidden many things under his clothes and those things started...

Chinese fireworks! So the whole village laughed, and those two said, "You rascal! You have died, but again you have defeated us. Your laughter is the last."

There is a cosmic laughter when the whole joke of this cosmos is understood. That is the highest; only a buddha can laugh like that. These three monks must have been three buddhas. But if you can laugh the second, that too is worth trying." ~ Osho; "Vedanta: Seven Steps to Samadhi"

So: is there an example in real life of this inner alchemy of laughter, of creating a new field of coherence in others?

Yes, there is.

THE LAUGHING MAN ON THE TRAIN

In a very powerful video, (available in the member's area) a man enters a train in France. Everyone looks tired, sad, deflated, and defeated. No one has the energy to even attempt to smile.

From Chaos to Coherence

Everyone is absorbed in their own miserable inner dialogue and train of thoughts (no pun intended).

That is the coherence in that space. The frequency field is gloomy. Everyone entering the train is simply aligning themselves with that energy and in this way reinforcing it, maintaining it, and unknowingly feeding it. Then a man sits down in the middle of the train car, and all of a sudden he starts laughing his head off!

At the start, this makes people uncomfortable, as it is disrupting their own set coherence, their own energetic, vibrational field; but then something starts to change. His laughter (coherence field) is so strong, so powerful, so overwhelming, that like a big wave, it embraces all. Little by little, like the metronome video earlier on, all the people in the train, even the ones with the deepest blues, start laughing.

The woman closest to him is the first one affected; she too starts laughing, then like a big tsunami, everyone is affected. We see this laughing master then exiting the train, smiling, knowing that he has made the life of others better, changing darkness into light, sadness into joy, tiredness into energy, and despair into hope.

But that's not all; he moves to another carriage. The first woman that was seated next to him puts her hand on her heart, thanking him for changing her inner state. We then see the man starting laughing again in the next moving train, in the opposite carriage, starting a new inner alchemy laughing process again.

This is a powerful message; if you can watch the video, it's inspirational.

Some of my readers have started doing actions like this in public, like wearing a shirt saying: "FREE HUGS! NO QUESTIONS ASKED" and hugging strangers. A few have put powerful messages on their T-shirts, endeavoring to help others; some give away USBs with these PDF book(s). All of us can make a difference; we can all be part of the solution rather than the problem.

Even with a simple smile or gesture of kindness towards a stranger.

A FEW CONCLUSIONS: LIFE IS NOT A MEANIGLESS EVENT

Life is not a random event, not a brief anomaly that has casually happened on Earth, but rather an intelligent, purposefully designed creation based on intent. The cosmos is not an accidental game of Russian roulette waiting for life to hopefully manifest, but rather a Divine expression of creative forces teeming with life, meaning, and potentiality. This is visible in the very small as well as the very large.

Which means, also, on a different scale, that: YOUR LIFE MATTERS, YOU MATTER, AND THERE IS AN HIDDEN PURPOSE, EVEN IF YOU MIGHT NOT KNOW WHAT IT IS!

If you look at your life and it seems that it lacks purpose, meaning, and direction, it's because you have not yet understood that this life is a soul school, designed to help you remember, explore, create, and evolve. A caterpillar has lessons to learn before it can morph into a beautiful light butterfly. Sure, life as a butterfly seems to be purer, elevated, ethereal, and even glamorous, yet it is not what the caterpillar needs to experience at the start.

There is a perfection, a planning in your life, even if you cannot (in most parts) see the hidden frequency-based Divine hand creating synchronicities and serendipities to attract people, places, things, times, and events that match your energetic blueprint and lessons.

As you read these books in this series, you'll understand more, uncover greater truths that will help you find your unique place in this world. My goal is to elevate your life, your understanding, and embrace you in the light that I have encountered, so that together, we can make a better world. This is one reason why I made the PDF of these books free, even though it costs me between $3,000 USD and $5,000 USD to edit each one of the 10 books (as English is not my native language).

Some people help by buying the physical books, and spread this message; others join the membership area online, which helps greatly. Thank you, thank you if you are one of these beautiful readers, champions of this message! It is a labor of love and light, because I feel that no matter who you are, or where you are, that you are indeed my brother, my sister, my father, my mother, my son or my daughter, my friend and my companion, and ultimately myself, experiencing a different adventure — at times lost and unaware of the beautiful, incredibly convoluted, and intricate yet elegant and dazzling creation we live in.

So remember that when we emit in any form, be this a thought, a word, or action, we become frequency-resonant too. We attract and amplify. So be light, be love, be kind, be compassionate, be joyful, be abundant, be hope.

A great video showcasing kindness can be found in the Members Area at PaoloTiberi.com.

And remember, be patient. Each soul level has its own lessons to teach you. This will be incredibly self-evident in the book *Many Lives, Many Lessons, One Destination* later in this series. Be patient with all the science and scientific case studies provided; all of these are designed to tame your logical, divisive, dualistic, analytical mind so that your beautiful, resplendent soul can breathe and find its own light and purpose. That is the only reason why they are in these books.

If from the very small to the very large, everything is based on intent and consciousness, then your life and yourself have been created by design. In a way, although assisted, this life is *your* design, based on what many Near Death Experiences (NDEs) and Past Life Regressions testimony have called the "Life Planning" stage of the afterlife.

All the obstacles, challenges, and painful meetings with individuals in your life that shake you to the ground are all "props" in your soul journey, designed to help you evolve, grow, and most importantly, remember who you truly are. You matter; you have a place in this Divine play. Your life is not meaningless. All of your challenges, handicaps, as well as talents and wisdom, play a vital role in helping you finding the truth...

Which truth, you might ask?

Simply that you are a Divine creator, on a life path to learn how to become unified, unplug from the matrix, and move from separation to unity, from duality to oneness, from matter to wave, from darkness to light; and from being the son of man to the son of the Divine Intelligence/God, as told in ancient Gnosis and religions.

YOU ARE LOVED.

Are you ready for more soul-expanding truths?

CHAPTER 20:
The Holographic Universe & Coherence

"Remember that your perception of the world is a reflection of your state of consciousness. You are not separate from it, and there is no objective world out there. Every moment, your consciousness creates the world that you inhabit." ~Eckhart Tolle

THE HOLOGRAPHIC NATURE OF REALITY

The universe is holographic in nature, meaning that all parts, even the smallest one, contains the all. Inside you is the entire blueprint of the universe.

The idea of the hologram was first introduced to the public *en masse* in the movie *Star Wars: A New Hope*, when Princess Leia sends a message to Obi Wan Kenobi saying: *"Help me, Obi-Wan Kenobi You're my only hope."*

Image courtesy of Lucas Films – All rights reserved

The Science of Consciousness

The idea is that the one tiny point, like the Primary Consciousness, has in itself the potential for all things to be expressed (remember, one cubic cm of vacuum has the power to create and sustain 39 different universes with billions of galaxies) and, at the same time, that any part of creation can contain all the information of everything that has ever been created.

If we follow the Hermetic Principle of Correspondence, we find: *"As above, so below; as below, so above. As within, so without; as without, so within,"* meaning that every aspect of life is a replica of itself, and contains a seed for all creation.

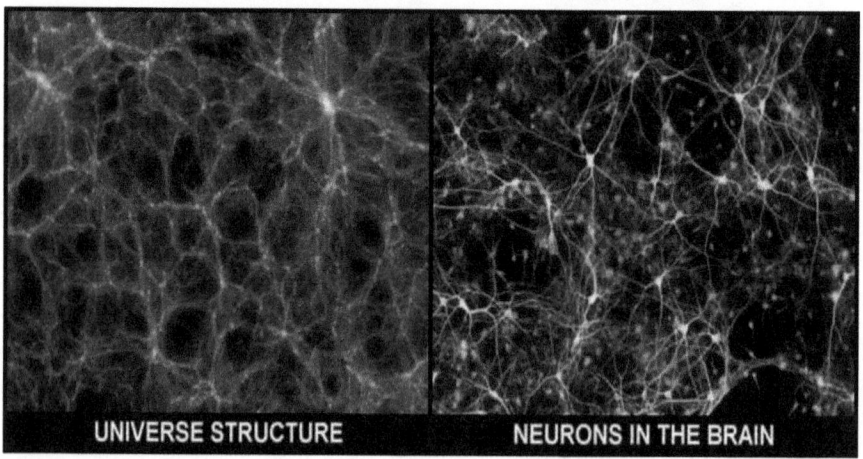

UNIVERSE STRUCTURE   **NEURONS IN THE BRAIN**

The solar system is a replica of the atom. Rivers follow the same patterns as the veins in our body. The neurons in our brain function and are similar in structure to the energy between planets, solar systems, and even galaxies.

This repetition of patterns from the very large to the very small can also be found in every aspect of nature, suggesting that the entire creation is built on mathematical, geometric formulas. We will expand this further when we cover the fractal aspect of the universe in the next chapter.

"Holography (from the Greek, Ὅλος-holos whole + γραφή-graphe writing) is the science of producing holograms, an advanced form of photography that allows an image to be recorded in 3 dimensions. The technique of holography can also be used to

The Holographic Universe and Coherence

optically store and retrieve information." en.wikipedia.org/wiki/Holograms.

THE NATURE OF THE HOLOGRAM

No copyright infringement is intended. Used for educational purposes only

Now if we put the last sentence in context with what we have learned so far, we can then come to the conclusion that consciousness and light are information; furthermore, that all of reality is holographic in nature. In other words, even the smallest particle we can think of contains the blueprint of the entire universe. Also, through entanglement, it contains all the history, knowledge, and information of the entire universe.

This concept will be explored further in this chapter.

So how is a hologram made, using current technology?

"A hologram is a three-dimensional photograph made with the aid of a laser. To make a hologram, the object to be photographed is first bathed in the light of a laser beam.

Then a second laser beam is bounced off the reflected light of the first and the resulting interference pattern (the area where the two laser beams commingle) is captured on film. When the film is developed, it looks like a meaningless swirl of light and dark lines. But as soon as the developed film is illuminated by another laser beam, a three-dimensional image of the original object appears. The three-dimensionality of such images is not the only remarkable characteristic of holograms. If a hologram of a rose is cut in half and then illuminated by a laser, each half will still be found to contain the entire image of the rose." ~ Michael Talbot

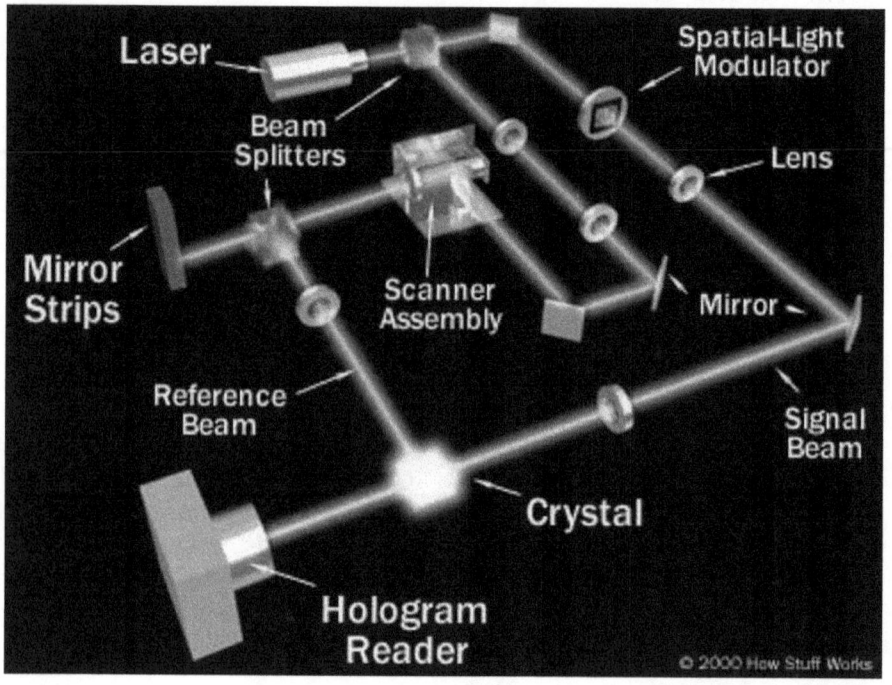

Image courtesy of *How Stuff Works*, Copyrighted 2000

So what does this mean in the context of this consciousness-based simulation we call reality? That the very small contains the very big as information; a mustard seed, if we use this analogy, could contain all the data, instructions, knowledge, and intelligence needed to create a majestic tree.

All that is in existence today came from one point of light, smaller then a mustard seed, what some scientists have called Point Zero. From one point of light, from Primary Consciousness, the primordial Divine seed, all creation has ushered out. Let's simplify this concept:

The Holographic Universe and Coherence

What do these foods have in common? Chocolate cake, chocolate bar, Tim Tam chocolate biscuits, chocolate ice cream, chocolate cookies, chocolate maltesers, and a chocolate drink?

They all originate from cacao seeds.

In the same way, all the known universe originates from *one* particle of light. This would have been hard to explain two thousand years ago, so parables were used instead. In the Gnostic text of the Gospel of Thomas, to make this parallel understood, Jesus mentions the smallest seed in Galilee: a mustard seed.

"30 And he said, Where unto shall we liken the kingdom of God? or with what comparison shall we compare it? 31 It is like a grain of mustard seed, which, when it is sown in the Earth, is less than all the seeds that be in the Earth: 32 But when it is sown, it groweth up, and becometh greater than all herbs, and shooteth out great branches; so that the fowls of the air may lodge under the shadow of it." Mark 4:30-32 KJV

Your entire body comes from the chromosomes of your father and mother forming a new DNA helix.

The Science of Consciousness

DNA, as we have seen previously, is a morphogenic field of energy and light. All nature is built on the same holographic, fractal, morphogenic principle. As above, so below; as below, so above. All things come from one point, a single particle of light, called in quantum mechanics Point Zero or "Primary Consciousness." All is one; we are all connected. What we do to another we do to ourselves. What we do to ourselves we do to another.

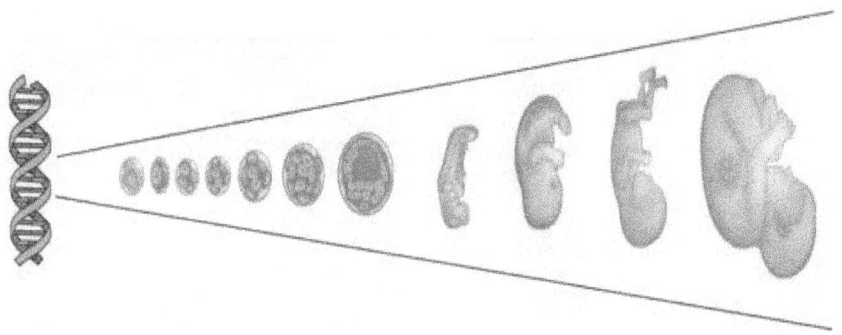

If we are all floating in the same sea of consciousness and energy, all thoughts, emotions, words, and action will influence, disturb, or enhance the coherence, the waves in this unified field — as with the laughing man in the train in France.

What this means is that potentially, your thoughts and emotions of anger could fuel the energy field of a robber, helping him finding the courage to commit a crime. In the same way, a thought and emotion of peace, love, and compassion could enhance and support the energy field of a nurse or a young man making the decision to help a fragile old lady cross the road.

The more coherent we are with something or somebody, the more in resonance with (in line with, connected with) it or them we are. Let's view this through a few scientific case studies.

CASE STUDY: DNA FOLLOWING COHERENCE

In a very fascinating experiment conducted in 2008, Dr. Sergey Leikin organized various types of DNA in a solution of ordinary salt water and tagged each type with a different florescent color.

The Holographic Universe and Coherence

These colored DNA molecules were scattered in this container randomly, after having been mixed and shaken repeatedly.

After a while, however, to the surprise of Leikin, the DNA self-arranged itself in groups coherent with their tagged color. Now, being extremely small, these DNA molecules would have to travel an equivalent of thousands of miles to reach one another.

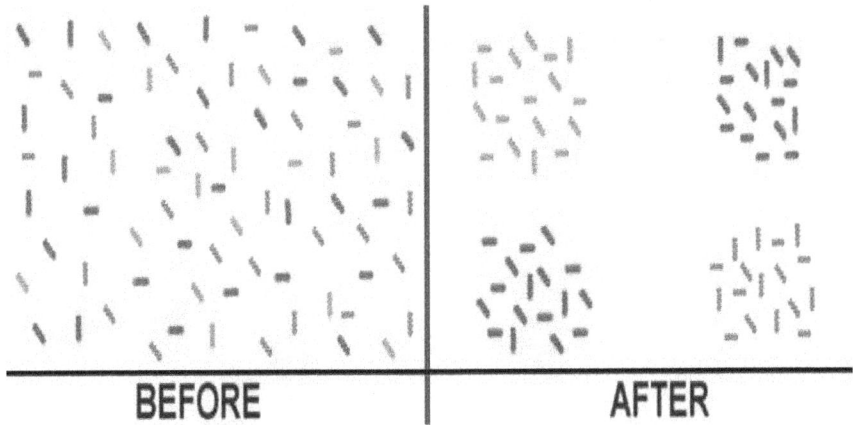

BEFORE | AFTER

It's as if the micro-gravitational fields and the exchange of particles of light allowed the DNA particles to communicate and rearrange themselves based on the only coherent command given. The color differential was the only coherent similarity. Even in small particles, in the lack of other coherent messages, they had the drive to move and travel to find all the DNA molecule with the same colors! Quite extraordinary, really![23]

CASE STUDY: LEUKOCYTES AND QUANTUM COHERENCE

In a 1996 experiment called, "Leukocytes Coherence at a Distance Based on Emotional States" by Glen Rein, Ph.D., a person's blood was taken. This blood sample was then moved to a different

---

[23] Charles W. Choi, "DNA Molecules Display Telepathy-Like Quality" *Live Science*, January 24, 2008 https://www.livescience.com/9546-dna-molecules-display-telepathy-quality.html

location, a lab a few miles away from the test subject, and tested for anomalies. No anomalies seemed to be present. Then the person from whom the blood sample was taken was shown at random either clips from horror movies and other scary videos, or calming, relaxing footage. Each time the test subject exhibited fear, surprise, or other strong emotions, the DNA in the white blood cells reacted, even if the participant and the leukocytes' DNA were 50 miles (80 km) away from each other.

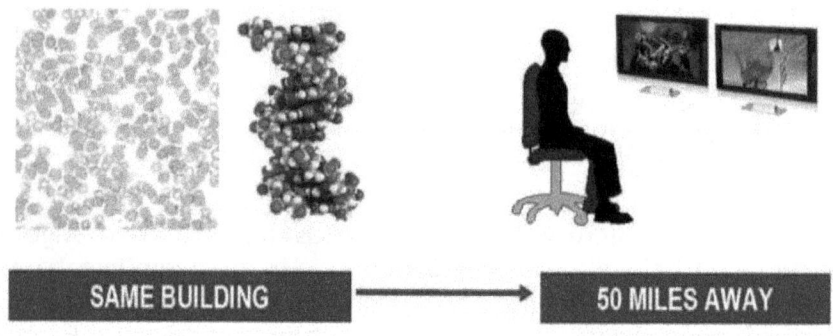

When fear-related footage was shown, the DNA of leukocytes in a Petri dish would contract, and when calming, peaceful images and footage was shown, the DNA strands unwound, even if they were separated from the subject. This shows that if there is any form of entanglement, of coherence, there is a response, even when separated by large distances — the same as when two photons become entangled with each other.

The cells in your body have your frequency resonance, and as a cellular hologram keep the entirety of what we call "YOU" as a potential state, a morphogenic blueprint. That's one reason why cloning is possible. What happens to one is felt by the other. The white blood cells were affected every time the donor was emotionally triggered. References to this case study can be found in the Member's Area as well as on the Web. In the Member's area it is under this chapter's resources:

http://www.paradigmshiftnow.net/human_energy_field/ConsciousIntentiononDNA.pdf

QUANTUM ENTANGLEMENT AND PLANTS

A similar form of entanglement happens with the plants you water and look after. The more individuals take care of the plants, the more the plants track the emotional states of their caregivers and even seem to try to help. This could be a reason why gardening is so good for one's health.

As we saw in an earlier chapter, every time you create coherence, you are creating a form of quantum entanglement, and a field of resonance.

Before I continue with this case study, I will expand a bit more on what a coherent emotion is. A coherent emotion is an emotion that is kept for a period of time without being tainted by opposing, conflicting, chaotic emotions. The more specific the emotion, the more it will function as a laser, a clear, direct, precisely targeted emission of light. The more convoluted, antagonistic, and chaotic the emotion expressed is, the less effective and disorganized the light and the results will be. The more coherent, in line with, you are with another, the more you can communicate on a deeper level, influence, or feel them.

Let me share with you three of my personal experiences with remote influencing, quantum entanglement, and coherence that you might relate to.

When I was eating meat, I used to imagine myself being my wife, focusing on her features, smiles, and eyes (identifying with the other creates coherence between the two fields), and I would visualize eating garlic salt chicken drumsticks with great pleasure and delight. Then, upon arriving home, my wife would look at me and say: "I don't know why, but I have a craving for garlic salt chicken drumsticks." And I would smile. Knowing that at the time it was one of my favorite dishes, she would ask: "Do you have anything to do with that?" I would smile cheekily, and proudly show her a bag full of chicken drumsticks, ready to cook. Did she pick up my intention? Did I transmit mine?

The reality is that quantum entanglement and coherence allowed us to communicate on a wave frequency, much like a radio transmitter and receiver. We were both receiving and transmitting signals and information.

Many times this was self-evident when I would sing a song in my head, only to have my wife starting to vocalize the same tune out loud. The opposite would also happen. Other times I would just have to think of her to get a phone call, and vice-versa.

Now that I have given you some personal context, let's move on.

CASE STUDY: MORE LEUKOCYTE QUANTUM COHERENCE

Like Dr. Glen Rein's research, but a bit earlier, Dr. Cleve Backster (the inventor of the polygraph) conducted a series of experiments in 1993 for the U.S. Army as part of an ongoing project. What is interesting in this experiment is that the effects of this coherence were proven to work at even greater distances, up to 350 miles (563 km), which seems to suggest that quantum coherence is not limited by time or space.

The project's first experiments looked at how human intention affects plants, but soon moved to the effect of emotions on DNA at a distance. His research and results were published in the journal *Advances*.

The DNA/Emotion experiment intended to test whether a DNA sample removed from a test subject would continue to respond to emotional (fear/joy/sadness, etc) stimuli even if separated and at a distance. To do this, the researchers started by collecting a swab of tissue and DNA from the volunteer's mouth. This sample was isolated in a vacuum container and taken to another room in the same building.

The volunteer then was sent into another room several hundred feet away, where he was shown a series of video images designed to create strong emotional reactions. The video footage ranged from graphic wartime and car accidents to erotic images and comedy, as with Rein's research.

Each time the DNA donor experienced emotional "peaks" and "dips," his cells and DNA in the room hundreds of feet away showed a powerful electrical response at the same instant in time. Although the distance was great, the DNA acted as if it was still physically connected to the donor's body.

Although the Army ended their experiments, Dr. Backster continued the investigations at even greater distances. At one point, a span of 350 miles (563 km) separated the donor and his cells without interrupting this communication. Like a radio receiving a message by being on a specific frequency band connected to a radio broadcaster, they reacted, no matter the distance.

The time between the donor's experience and the cell's response was zero. The communication was faster than the speed of light, with the effect of this communication being simultaneous. No matter the vicinity or distance, the results were the same. As a colleague of Cleve Backster, Dr. Jeffrey Thompson, states so eloquently, from this viewpoint: *"There is no place where one's body actually ends and no place where it begins."*

CONCLUSIONS

First of all, these experiments tell us unequivocally that we are all connected by a field of coherence, what Rupert Sheldrake calls "The Morphogenic Field of Resonance."

Second, cells and DNA communicate through this morphogenic field. This also has great implications for organ transplants, as we discovered in an earlier chapter. Our blood and any part of our body is in a state of a quantum coherence with us.

Third, human emotions have a direct influence on living DNA, cells, organs, and the human body on a physiological level; and the outside world on a macrocosmic one, as proven now through epigenetics.

Fourth, when it comes to consciousness, time and space are irrelevant.

Fifth, each time we create a coherence with someone or something like a plant, we become linked to them. This applies to the people we love, and to the people that we have come to resent or hate.

In their quantum state, each particle cannot be described independently from the state of the other(s), even when the particles are separated by a large distance. What you do to one, you do to the other.

Now that we have covered how everything is connected, one of the following up questions is, how does this universe operate? If this creation is truly so marvelously designed, perfectly intricate, and flawlessly precise, is there any proof that this life we live in follows specific laws, even mathematical formulas? In other words, is there a mathematical code to creation?

This will be the subject of the next chapter.

CHAPTER 21:
The Fractal Nature of the Universe

"The Fibonacci Sequence turns out to be the key to understanding how nature designs... and is... a part of the same ubiquitous music of the spheres that builds harmony into atoms, molecules, crystals, shells, suns and galaxies and makes the Universe sing." ~ Guy Murchie

If you think fractals are useless, you might want to rethink this opinion, as it is thanks to the fractal design in your mobile phone, designed by Nathan Cohen, that you can receive phone calls (Using the Menger Sponge Fractal Antenna Design).

Fractals are everywhere in nature; in fact, they form the coding, the mathematical basis, of this entire reality, life, and universe. The reason why we are covering this topic is because it provides the basis to understanding how frequency and vibration creates matter. Furthermore, it will help us also understand how all nature follows the same mathematical, geometrical rules and laws. By understanding this, we can see that beauty, order, and perfection abound everywhere around us.

So, what is a fractal?

Think of a fractal as the mathematical and geometrical formula the universe uses to express itself. Whether scaling up or down, the same mathematical and geometrical rules apply. The way the universe moves from the very large (like a planet) to the very small (like a cell), and vice-versa is based on this division and cohesion of geometry.

Most fruits have a spherical shape; so do planets, cells, atoms (as a spherical cloud of potentiality) and quarks.

The Science of Consciousness

Take the structure of the universe as we saw earlier; it looks like the expanding branches of a river seen from above, or the branches on a tree, the veins in your body, and the neural net in your brain. Every aspect of your life follows the same patterns. This is the mathematical frequency language of God.

On a certain level, geometry is based on frequency. Let us review for this purpose the science of *cymatics*.

CYMATICS: THE STUDY OF HOW SOUND AFFECTS MATTER

Ernst Florens Friedrich Chladni was a physicist and musician interested in the effects of vibration on matter. His work includes research on vibrating plates and the calculation of the speed of sound for different gases. For this, some call him the "Father of Acoustics."

To see how we could make these wave frequencies visible, he placed some fine sand on a metal plate, and used a violin bow to create different sound wave frequencies, as shown in the below picture.

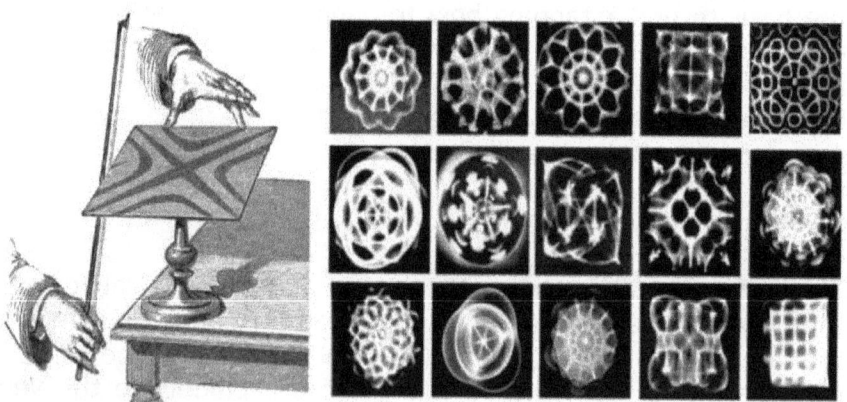

What become obvious was that low tones resulted in rather simple and clear pictures, while higher tones formed more complex structures.

The Fractal Nature of the Universe

More harmonious music like Pachelbel's *Canon in D* produce beautiful harmonious geometry, while harsher music like heavy metal produces more chaotic patterns.

Later on, in 1967, Hans Jenny published the first volume of *Cymatics: The Study of Wave Phenomena*. This book was a written and photographic documentation of the effects of sound vibrations on fluids, powders, and liquid paste. He concluded, *"This (sound vibration) is not an unregulated chaos; it is a dynamic but ordered pattern."*

Jenny made use of crystal oscillators and his so-called tonoscope to set plates and membranes vibrating. He spread quartz sand onto a black drum membrane 60 cm in diameter. The membrane was caused to vibrate by singing loudly through a cardboard pipe, and the sand produced symmetrical Chladni patterns.

Dr. Robert Moon, one of the people involved in the creation of the atomic bomb and a participant in the Manhattan Project, discovered that atoms too have geometrical structures. He came to this conclusion by substituting the protons in the atom with a corner in a geometrical shape. This means that different elements/particles with different amounts of protons can be distinguished among each element based on their geometry.

In Moon's model, many quantum physics problems can be solved if this geometrical pattern is included. For example, oxygen has eight protons, and a geometrical shape with eight corners is the cube. So geometrically, oxygen could be described as a frequency cloud that resembles a cube. This can explain why atoms can appear as both particles with protons or as waves with a cloud of potentiality oscillating in specific geometrical positions.

This also suggests something else: that by now, we should know quite well that everything in the universe is energy in different forms of vibrational expression or geometry. There are no solid objects, just different states of fluctuating energy taking different geometrical shapes based on their elemental nature, and nothing else. Change the geometry and you'll have a different element. Change the cubic energy signature of oxygen into a

The Science of Consciousness

pyramid (with five angles or protons), and you'll transform a gas like oxygen into a metal like boron.

Which brings us to consider the most universal geometry symbol ever discovered: the Flower of Life.

THE FLOWER OF LIFE

The Flower of Life symbol is believed to represent the base structure and element of creation. It is believed to be a sort of blueprint for all life, containing the fundamental patterns for everything from atoms to planets and everything in between.

Within the Flower of Life, many geometrical shapes can be included, including all five Platonic solids: the star tetrahedron (Star of David), hexahedron (cube), octahedron, dodecahedron, and icosahedron, which are found in life forms, minerals, music, sound, and language, as seen in the next image. More complex geometrical shapes like Metatron's Cube, the Merkaba, and even the Kabalistic Tree of Life can be found within the flower of life.

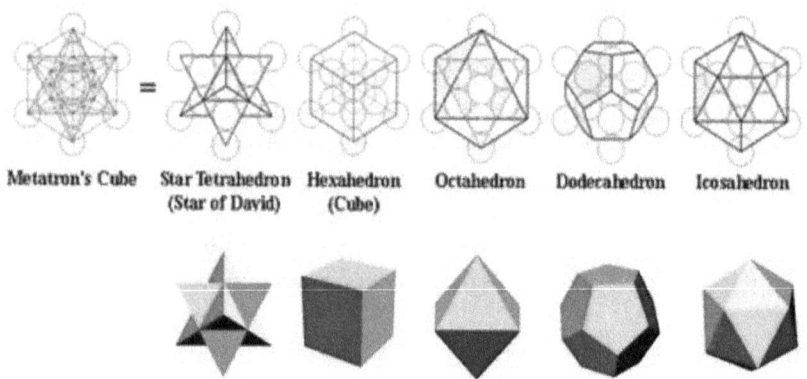

The image on the left, on the next page, is the Flower of Life as a 2D representation.

The importance of this geometrical shape was well known in many Gnostic circles and esoteric paths and can be found all over the

The Fractal Nature of the Universe

world, as seen in the two images on the right from Leonardo da Vinci's notes.

It is also the geometrical representation of how the cell subdivides in the womb, and how from Primary Consciousness the rest of creation was created. One becomes two, two become four, etc., which is called the Binary Sequence, as seen below.

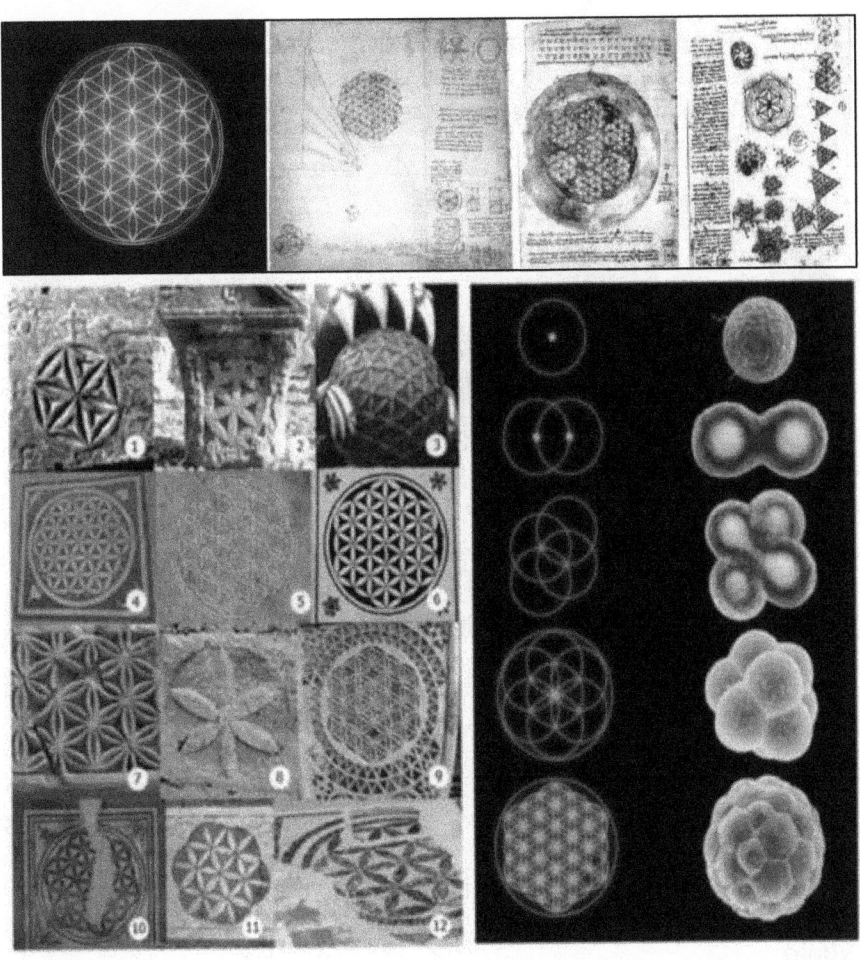

These images come from Scotland (1), Israel (2), China (3), Turkey (4), Egypt (5), India (6), Germany (7), Bulgaria (8), Sweden (9), France (10), Czech (11), Greece (12) and at least 14 other places. The oldest known example dates from the 2nd century B.C. It is both known as "The Seed of Life" and "The Six-Petal Rosette".

The Science of Consciousness

FRACTAL MATHEMATICS, THE UNDERLYING PROGRAMMING LANGUAGE OF THE UNIVERSE

Like a Russian nesting doll (matryoshka), in which smaller wooden dolls of decreasing sizes can be placed inside the other larger ones, reality itself seems to be formed as a cascade of fractals (different realities/universes), one nested inside the other.

For most people, this reality is hard to conceive or recognize, because all they can see is the world confined within one reality (one doll, one fractal, e.g., one religion), or one singularity.

This unfortunate, incomplete view invariably leads to a vast amount of misunderstanding, confusion, misjudgment, divergence, schism, and clashes as a result of the attempt to understand the self, society, and this universe as part of a larger, more inclusive whole.

If this existence is really based on a consciousness simulation, as we are discovering more and more, then it would need to have an underlying programming language, coding that should be applicable to both the universe (the very large) and the subatomic particle (the very small). If this programming language is based on mathematics and geometry, as the fractal nature of the universe suggests, is there anyone who has ever been able to see these patterns? Is there an unbiased witness?

MEET JASON PADGETT

Futon salesman Jason Padgett's life changed completely one fateful night on Friday 13 September 2002. While out with friends, Padgett was attacked and robbed by two men outside a karaoke bar.

"I heard as much as felt this deep, low-pitched thud as the first guy ran up behind me and smashed me in the back of the head," he recalls. *"And I saw this puff of white light just like someone took a picture. The next thing I knew I was on my knees and everything was spinning and I didn't know where I was or how I got there."*

After the attack, Padgett's behavior changed quickly and dramatically. The anxiety of the attack made him develop OCD and an irrational fear of germs, which prompted him to isolate himself from any type of social life.

"I just remember nailing blankets and towels over all the windows in the house... I remember actually using this spray foam and gluing the front door shut."

But while Padgett was experiencing all these negative consequences from his attack, something incredible was happening too. The way he saw things changed. Because of his concussion, a different part of his brain was activated, allowing Jason Padgett to see geometrical patterns everywhere.

"I was very shallow," he laughs. *"Life rotated around girls, partying, drinking, waking up with a hangover and then going out and chasing girls and going out to bars again.*

"I used to say 'math is stupid, how can you use that in the real world'? And I thought that was like a smart statement. I really

believed it. Then it all changed. Everything that was curved looked like it was slightly pixelated," he explains. "Water coming down the drain didn't look like it was a smooth, flowing thing anymore; it looked like these little tangent lines."

The same thing happened to him with many other natural phenomena, like clouds, sunlight streams, tree branches, traffic, etc. All seem to form pixels, like "realities" you could experience in an old video game from the 1980s.

ENCOUNTERING FRACTAL GEOMETRY

While searching for geometrical and mathematical patterns in life, Padgett stumbled across fractals. In trying to visualize how a fractal works, we could say that at its most basic level, a fractal is akin to a snowflake. If you take a snowflake and zoom in, you will see it is made up of smaller snowflakes connected together; zoom in again and you will see that those snowflakes are made of smaller snowflakes, and so on until infinity.

This is called the Koch Fractal — where the perimeter is infinite while still defined in a finite area, like the picture below, where the fractal fragmentation is still limited by the size of the main triangle. The infinite fragmentation happens within a definite space, which does not change. This is can be seen easily with the Sierpinski Triangles model, where the fractals are built within the triangle itself.

As the fractal fragmentation (iterations) happen, you go from one triangle to five (the four visible plus the bigger triangle itself) in iterations of two to 16 triangles (four white triangles and nine black, plus the bigger triangle itself).

These iterations or fragmentation can go on and on to infinity, yet the perimeter, the original form of the triangles, never change.

The Fractal Nature of the Universe

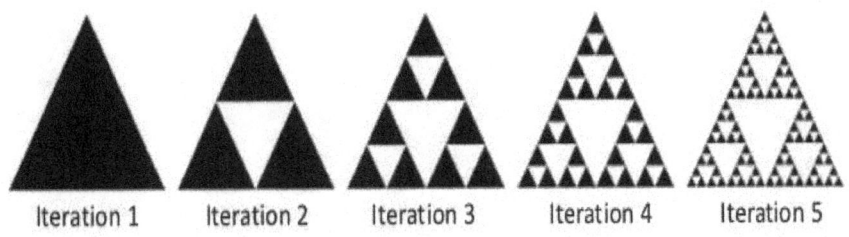

The same idea of infinite fractals can be done by creating extra fragmentation or iterations from the outside.

If the fractal is placed in a circle, its fractals will never become bigger than the circle itself, keeping the Koch Fractal rule intact.

A good video that explains what a fractal is can be found on YouTube by searching: "What Is a Fractal (and what are they good for)?" or in the Members Area.

The Science of Consciousness

Padgett was fascinated by this concept, but could not describe it until one day his daughter asked him how the TV worked.

"When you're looking at a TV screen and you see a circle, it's really not a circle," he says. *"It's made with rectangles or squares and, if you look close, the edge of the circle is really a zigzag. You can take those pixels and cut them in half and cut them in half and you get closer and closer to a perfect circle, but you never actually reach one because you can keep cutting the pixels in half forever, so the resolution gets better but you never have a perfect circle."*

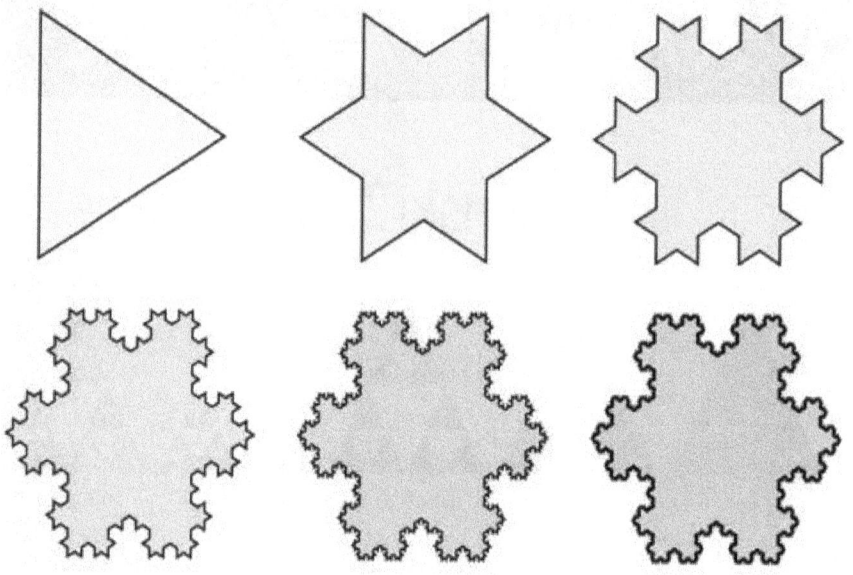

This is the same as the pixel on a computer monitor, a television screen, or our consciousness-based simulation.

Padgett felt compelled to explore the intriguing concept further by drawing what he saw. *"I had literally a thousand or more drawings of circles, fractals, every shape that I could manage to draw. It was the only way I could manage to communicate effectively what I was seeing. I'm trying to describe the discrete*

The Fractal Nature of the Universe

PIXELATED   CUBES-LOW RESOULTION   NORMAL RESOLUTION   HIGH RESOLUTION

structure of spacetime based on Planck length (a tiny unit of measurement developed by physicist Max Planck) and quantum black holes."

Interesting that he is referring to the Plank Scale, which is what Nassim Haramein has found was the mathematical base of the universe, from the very small to the very large.

After further analysis, and the recommendation of a physicist who observed his highly structured drawings, Padgett took math classes, to better explain his drawings from a mathematical perspective. Wanting to discover how the changes in his brain enabled him to see geometrical fractals everywhere in nature, he explored the internet and came across Berit Brogaard, a cognitive neuroscientist now at the University of Miami.

After many phone conversations, Brogaard brought Padgett to the Brain Research Unit of Aalto University in Helsinki, where he underwent a series of MRI scans. While in the scanner, hundreds of equations, including fake ones, flashed on a screen in front of Padgett's eyes; this was done to see which part of his brain would light up in response. These tests brought Brogaard to conclude that Padgett had synesthesia — essentially a cross-wiring of the brain in which the senses get mixed up. Synaesthesia is caused by the connection between parts of the brain that do not normally link together in normal people. In some rare cases, you can be born with this condition; however, synaesthesia can be the result of some type of trauma, an injury, a stroke, or an allergic reaction. Or a concussion, as in Padgett's case.

The Science of Consciousness

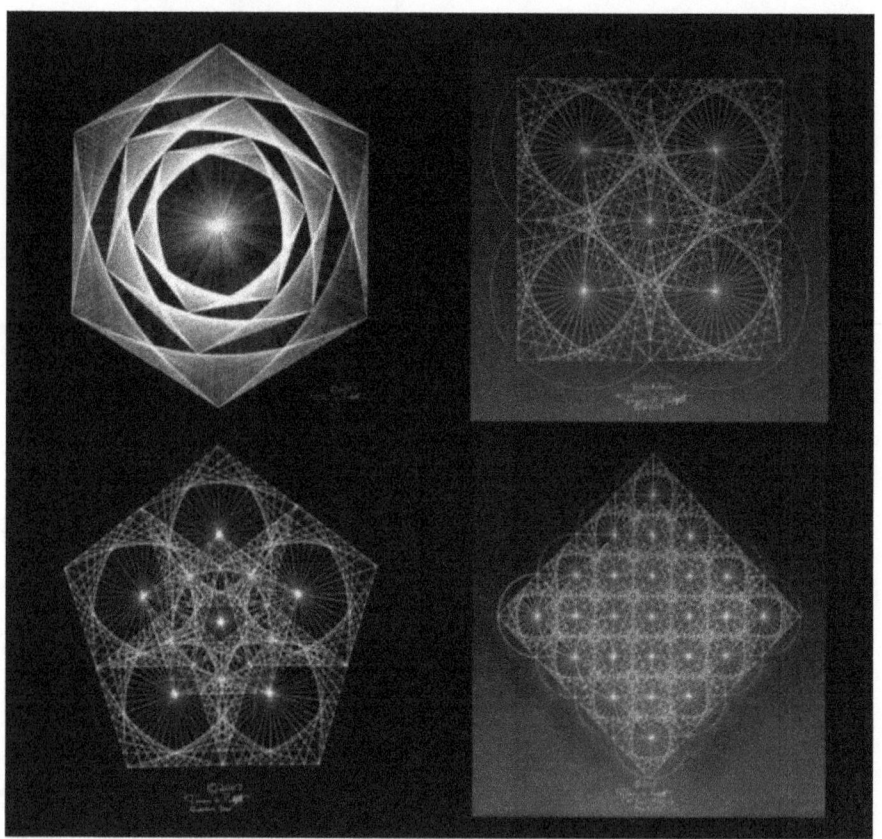

Images courtesy of Jason Padgett

"Most of us don't have that kind of insight, because we don't visualize mathematical formulas," says Brogaard.

"They found that I had access to parts of the brain that we don't have conscious access to, and also the visual cortex was working in conjunction with the part of the brain that does mathematics, which obviously makes sense," says Padgett. *"I'm a completely different person. When I look back the abysmal person that I was in the past, I just don't see how I existed on that level."*

This geometrical shapes and forms are at the base of nature, it is just that our brains are normally not wired to see them, and therefore we assume they are not there. Once you realize the beauty and perfection of this creation, you cannot help but be in awe, mesmerized, and amazed at the incredible complexity, artistry, elegance, and refinement of God's creation.

"I see it [beauty] everywhere," he says. *"You should be walking around in absolute amazement at all times that reality even exists,"* he says. *"I'm having this mathematical awakening, and all around us is absolute magic or about as close as you can get to magic."*

We can see this fractal infinite fragmentation, like the universe expanding constantly, visually using the Mandelbrot Set Fractal.

THE MANDELBROT FRACTAL

The idea of fractal reality is just an expansion of the holographic aspect of this universe, all is based on the mathematics of the Phi ratio and number 1.618 (also called the Golden Ratio), which we will cover in one of the next chapters in more detail.

Everything from the very small to the very large follows this golden ratio and geometry. In physical cosmology, fractal cosmology states that the distribution of matter in the Universe, or the structure of the universe itself, is a fractal across a wide range of scales from the very small (subatomic particles) to the very large (galaxies).

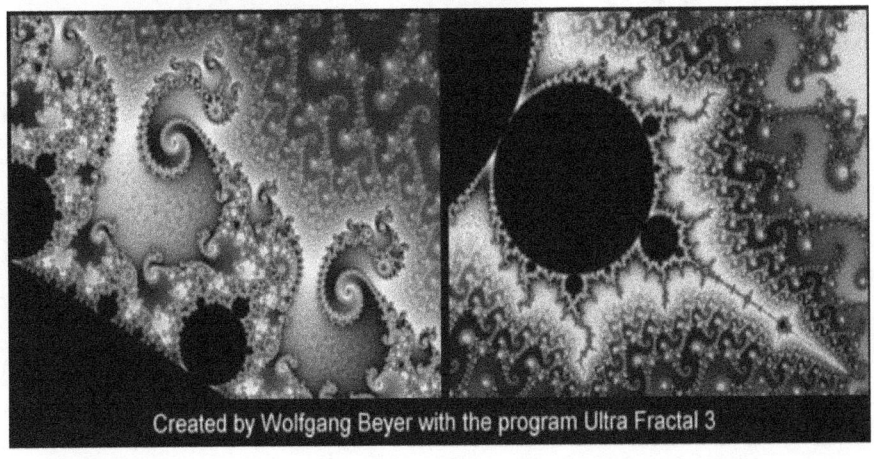

Created by Wolfgang Beyer with the program Ultra Fractal 3

The Science of Consciousness

"The mystery of the universe is hierarchic in structure. There are graded orders, one supervening upon the other." ~ Meher Baba

"The laws of nature are written in the language of mathematics... the symbols are triangles, circles and other geometrical figures, without whose help it is impossible to comprehend a single word."
~ Galileo Galilei

On the next pages are a few images of how this fractal geometry is manifested in our world.

The planet gets seeded by ice comets (panspermia) full of life; the ovum gets seeded by the sperm. The Earth's structure is similar to the cell in the body. As above, so below; as below, so above. Same design, same laws, same language.

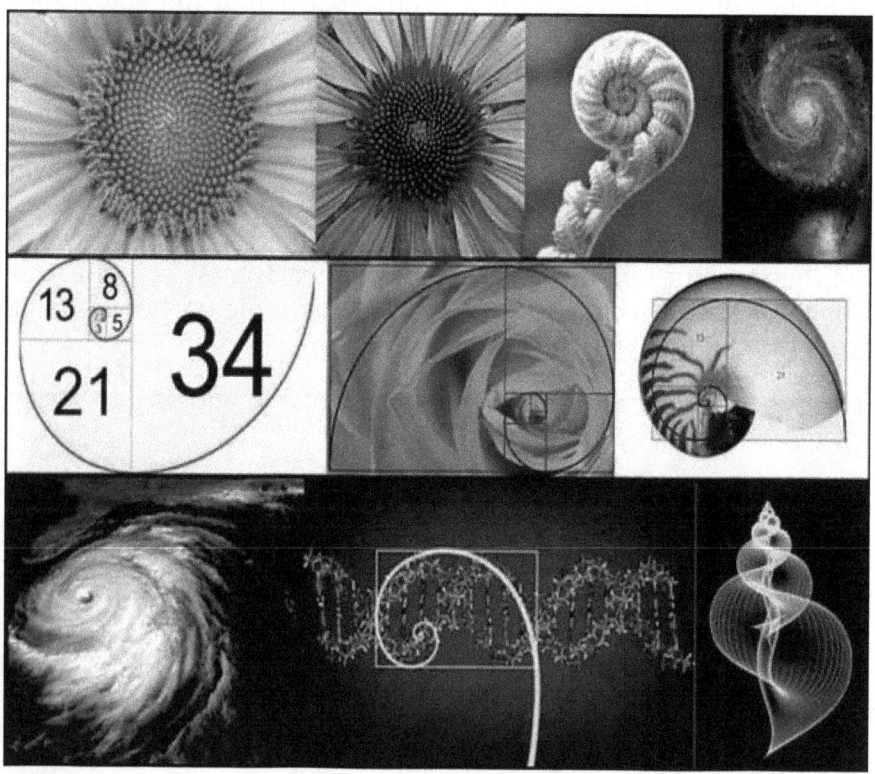

The Fractal Nature of the Universe

GEOMETRY: MATHEMATICS IS HIDDEN IN ALL REALITY

Again we can see this geometry in all aspects of nature. As above (the Macrocosm, solar system, Earth), so below (the Microcosm, cell, atom).

You cannot have a rule for one aspect of nature and another rule for something else. This would create complete chaos and destruction. Just a small variant in temperature on Earth, for example, and there would not be any life on this world.

If this is a holographic reality, with fractal mathematics for its contraction and expansion, and if life grows through the reconciliation of polarity and duality, through emotions and intent, then it means, really, that we live in a "consciousness/light" simulation design to help us express, discover, and advance.

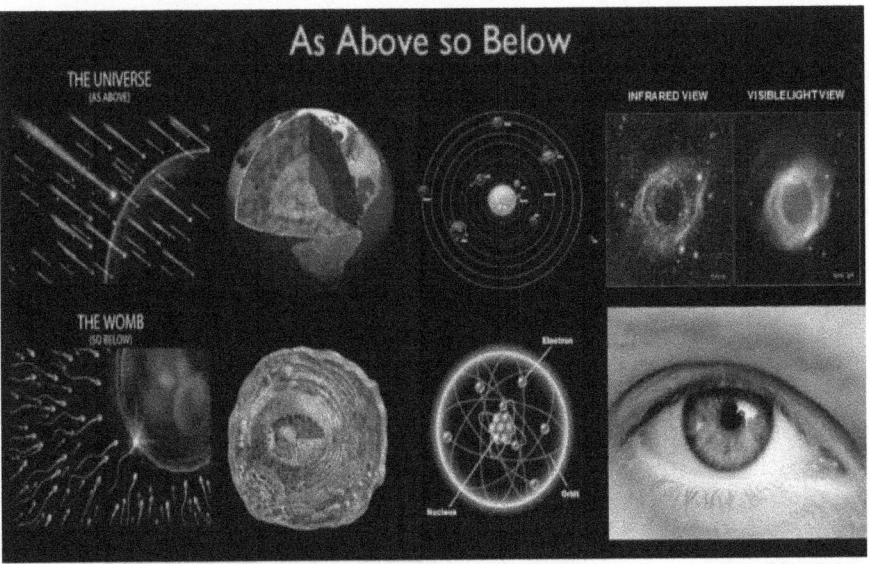

So why did I cover such a boring topic as the nature of a fractal, mathematics, and geometry? Because I want you to start recognize that behind all the chaos and disorder that you might experience in your life, there is a magnificent uniformity, arrangement, methodology, intelligence, and intention at play.

The Science of Consciousness

The pain and chaos that you might be experiencing in your life is not based on punishment, judgment, or retribution, but is a result of the ignorance of certain people misunderstanding the creative power of intention and free will. Furthermore, as creators ourselves, our own thoughts, emotions, beliefs, words, and action draw and invite specific lessons we need to confront and overcome.

Intent through thoughts and emotions creates our reality. If we have chaos, disorder, and negative emotions within ourselves, this is what we are going to attract and experience in our reality. There is nothing personal about that; is just like the law of magnetism, or gravity. It just a law; it does not discriminate or judge. What you believe, and are polarized towards (love or hate), you attract.

All of the outside people, places, things, times, and events are nothing more than players showing on an energetic level what we need to overcome and resolve.

CONCLUSIONS

These few last chapters bring us to a few conclusions...

1. Based on the Big Bang Theory, all the universe originated from one point, "Point Zero" or "Primary Consciousness."

2. As Primary Consciousness expanded, it created different levels of density, consciousness, and expression, which we can call involution and evolution, or heavens.

3. The universe is not empty; emptiness is filled with consciousness as "dark matter," waiting for a coherent intent to manifest and create.

4. The Universe is holographic in nature, meaning all parts, even the smallest, contain the whole. The very small contains the blueprint of the very large. The creative force of primary consciousness, the Divine seed, is in all things.

The Fractal Nature of the Universe

5. Nature always follows the stronger coherence. The stronger the intent and coherence, the greater the magnetic vortex, attracting or/and repelling people, places, things, times and events in our lives.

6. The Universe is fractal in nature, meaning all nature follows the same mathematical rules/program of expansion and contraction, which also suggests there is an intelligence at play, an order, a structure, a method on how consciousness expresses itself.

7. The universe and life is a consciousness- and frequency-based simulation.

The Science of Consciousness

Part V

PART V: CONCLUSIONS

The Science of Consciousness

CHAPTER 22:
From Caterpillar to Butterfly

"There is a world within - a world of thought, feeling, and power; of light and beauty, and although invisible, its forces are mighty." ~ Charles F. Haanel

In the same way a butterfly leaves the heavier, denser body of the caterpillar behind, the path of the initiate involves moving through the denser level of physicality which include survival, procreation, power, and ego to higher states of consciousness.

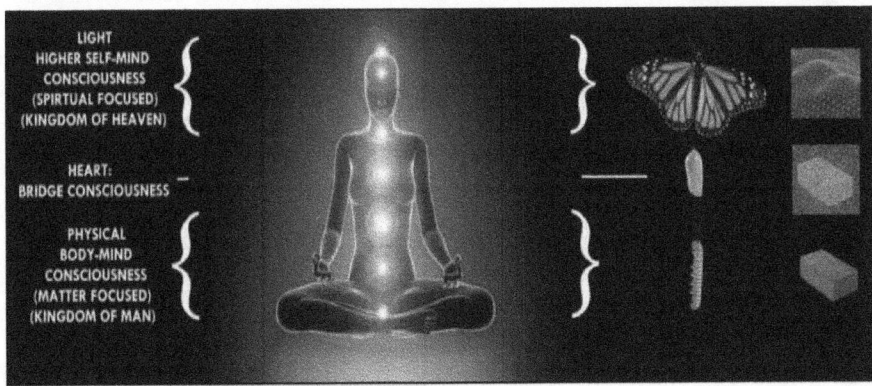

At the start of your evolutionary path, you are lost in the density of physicality (the caterpillar stage), where all you desire are the many pleasures of life, as well as the security you believe you can have through wealth and physical possessions. For many of us, it's only during our golden years — when all of the more physical goals and gratifications have been fulfilled — that we start asking deeper and more meaningful questions.

This is one reason why, in Hinduism, we find the concept of "Ashrama," which discuss four stages of life. These four are: Brahmacharya (student), Grihastha (householder), Vanaprastha (retired), and Sannyasa (renunciate). It is believed that only when you have done all that you want to do with the world of appearances and possession that you finally ask deeper question and look for more meaning in your life.

Of course, this does not have to be the case. You can start wherever, whenever you are on the path. When this inner transformation occurs, you can then move from the denser, physical reality, which in some Gnostic circles is called the Kingdom of Man, through the bridge of the heart into the more refined light- and frequency-based Kingdom of Heaven.

While you are attached to the life of the caterpillar and all its amusements, contentment, gratifications, and thrills, you are kept in a state of self-imposed entrapment and hypnosis. It is only when you make the conscious decision to operate from the perspective of being a creator, a light-frequency being, when you start seeing the other as yourself, that you as the caterpillar can move into the pupa/butterfly stage of development.

The pupa is the representation of the caterpillar's dream of becoming something more beautiful, radiant, and ethereal in nature. This is the heart, the desire for something greater. All activities stop, the body of the caterpillar dissolves, and a new, subtler, polished body is created.

MOVING INTO THE HEART AND THE SOUL

Your life is a construct: a mixture of all your past life lessons, soul contracts, beliefs, internal blueprints, and decisions you have made. You are light, expressing yourself though thoughts and emotions. These give rise to an electromagnetic field of feeling, words, and actions.

The ancient Gnostics and Essenes taught us that if you are one with and resonating in harmony (coherent) with your desires, then you can ask a mountain to move, and it will move. Through this coherence, and aligned resonance, you can affect matter and reprogram this consciousness-based simulation to fit your new blueprint of reality.

From Caterpillar to Butterfly

When you operate from the body-mind-consciousness, the ego, you tend to fragment your experience, to divide, judge and analyze with rigorous fervor all aspects of your life. When you are in the ego-mind, you become swept up by social programming, the sense of separation, and lose track of your real purpose and nature. This tells you in a second that you are not functioning from a place of unity, you are not functioning from the heart, you are not going with the Divine flow. The heart does not judge, does not separate.

"4 Love is patient, love is kind. It does not envy, it does not boast, it is not proud. 5 It does not dishonor others, it is not self-seeking, it is not easily angered, it keeps no record of wrongs. 6 Love does not delight in evil but rejoices with the truth. 7 It always protects, always trusts, always hopes, always perseveres. 8 Love never fails. But where there are prophecies, they will cease; where there are tongues, they will be stilled; where there is knowledge, it will pass away." ~ Corinthians 13:4-8 NIV

Now that we understand a bit more that this life is a consciousness- based simulation, that we are all one, quantum-entangled from the first particle of light, that when something crosses our path that causes us frustration, stress, pain, and suffering, we don't need to move away, but rather we can embrace the experience with less or no judgment — now we can ask with compassion: "What is this experience here to teach me?", and "Why did I attract it in my life?"

You can't expect others to be like you. All souls are at their own level of development. A caterpillar will never understand the wisdom of a butterfly, as I mention at the start of this book. This understanding should bring you great compassion, and a sense of peace. After reading this book, you will hopefully have gained a deeper understanding and a greater tool box for living in this reality, with the ability to transmute negative experiences into opportunities for transformation and growth.

Other people in your circle might need to experience for themselves the knowledge in this book, and making it available for free as a PDF can mean that my gift to you can be a light offering that keeps on giving, transforming your life and the lives of the people around you, turning them from caterpillars to stunning, vibrant, beautiful butterflies. You also have to respect the ones in your life who do *not* wish to know, understand, grow, and evolve, as their path might be different, and they might have to experience the dark night of the soul, their own tempering fires, pains, and tribulations, before they can be open to something new, something greater. To those people, you can be a beacon of light and support, a reminder of what is possible, a shoulder to lean on in times of need. You can lead by example: be light, be love, be compassion, be kindness.

"Those who don't want to change, let them sleep." ~ Rumi

If you can move into your heart and grasp that any villain in your life, or the situation that is creating stress and heartache is only a messenger, providing lessons you directly or indirectly attracted, then and only then can you truly transform darkness into light. When this happens. miracles unfold. You are able to transform hate into love, destruction into creation, ugliness into beauty, aggression into kindness.

EGO-MIND-SEPARATENESS VS. THE SOUL

We are near the conclusion of this first book. One of the questions that I get a lot from my readers and attendees of live events is: "How do we know if and when we're on the right path, having learned all this?"

You can look at yourself in a mirror, and recognize how your thoughts, words, emotions, and actions are closer or further away from the path of light, using the following map.

The Ego/Mind seeks to serve itself;
The Soul seeks to serve others.

The Ego/Mind seeks outward recognition;
The Soul seeks inner authenticity.

The Ego/Mind sees life as a trap, prison, or competition;
The Soul sees life as a gift, a blessing, and an opportunity for growth.

The Ego/Mind seeks to preserve itself;
The Soul seeks to preserve, help, and support others.

The Ego/Mind looks outwards;
The Soul looks inward.

The Ego/Mind always feels incomplete, in a state of lacking.
The Soul feels complete and in a state of grace.

The Ego/Mind is scared, as it knows its mortality;
The Soul is at peace, as it knows its immortality.

The Ego/Mind and body are drawn by impulse and lust;
The Soul is drawn to lasting love.

The Ego/Mind desires knowledge to overcome insecurity;
The Soul seek inner wisdom.

The Ego/Mind looks for instant gratification, the price;
The Soul enjoys the Journey, as it knows this never ends.

The Ego/Mind identifies with separation, the cause of all suffering, loneliness, fear, and pain;
The Soul seeks unity, wisdom, love and healing, knowing that we are all one.

IMPORTANT; WHY MOST SELF DEVELOPMENT AND SPIRITUAL KNOWLEDGE <u>DOES NOT</u> TRANSFORM ONE'S LIFE

This part of this book is extremely important for you. It will be vital on your journey to fully understand and internalize this message in your life, so please pay full attention. It is one of the keys for personal alchemy and transmutation.

The reason why most self-development/spiritual courses and awakening books like this one leave a beautiful afterglow for a period of time after the event, but do not offer lasting effects, is because the knowledge acquired has not become internalized as a state of being. Being light, unity, compassion, kindness, and love is not something you do once in a while, after the bills are payed and the kids are in bed; it is something you have to become.

Any state of being, any feeling including happiness, is a chosen state. You have the power to endorse one polarity over the other at any time. If something throws you out of balance by triggering you and your emotions, thus gaining power over your state of being, this means that there is a lesson for you to learn. Otherwise, you would be in a state of peace, calm, love, and grace; you would not have been triggered.

I hope that what you have read up to this point has made you realize that life is a school for the soul. The relationships, the money, the possessions, the shiny toys, even the family are just props in this consciousness-based theatrical performance we call life, designed to make you more complete, unified, and light.

Everything is upside down. The props have gained central stage and our spiritual development has been hidden, opposed, and/or at times negated. Your life will change in an instant once you truly realize the true purpose of your life.

The knowledge in this book, if fully understood, has the power to completely change your life, as it has done for many others before you. But this only works if it is *not* something you do in your spare time, but is something you learn how to become, a higher state of being that you have learned how to integrate into every aspect of your life. This takes times and patience, and a lot of trial and error. This is nothing to be concerned about; it is all part of this journey of light and unity.

Your life becomes your initiation, and every aspect of your existence becomes part of your training — everything from brushing your teeth, to making a phone call, to preparing food for your dinner, to not getting upset with the person who has just cut you off on the road or who has been unkind.

From Caterpillar to Butterfly

MY TRANSFORMATION

When I first realized this a few years back, I was down and in a state of depression, feeling that my life meant very little and that I was not fulfilling my purpose. I had so much love, light, and knowledge to give, yet I was focusing on paying bills, loans, and credit cards. I felt a bit dead inside. My light and life force were dim, and I was barely surviving rather than living.

I realize that wherever I am, there I am. I did not need to be in a cave in the Himalayas, or in an Ashram in India, or in a monastery somewhere in the hills of Tuscany to create an inner space for this light, for this Divine energy, for what we call God. I could do it anywhere, at any time, no matter my job, no matter the environment I was in. I just needed to remember what I truly was: Light in human form; a son of the Source of all things; love yet unexpressed; a singularity of consciousness.

Armed with this awareness, I started looking at being a flight attendant for Virgin Australia in a completely different way. While serving drinks and food, I would smile at the person before serving them, and I would think: *I am facing a Divine self, another me in another physical vessel. I am honored and grateful to be at service to you and to be part of your journey.*

When serving an item from the cart, and seeing a fragile or angry person, I would imagine and say internally: *I give you light and love; may this item heal you, give you strength, and bring life and light into your body,* even if what I was offering was a soft drink full of sugars and toxins. As I performed the safety demo manually, I would imagine myself as an angel of light and, with my wings swinging forwards and backwards, I would visualize removing all the stress, frustration, anger, and darkness from all the passengers in front of and behind me. I would see these darker emotions as shadows being dissolved and transmuted in my light.

As I was driving to work, I would focus on the "Awareness Gratitude" meditation taught at my live events, or on a mantra. One that I created a long time ago is, "All is God, All is Light, All is One, All is Love; I am light, I am one with all, I am Love, I am one with God." Sometimes I would just focus on one for prolonged periods of time and see everything as examples of light — the car, the road, the trees, etc... Like Neo seeing the Matrix wherever he looked.

As I went to bed, I reviewed my day and blessed all the experiences I had been triggered by, to see what lessons I could learn. I also created my day (a practice I learned from Ramtha, a channel entity I learned from 1994 to 2009) and wrote down the tasks that I would like to accomplish the next day.

Now, you might think this is a lot of work. But do you consider driving home from work as hard work for you? Probably not, because it has become second nature. You have internalized it. If you have ever gone to the gym, you'll know that at the start it is hard work, but once it becomes part of who you are, then *not* going to the gym becomes hard work. This is not something that you do any longer, but something you have to become. Once you have become it, it is second nature; there is no effort, no thinking about it. For me, it is now a state of being; light is my natural state, and the more I increase this light and love inside myself, the more I have transcendental experiences, realizations, and awakenings.

The reason why I am telling you all this is because all of your life, even the most trivial parts, like serving a cup of coffee, can become an act of light and love, a form of meditation and prayer, and act of spiritual revolution and awakening. Your life is your initiation, after all!

CELEBRATE TODAY, THE NOW

Instead of focusing on a goal far into the future, you can enjoy the journey and be a light to the world wherever and whenever you are, while you are getting to where you want to be. You can stop delaying your fulfillment and happiness by attaching it to a thing, or an acquisition, or a state — one of the main reasons for depression.

You could stop saying, *I will be happy when I am out of my parents' home.* Or, *I will be happy when I have a good job*, or *I will be* happy when I find the love of my life, or *I will be happy when I have happy and healthy children*... and the *I will be happy when the children have stable jobs*, etc., etc. This never ends.

At the root of all desires is the desire to be loved and express love. It is the interaction of love in light that creates free will.

We really are light (as will become obvious in the book *You are Light* in this series), but it is through love that we express our light — as the following story will showcase, where I coach a very successful woman (by modern standards) around 38 years of age with no children or partner. I do One-on-One Coaching session when I have time. She came to me after having a few painful relationships and two broken marriages, feeling empty inside, depressed and purposeless.

(P will stand for Paolo and C for coached)

STORY: LOVE AND CHILDREN

After talking for about 20 minutes about her life and past experiences, I asked...

P. Why are you depressed? Why do you feel your life lacks purpose?

C. I have achieved financially all I could desire, but I still feel empty inside. I have no relationships and no children. I thought having all these properties, businesses, cars, and assets would make me happy, but it didn't; I still feel like something is missing.

P. So what do you think would make you happy? What is missing?

C. Having someone to love, who can love me back.

P. So you are looking for love?

C. Yes.

P. So love is what you are missing?

C. Yes, I guess.

P. Do you have love in your life right now?

C. Some, but not enough.

P. Is that the case, or are you so fixated on how this love *should* manifest in your life that you cannot see the love present in your life right now?

C. What do you mean?

P. Do you have family members who love you?

C. Yes, I do, and I am also lucky enough to have some good friends.

P. Do you spend very much time cultivating these relationships so that love can be expressed?

C. Not as much as I should.

P. So, potentially, you could have lots of love in your life, if your perspective and attitude changed.

C. Yes I could, but I believe it is not enough. I want children of my own, and a loving partner if possible.

P. Why?

C. So I can feel than that I am leaving something behind me, and when I am older, I have someone to look after me.

P. As you might have experienced indirectly, especially in Western society, having children is not a guarantee of them looking after you in your older days. Most elderly people are in fact left in nursing homes, and seldom receive visits. True legacies live in people you have inspired and helped, but your name will most likely be forgotten in the mists of time, like most all names are. We are not here to imprint our names in history books, but rather to complete a soul mission. Our legacy is not in the doing but in the being. These soul lessons are different for each one of us;

some might need to express it in a relationship, as a mother and wife, while others might have to experience a relationship with themselves to learn how to love themselves unconditionally.

But I want to know, are you looking for security, leaving a legacy behind, or for love? What is your primary desire?

C. Love. The resources, assets, and wealth I have could become the security, I guess. The legacy I thought would be my children.

P. You have attended one of my live events, right?

C. Yes, I did.

P. Great. So do you think your children are *your* children? Or are they just souls who have decided to come down to help us in this specific life?

C. I understand that conceptually, but there is a magic in growing a life inside of you.

P. As a man in this life, I can't fully understand that; however, I remember my other lives and the experiences as a woman, a mother and a wife, so I can relate to all you are saying at some levels. I understand the indescribable feeling of having another life inside of me, a little heart pulsating in unison with mine, and feeling this little life presence through the slightest movement, reminding me each time of the beautiful miracle and life I am carrying within myself.

So, I will ask again, why do you want children?

C. I believe it is because I am not experiencing love in my life.

P. Okay, we are getting somewhere now... If love is what you seek, if this is truly the cause of your deepest desire, then why don't you start recognizing that love is your natural state of being?

You are, at the core, light expressing love. When your life is based on fear or the mundane, you diminish this spark inside you, and naturally you feel empty, sad, as your light cannot express itself.

C. Why am I feeling this way if love is what I am? How can I get this spark back?

P. What happens if you put a beautiful bird in a cage?

C. What does our conversation have to do with birds?

P. Everything. So, what do you think?

C. Well, it would get sad, maybe stop eating, and maybe even die.

P. Why?

C. Because its nature is to fly, to be in nature and be social.

P. And what is your nature?

C. To be a mother?

P. This is an instinct, but at your core, are you really a mother? Or is this something that you might or might not do in this life? In the next life you could be born as a man, if that is what your soul needs.

C. I guess it's a role, not who I am.

P. Okay, so if being mother is something that you do, then what is your true nature, beyond genders, appearances, and roles?

C. Light, Love?

P. Yes, if you are love, then what would happen if you don't express love?

C. I would feel dead inside.

P. Like you are feeling inside now? Like a bird that cannot fly?

C. Ah yes, I understand your analogy now.

From Caterpillar to Butterfly

P. Do you know why you feel this way?

C. Because I am not flying? Not expressing my true nature?

P. Exactly. Because the cage you have created for yourself is the specific form you have decided this love has to show itself as. You are saying to life and the universe: *"Unless love comes through a baby of my own, I will feel empty, loveless. Love is nonexistent in my life."* Thus, belief in how this love should appear in your life has created the bars in your prison, your cage, as you have made the limiting decision that only through this experience can you receive love. Truth is, you *are* love. This is your natural state. All desires, in fact, go back to this: Express, be LOVE.

Everything around you is possible because of love. Without love, nature will die, mothers of all species will stop caring for their babies, and men would stop having lasting and stable relationships with the opposite sex. The car you are driving is the result of the imagination and love of engineers, designers, and mechanics. The cup of coffee you have is the result of the labor of love of a potter, who cared for his work, and the love of a coffee farmer.

Love is the engine of creation and life. Without it, nothing exists. So could it be possible, then, that by expressing love, you could rekindle the spark of light within yourself again?

C: Yes, I understand now.

P. You don't need to depend on someone outside of you to be who you already are; you just need to spend time being that. Feel, express, and nourish the love you are and have now in your life. Then, if your soul purpose calls for the experience of a partner and children, or even just a child, the universe and the soul contracts you set in place before your descent into this physical reality will come to fruition by their own accord.

Be love, be what you most desire, give to others what you are, express kindness, donate time in an orphanage, feed the homeless, take care of a garden, spend time with your pets if you have any, or feed and love abandoned, forgotten dogs and cats in shelters.

The Science of Consciousness

Spend time with your family and friends, and become a greater part of their lives.

What you express, you become. By focusing on what you lack, you are only reinforcing your unhappiness and lack of love. Be love, and love will flow in your life from all directions. The secret to having anything is to become what you seek. If you want wealth, have a wealth mindset; become wealth. If you desire unity, become unified in all you do. If you desire love, be love.

At the root of all desires, including purposefulness and happiness, is love. All of that can be achieved now, today, this minute, by simply changing your inner perspective of how you are supposed to experience love. If you wait for a partner or a child to make you feel love, you are powerless, as you are waiting for something outside of you to fulfill you. That was and is your sole responsibility; what a partner or a child does is just mirroring you. Do you understand?

C. Yes. So I don't need anything; I can have love now.

P. Yes, you can have love now, by being love now.

C. Thank you, I understand.

END

The Ego-Body-Mind can never be fulfilled. Only the higher self, the soul, can. If you truly want to seek lasting fulfillment, your focus has to shift.

If you think that you want to leave something behind for your kids, and you also understand that this is a soul school, then you can see that it's not what you give to your children, not what you leave to your children that makes them great, but rather what you LEAVE IN them that makes all the difference. Your legacy, if you have kids, consists of the wisdom, the lessons, the values, and the morals that you have left as seeds in their consciousness. It is how much you have allowed and nourished their own light.

From Caterpillar to Butterfly

I love Kahlil Gibran's poetry, in which he explains so well what children really are:

"And a woman who held a babe against her bosom said, "Speak to us of Children." And he said: Your children are not your children. They are the sons and daughters of Life's longing for itself.

They come through you but not from you, and though they are with you, yet they belong not to you. You may give them your love but not your thoughts. For they have their own thoughts. You may house their bodies but not their souls; for their souls dwell in the house of tomorrow, which you cannot visit, not even in your dreams.

You may strive to be like them, but seek not to make them like you. For life goes not backward nor tarries with yesterday. You are the bows from which your children as living arrows are sent forth.

The archer (God) sees the mark upon the path of the infinite, and He bends you with His might that His arrows may go swift and far. Let your bending in the archer's hand be for gladness; For even as he loves the arrow that flies, so He loves also the bow that is stable."

From the book *The Prophet* by Kahlil Gibran, FREE inside the Members area or $12 on Amazon and $12.62 on Book Depository.

(AM: https://amzn.to/2uwuh2y; BD: https://tinyurl.com/t5go8sx)

Your legacy if you have no children, like myself and my wife, is the light, love, kindness, wisdom, and knowledge you leave behind.

This life's purpose, however, is not to leave a legacy behind; most of the greatest people in history have been forgotten, unless you come across a biography or history book sharing their story. Have you ever read about Apollonius of Tyana, a spiritual teacher, contemporary to Jesus, who accomplished all the miracles that Jesus did? Have you read of the Stoic Philosophy and of Marcus Aurelius, the most enlightened leader and Caesar in Roman history?

The Science of Consciousness

Nikola Tesla is now known by many, but just a few years back, no one knew who he was, even though the entire world uses his electricity patents to light up the world we live in.

This life's purpose is to become more complete, more light, more love, closer to your natural Divine state. This is why you face so many challenges and tribulations in this life. All of these are there to forge the sword of understanding, strengthen the self, and develop wisdom, so that one day you can remember your true nature.

Celebrate life; celebrate yourself and others as Divine lights. In this way, your life becomes an extension and an expression of this stunning, marvelous Divine intelligence that is all around us and within us. It becomes the meditation, the contemplation, the prayer. This is how you can transform your life and enter a state of peace and grace beyond any of the storms of life.

THE NEXT STEP:
Book II in the AWAKENING Series:
How to Create Miracles:
A Practical Guide into the Extraordinary

"There is a difference between knowing the path and walking the path." ~ Morpheus, *The Matrix*

This first book has all being about helping you navigate this current Life Matrix. The problem, as Morpheus said in *The Matrix*, is: *"You have to understand, Neo. Most people are not ready to be unplugged from the Matrix, and many of them are so injured, so hopelessly dependent on the system, that they will fight to protect it."*

Fighting and arguing to protect one's limitations is why I covered Cognitive Dissonance at the beginning of this book. Minds are like parachutes; they work better when they are open. Hearts, too, can only feel when we allow them to be open and receptive.

This book was the first step in helping you realize that we live in a consciousness-based reality that I call the Life Matrix and the Source Field. Your thoughts, beliefs, emotions, words, and actions attract the reality and destiny that best resonate with your perceptions. Realizing this brings you to the understanding that we are creators rather than victims.

This is not a book that you can read just once, as you have probably realized by now, but one that needs to be reviewed, internalized, discussed, and applied. Only then it will truly and fully transform your life from within.

There is a hidden war being waged on your consciousness, mind, and heart in this society. It is a war between the forces that want to keep you entrapped in this illusion (plugged in, like in *The Matrix*), making you feel that you are powerless, a victim of circumstances, a slave of the system; and the ones wanting to reconnect you to the truth light, re-awakening you to your Divine heritage.

If your consciousness is a Field, then looking at how you SPEND YOUR TIME, what you PAY ATTENTION TO and where you INVEST YOUR ENERGY (the three human currencies of time, attention, and energy) will showcase what direction your life will take and what destiny you'll attract.

If you have wisely spent time reading this book and have come this far, it means you are one of the few who is on the path of awakening, on the path of understanding your true light, heritage, and purpose. YOU ARE AN ADVANCED SOUL.

The messenger is irrelevant; it is the message that counts. You could have spent time in other spiritual endeavors, of course, which will have still mattered, but I am happy that you took this journey with me. For this, I am truly grateful.

You looked at your life, and affirmed loudly:

"There must be something more than this!"

And by doing so, you started questioning life, and your life quest began.

"I was not born to pay bills and spend my life in the quest of paying off a house, which I might not even enjoy in the end!"

"Life expectancy is 78; retirement age is around 65, if not later. Did I work for over 50+ years to spend my last 10 between doctors, hospitals, and nursing homes? Is this what life is about? It can't be."

"I have followed what the system told me I needed to do to be happy and fulfilled, and yet I am stilling feeling empty, drained, and depressed. Why?"

The Next Step

"Why are we living in a society where we are taught that it is OK just to survive, instead of thrive? Where we are told that we do not matter, that we are insignificant? Why do we have a depression epidemic? Why are we told that chasing impermanence is the key to fulfillment and happiness, when it clearly is not?"

"Why are we not spending time doing the things that bring us joy and that we love doing, and instead are trapped in a never-ending hamster wheel of survival?"

"Who are we... truly? Why are we here? What is our purpose? What are we supposed to do in this life?"

And again...

"There must be something more than this!"

Hopefully, some clarity has been provided in this body of work. But this is just the beginning.

The books in this series will continue to take you on more outrageous journeys, more mind opening and exhilarating discoveries.

What You'll Learn in the Next Book: *How to Create Miracles: A Practical Guide into the Extraordinary*

All the knowledge we have covered so far points to something incredible: the fact that there is exists a UNIFIED FIELD where all matter, all that exists, is connected on a subatomic level, exchanging information through light, resonance, waves, and frequency.

This suggests, therefore, that even we humans are nothing more than coagulations of light, and information interacting, resonating, and pulsating at all times with all that exists.

The Science of Consciousness

The Laws of Physics, like motion, first published in the *Principia* in 1687 by Newton, describe a universe with self-contained, unchangeable laws. But they are no longer fixed, rigid, and inviolable; rather, in the light of quantum physics and consciousness experimentation, they take on a semblance of a dynamic sea of consciousness, manifesting itself through diverse layers of expression and density.

The more we understand consciousness and the role it plays in this co-participatory universe, the more we have to tear up the old rulebooks of what we *believed* to be real and possible, and burn them in the fires of awareness, scattering the ashes to the winds of change.

"A human being is part of the whole, called by us 'universe', a part limited in time and space. He experiences himself, his thoughts and feelings as something separated from the rest — a kind of optical delusion of his consciousness." ~ Albert Einstein

Matter is no longer a rigid, unchangeable block or thing, but rather a cloud of potentiality that can no longer be viewed in isolation, but rather as part of the fabric of life, dynamically exchanging information and interacting with everything around it. On a subatomic level, therefore, matter does not appear to be isolated particles, but starts to look like droplets of water in one unified field similar to an ocean, involved in a continual exchange of light, frequencies, and information, constantly changing, adapting, and responding to the overall matrix of reality.

Armed with this knowledge, your entire life can be transformed.

Knowing full well by now how the observer influences the quantum field and is the driving force, the coagulant of reality, we can recognize that what we call life is malleable, fluid, responsive, and subject to our creative commands. The power of intent and coherence, in hundreds of consciousness-based experiments and case studies, also proves that consciousness is at the base of all that exist. Thoughts, especially when coherent and directed, have the power to create reality and affect matter at all levels.

The Next Step

Thoughts, emotions, and intent have the power to not only change our reality, but potentially the world at large. It appears that coherent intention functions like a huge tuning fork, causing anything that is frequency-specific, in tune with it, to resonate in the same way. What we resonate with, we become and attract in our field of experience. This is becoming more and more obvious with each passing page in this book and with each scientific case study under our belt, proving that even space and time are no obstacle or limitation.

In fact, all of this book was focused on making you, the reader, unveil how consciousness is at the base of all things, and how the act of focused, coherent attention can affect physical matter. Which means that we are not only creators but also influencers, able to influence people, places, things, times, and events, which brings in itself a sense of purpose, and great potential and opportunity to change your life in any given moment.

Can someone believe so much in an outcome that they create miracles? If so, how, why, and what happens when a person produces a miraculous healing? Or, to rephrase, how do you create miracles in your life?

Does a group of coherent people, focusing on one intent, have more power and efficiency than a single person?

How do you affect your present reality, life, and the world in a practical way? Is there a methodology, a science to it?

These will be the subjects of the next book in this series, *How to Create Miracles: A Practical Guide into the Extraordinary*. This is no ordinary book; it is a book where you can have a direct co-participatory influence, if you wish to do so (it is not mandatory) by participating in The Intent Coherence Project online. This is not dissimilar to many such coherent consciousness projects popping up everywhere, as the efficiency of this knowledge comes to full view.

I have been using group coherence since 1989, and have come to fully appreciate its power in changing people's lives. If you want to take part, you will just need to check periodically for experiments, results, feedback, and announcements on the website and the other social media platforms.

You, like all readers of these books, have the power to be part of something greater, a life purpose designed to help yourself and increase your love and light by giving others light through the power of coherent intent. This includes creating groups with one intent, focusing as one mind and one heart on healing a person at a distance, manifesting wealth and abundance where there is none, reducing crime, or sending rain to an area affected by drought and fires, as has been done during the summer of 2019-2020 here in Australia.

What you will discover is that the more you give a specific frequency like healing, the more healing you will get in your life. The more you help another to attract wealth and abundance, the more money will flow into your life. What you focus on grows; what you entertain, you become. Thoughts and intent matter; they change and influence physical objects, people, and situations, small and large. This next book will be a practical manual on how to accomplish the extraordinary in your life.

You will also discover how to heal broken relationships, and how to change world politics and economics without even interacting with another person, and much more. Truly, it is a book on HOW TO CREATE MIRACLES in your life, and the lives of others.

In Book 3 on this series, *You Are Light*, we will start to unveil the light coding behind the matrix, and finally have the scientific evidence to prove that we are truly beings of light, living in a simulated reality based on duality. I will reveal the sacred code and sacred Gnostic knowledge contained in Leonardo da Vinci paintings and the works of other esoteric adepts. We will review some more of the hidden, repressed, and lost teachings of Joshua Ben Joseph, also known as Jesus.

You will learn why there is a food allergy epidemic, and how and what the ancient masters, philosophers, and initiates ate. If you know of anyone with food allergies, this is a must-read book. We will also delve into the mystery of why so many ancient civilizations focused on the Sun, how humanity's evolution has followed sun cycles, the flow of nature through the understanding of the Tao, the Yin and Yang, and much more.

In Book 4 on this series: *Many Lives, Many Lessons, One Destination*, we will start to unraveling even further the truth about who you are, your life purpose, and how the engine of evolution truly works. Concepts like Hell, the idea of one life only to get it right, and the concept of a judgmental, chauvinistic, self-absorbed, egomaniacal, psychotic, and selfish God punishing its creation will be put aside for a more inclusive, compassionate, all-loving Divine principle. Reincarnation was in fact one of the main tenets of Jesus Christ's original teachings, which was removed to adapt it to the Sol Invictus faith and Mithralic, Egyptian cults of the time in the Roman Empire.

To see which books are in the pipeline, please visit this webpage: https://paolotiberi.com/books/paolos-books/

As our journey continues through all the books in this Awakening Series as well as the other, related series, as many readers and students of the great work have attested, you will be transformed; and as a result, your life will become increasingly based on light and higher frequency vibrations, making your life fuller, more complete, more peaceful, and happier — moving you from the ordinary to the extraordinary, from physicality of the body through the light of the higher self, from the natural to the supernatural.

The Choice Was Mine Once; Now It Is Yours

This was part of the end of my NDE experience, before returning to my body. There was so much more that has not been discussed here, as it is more relevant to other books in the series, and it will be included there. I have inserted this here because it is fitting for the ending of this book.

"You are indeed a creator, and one with the all. Everything is you. Once you fully realize this, the Ego, the limited self, will dissolve as you start seeing the other person as yourself. All the sense of importance, all the sense of superiority, all the insecurities and

fears will dissolve when you fully understand that you are part of this creation and one with God, a singularity of light and consciousness living a physical experience. After the experience you are having right now, you will forget.

"*You will be lost for many years. Some of the knowledge shared in this Near Death Experience will stay with you, but most will be sleeping in the recesses of your memory, waiting for a day where you are ready to be light again. Many questions you will still have, some which have been answered to you before, but never fully comprehended, internalized, or lived.*

"*The illusions of life will take precedence; the lacks, the fears, the confusions will make you take many different paths. You will enter forgetfulness, and you will become entrapped in its grasp of illusions, tricks, and trinkets. This is because you have learned some of the knowledge, but will have missed becoming the knowledge, internalizing what you have this far comprehended.*

"*Then, one day, after searching everywhere, to the other side of the world and back for answers to reconcile your doubts, fears, and misunderstanding, you will start, little by little, to reconcile the paradoxes of life, duality in unity, physicality in energy, matter in wave, and darkness in light; and finally, you will remember this experience.*

"*On that day, when you are able to find a point of centeredness and silence within you, without outside distractions, then I will talk to you again. But not before you have made a decision.*"

"What decision?" I asked.

He continued, "*An important decision has to be made... Are you going to live your life like a powerless nobody, a son of man, or are you going to reclaim your rightful position as a son of the light, a creator in his own right, and a manifester of reality? Are you going to allow life to happen to you, or are you going to create and manifest your desires through the sacred laws of the Divine?*

The Next Step

"All of us are given the same gifts, the same tools; all of us are subjected to the same laws; all of us have the same potential and birthright. Your thoughts, emotions, and intent create the nature of your reality. Consciousness, light, and love are all that exist, in different states of manifestation and density.

"The choice is yours.

"Are you going to live like a bright star, shining its loving light and knowledge on all that you encounter, living a positive imprint on all... or are you going to live like a small candle left in a dusty, forgotten room in the corridors of life?

"You don't need to become a writer, a public speaker, a president, a famous actor, or powerful magnate; this is not what I am saying. You could live in a poor village in a remote area of a Third World country, but still be a light to that entire nation, even if only a few people know you and your name. No matter how humble your work, or how unglamorous it might appear, you can still grow, evolve, and make a difference. Wherever you are, there you are. As we are truly all one, helping just one person means helping all.

"There is a beautiful story that you are familiar with, so I will use it here to give you context.

"There was once a little child walking on the beach with his grandfather, a very renowned and wealthy person in his community. At the time, there were thousands of starfishes on the beach after a recent storm and high water currents. There were so many starfishes that it looked like the sand was moving, with all the erratic creatures trying to survive, and struggling to go back into the water.

"While the grandfather was thinking deeply about his assets, and company issues, and legacy, the little child was busy running around, looking at the liveliest starfishes, and throwing them back into the sea. The grandfather looked at the child with content and judgment. "How cute... he has no clue," he thought within himself.

The Science of Consciousness

When the child came closer to his grandfather again, the old man asked: "Why are you doing this, my child? Can you not see that there are tens of thousands of starfishes on the seashore, if not more? How do you think you can make a difference, when there are so many?" The grandfather thought that he was wise, and was teaching a valuable lesson to the young boy.

The young buy looked at his grandfather with a big smile on his face, and put both his two little hands on his heart. After collecting his thoughts, he responded: "I might not be able to make a difference to all of them, but for the few that are back into the water, I made a big difference! For them and maybe even for their children, and the children of their children after them!"

"Paolo," said the light entity, "What you do to one, you do to all. Make your life a testament to your inner beauty, your light, your love for others, and your greatness of spirit. Make your thoughts a seed of light, your words a gentle, loving caress that nourishes the souls of those in your presence; let each of your actions, no matter how small, be a majestic act of kindness, compassion, light, and love. Then your light will be mightier than a king, and more beautiful than the greatest Hollywood star to have graced the silver screen.

"Share your knowledge and the lessons you have learned, no matter in what capacity — no matter how much you might be ridiculed, judged, or repressed. Write, and write more, speak, and speak more, and share your awareness and awakening with as many people as you can, so that the other you in a different body can also be transformed by the same realizations.

"I am your higher self. I am you, and you are me. We are Light, we are Love, we are One.

"So it is, now and forever."

The Next Step

Closing Affirmations

I am content, I have arrived, I am home. What I am looking for is right here, right now. I have a loving wife, a roof over my head, food in my belly, people who allow me to express gratitude and kindness, and I have love in my heart for all. All I have left to do is to be light and share light with YOU and others, wherever and whenever I am.

That is the greatest secret I have learned: be what you wish to become.

My hope is that this book has given you some insight, increasing your light, love, and compassion, and has helped you in your journey.

If you decide to send this entire book or a chapter or small part of this book (in any format — video, audio, text, or live event), I ask you to please include the source (the book title), and the authorship of the work (myself), so that the reader can expand on the knowledge you have shared if they wish to do so. This is the only requirement I have.

If you would like to purchase this book in physical format, or have a few copies to share around, as this will help me greatly and support this cause, you can get it from the links below.

BOOK LINKS

To purchase this book in physical form please visit http://www.paolotiberi.com or search on Amazon or online book sellers

---

The Science of Consciousness

If you would like to help further, please look over the next pages. There are many ways you can make a difference, and in doing so, you can make this endeavor a part of your life, purpose, and path.

Thank you once again for taking this journey with me. I leave you with a series of affirmations that I normally use at the end of my live events.

"In the face of great obstacles, difficulties, uncertainty, and conflicting sensory information, I recognize more and more the magical, infinite, nurturing reality that I live in. I am the son, the daughter of Divine Intelligence. I was never abandoned, never separate from its loving embrace.

"I understand now that I am neither the events of my life, nor the roles of each passing reincarnation. And even if I may feel otherwise, trapped and triggered by the storms of life as well as the heroes and the villains in my play of life, I recognize that I am that which transcends all the borders of life, death, and limited identities.

"I am consciousness; I am light in human form, and I have the power to create any reality I wish to manifest. I further recognize that living within this magical reality, as a Creation among my Creations, is the ultimate adventure.

"All I have to do is be the light that I always have been, be the love that runs through every cell in my body, and express my inner beauty, kindness and understanding to all beings, big and small.

"Duality is just a game of consciousness playing hide and seek in order for my soul to learn, grow and move above the realm of illusion, separation and duality. Not good, not bad, it just is.

"I will no longer fall for the illusions of separation and duality, seeking to have rather than be, to be trapped by the wheel of pain and pleasure, but rather to recognize the light, love, unity, and perfection of this great consciousness-based reality, and in doing so freeing myself from the grasps of suffering.

The Next Step

"I realize that in this loving and magical creation, my intent, thoughts, and emotions create my experience, and allow my nightmares as well as my dreams to come true. My hell or my heaven... It is my choice, my command, my creation.

"I recognize that love is the engine of creation and is the base and the Divine glue of all that exists. Love conquers all, because Love is the driving force of all that exists. In this light, all that we perceive as wrong is a result of lack of love, as how could you have true unconditional love and still have suffering?

"Therefore, as I recognize more and more the power that is within me, I pledge to use this power, wisdom, and knowledge for love, compassion, kindness, light, and the benefit of all beings.

"Finally, I promise to myself to love and be at peace, in the better times and in the darker times, no matter what I face, as I realize the bigger picture and the plan behind my life and all that exists.

"I chose to love myself, appreciate myself, and respect myself in this new light of understanding.

"All is Light, all is Love, all is One, all is God.

"With love, light, compassion, and kindness for all, I will express my life, now and forever.

"So be it."

I am extremely grateful that you have shared this journey of knowledge and love with me.

Closing Prayers

"Layer by layer I removed all that I thought I was, all that I thought I had been, and in the moment I was left standing naked and vulnerable without identities and labels. Then I remembered: I am light, I am love, I am all, I am that I am." ~ Anonymous

"Pachamama, Mother Earth, sweet Mother,
We come here for the healing nourishment of all your children; the Stone People, the Plant People, the four-legged, the two-legged, the creepy crawlers, the finned, the furred, and the winged ones. All our relations that are here to teach us."
~ Native American Prayer

"Lord, make me an instrument of your peace
Where there is hatred, let me sow love
Where there is injury, pardon
Where there is doubt, faith
Where there is despair, hope
Where there is darkness, light
And where there is sadness, joy
O Divine Master, grant that I may
Not so much seek to be consoled as to console
To be understood, as to understand
To be loved, as to love
For it is in giving that we receive
And it is in pardoning that we are pardoned
And it is in dying that we are born to Eternal Life.
Amen." ~ Saint Francis of Assisi

THANK YOU

Other Books by Paolo F. Tiberi

GET INVOLVED:
Share Your Light and Understanding

This specific book has come to an end. It was a pleasure having you come on this journey with me, page by page, moment by moment, day by day. In this time, I shared with you my knowledge, my personal experience, my vulnerabilities, my mind, my heart, and my soul — without filters, without conditions, without concerns. It was me and you, connecting on a deeper consciousness- and light-based level.

You could keep and forget this PDF book and even delete it now, or treasure the message so much that, like a seed, it can grow into the consciousness of others as a beautiful tree providing shelter and hope, at many levels, to those who are still lost.

I am extremely passionate in spreading this message to the world and seeing you grow, awaken, heal, and create the miraculous in your life.

If you would like know when new books become available, join my social media, links are provided below.

BOOK MAILING LIST: http://paolotiberi.com/books/book-mailing-list/

This will make sure you are notified if there is a live event in your area or a new book release is scheduled, as well as notifying you about group awareness activities you can participate in. You are not alone; you can join this family of light in whatever way you like. You don't need to join them at all, or join them all, just the ones you use the most if this is what you feel resonating with you.

I believe it is time for a more enlightened society worldwide to emerge, and a perfected human being to be nurtured and assisted in his or her personal journey. For this reason, I have included many possible ways in which you can play a role, bringing these concepts, ideas, wisdom, and practices to the people around you.

The Science of Consciousness

You can make a difference; you can bring a sparkle of life, hope and magic into other people's lives. How little or how much you want to be involved is up to you. Below are some suggestions, a couple of which I have already mentioned.

How many people suffering depression or struggling to live do you know who could benefit from reading this book? Share it with them; it's free in PDF format, and because is below 5 MB in size, is easy to send to almost any email account. It only takes a few minute to do so.

If you have a beautiful, inspiring email you would like to share with others to help them read the book, I can post it on the awakeningfromthematrix.com > resources > email suggestions.

If you want to send me an email to share how this book has transformed your life, please do so; I would love to know how it has helped you.

I have listed in the next section a few possible ways you can be part of this light/change movement.

To see other ways in which you can get involved and support this book and message please visit:
https://paolotiberi.com/books/get-involved/

Information on how to become a volunteer or an organizer can also be found at the above URL address.

ABOUT PAOLO F. TIBERI

Born in Rome, Italy, Paolo has dedicated most of his life exploring the subject of the self, human nature, and the unlimited potential of human beings. After having seen, at the age of 5, his grandmother successfully heal individuals with terminal diseases, and his mother leading people into a state of trance, speaking ancient languages, and reliving their past lives, Paolo's curiosity in unraveling the mysteries of the unknown brought precedence over everything else in his life.

Between the age of 12 and 23, Paolo embarked on his own Self Development journey, and during this period he become a certified Kinesiology Practitioner, Crystal Therapist, Aroma Therapist, Chromo Therapist, Auric and Prano-Therapist, and Reiki Usui Master. Through these disciplines, Paolo realized that there were still many aspects to life and learning that were missing. He therefore branched out to study the mind and the body in more details and therefore become a certified Neuro-Linguistic Programming (NLP) practitioner, Hypnotherapist, Past Life Regressionist (with Dolores Cannon), Gym Instructor and Personal

The Science of Consciousness

Trainer (Level IV). To better integrate and understand the soul-body-mind paradigm, Paolo decided to branch out more and study quantum physics, neurology, cell biology, chemistry, physiology, psychology, and other related sciences, which eventually led him to put more pieces of the puzzle together.

In his quest for knowledge and understanding (and thanks to his mother being a flight attendant for Alitalia, and providing cheap tickets) he was able to travel extensively by himself from the age of 15 throughout Europe, Africa, Asia, India, and North and South America, encountering some of the best thinkers, teachers, and masters in the areas of spiritual education, human behavior, and self-mastery with whom he spent as much time as possible.

During this journey, Paolo studied many different types of esoteric and spiritual traditions and religions, including Hermetic, Egyptian, Sufism, Shamanistic, Indian (Advaita, Kashmiri Shivaism, Vedas), Tibetan (Nyingma-Dzogchen), Zen, Greek Philosophers, Christian, and Essene.

Then, while in Italy in 1994, Paolo began studying other channeled material like the Ra Materials (*The Law of One*), Seth, Esther Hicks, and Ramtha's materials, which eventually led him in 1999 to participate in some of his events until 2007.

There, he learned some core knowledge like: creating your day, body-mind-consciousness, the somebody to nobody to everybody concept, the neuronet and its formation and operation, arguing for your limitations, becoming greater than your body and environment, how you create your personal reality, making known the unknown, the different states of awareness, brain wave states, victim to creator, matter to wave, natural to supernatural, ordinary to extraordinary, involution and evolution of the soul, Newtonian perception to quantum perception, philosophy to wisdom, the "Neighborhood Walk" to change neurological neuronet and reality (walking while identifying being a new person, with new traits one wants to have), and C&E or Consciousness & Energy Breath Process to elevate the lower energy and change to higher brain/frequency states. The knowledge he received was pivotal to his progress at the time, and therefore he likes to acknowledge it and honor it.

About Paolo F. Tiberi

For many people looking for answers or starting out, looking in unusual and mysterious places might result in a loss of credibility and trustworthiness in the knowledge offered. That's why many public speakers present today who come from that gnostic, esoterical background and from mystery schools have opted to negate, refuse, and reject any direct association and connections to that type of legacy, whenever it might appear to be unusual, bizarre, peculiar, weird, different, and/or non-scientific.

People learn from different sources and make other's knowledge their own. Some great teachers who are doing great work on this planet, like Dr. Joe Dispenza for example, have simplified, expanded, modified, and redeveloped older concepts and given them a more scientific flair. This allowed Dr. Dispenza to bring ancient esoterical knowledge from Gnostic Schools, like J.Z. Knight's Ramtha School, to a larger audience and avoid the backlash from more scientifically minded people and communities. This approach also allowed him to rename and repackage some of the practices learned at this school, and in doing so give them a modern twist.

Although he is no longer in that school, Paolo will be forever thankful for the awakenings, learning, and even the challenges he was given while he was there. All made him who he is today—the good, the bad, and the ugly.

His passion to share his unique ideas with a wider audience moved him toward the public speaking arena. He began transmitting the knowledge and personal experience of self-discovery and awareness and life strategies he had acquired to people of all backgrounds and ages in Italy, starting at the age of 17, and eventually Australia, where he now resides.

During his life, he has been invited to appear on different television shows in Italy, and had his own television program for a few months on a small, regional television channel in Rome at age 19, before he decided to move to Australia. In Australia, he has been invited to teach in different organizations, such as Salvation Army Employment Plus, where he was asked to inspire unemployed people. He also had a 30-minute section on Radio

The Science of Consciousness

Italia, an Italian radio station broadcasting to 250,000 Australians nationwide.

During a period of over nine years of inactivity from the public speaking arena, Paolo worked full-time as a flight attendant. Today, Paolo continues to run seminars, day events, and coaching sessions with private clients. Through his message, Paolo endeavors to integrate science, medicine, and Western and Eastern philosophies, bringing the mind, body, and soul together. His unique way of communicating information allows for quicker and higher retention while keeping you attentive and involved.

Already having inspired and motivated many others around the world to make significant and positive changes in their lives and in their relationships, Paolo helps you rediscover your higher self by empowering you to choose to embrace your higher life/self's purpose instead of your limited personality. Paolo's approach is highly interactive, compelling, and extremely impactful.

Lately he has been working on completing his Awakening Series, which has been offered in PDF format for free, in order to help a wider number of individuals in their personal journey to self-discovery.

"All knowledge and keys are already within us; the only effort is to unveil our true light and decide to be it," he shares with his audience.

"In times of crisis and confusion, what you need most is to re-awaken your inner power and awareness. When you start re-aligning yourself, then all is revealed and you reunify yourself. Your life becomes a great adventure instead of a continuous challenge. Experiences are seen in a different way, and a profound sense of belonging—peace, harmony and love—start to become more and more part of your reality and life. Then you are able to move from surviving to thriving, from the ordinary to the extraordinary." ~ Paolo Tiberi

The messages offered during Paolo's events are provided in a way that is not dogmatic, religious, or structured. Instead, they offer

About Paolo F. Tiberi

you the opportunity to expand within your own paradigm of understanding and knowledge.

For more information, please visit:

www.paolotiberi.com

And remember... if you have ever felt like you did not fit in this world, it is because you are here to help create a new one.

The Science of Consciousness

Suggested Readings

SUGGESTED READINGS

These are some of the books mentioned in this book, as well as other books that have helped me awaken further.

Chapter 1
The Art of Peace by Morihei Ueshiba
Book Depository Link (BDL): https://tinyurl.com/syzt3p6
Amazon Link (AML): https://amzn.to/2RuFg5B

Chapter 8
Molecules of Emotion by Dr. Candace B. Pert
Book Depository Link: https://tinyurl.com/u3t4plu
Amazon Link: https://amzn.to/37uLqbp

The Heart's Code: Tapping The Wisdom and Power of Our Heart Energy by Dr. Paul Pearsall
Book Depository Link: https://tinyurl.com/r4krdpq
Amazon Link: https://amzn.to/2uELV3V

Chapter 9
This Book Will Change Your Life by Ben Carey
Book Depository Link: https://tinyurl.com/yx6ct9e7
Amazon Link: https://amzn.to/37tmXTH

Programming the Universe: A Quantum Computer Scientist Takes on the Cosmos by Seth Lloyd
Book Depository link: https://tinyurl.com/vm8bkpp
Amazon Link: https://amzn.to/2RP1bmZ

Chapter 11
The Energy Cure by William Bengston
Book Depository link: https://tinyurl.com/s7t84cm
Amazon Link: https://amzn.to/38KLBQb

The Intention Experiment by Lynne McTaggart
Book Depository link: https://tinyurl.com/r5ozk79
Amazon Link: https://amzn.to/37t8qXl

Chapter 15
New Testament Origin by Dr. George M. Lamsa
Book Depository Link: https://tinyurl.com/sbbsd2h
Amazon Link: https://amzn.to/38CQ86U

Prayers of the Cosmos by Neil Douglas-Klotz
Book Depository Link: https://tinyurl.com/u3vohhk
Amazon Link: https://amzn.to/31UXYH7

Chapter 17
The Interconnected Universe: Conceptual Foundations of Transdisciplinary Unified Theory by Erwin Laszlo
Book Depository Link: https://tinyurl.com/wlm5efy
Amazon Link: https://amzn.to/38IpWbm

Chapter 21
Cymatics: A Study of Wave Phenomena and Vibration by Hans Jenny
Book Depository Link: https://tinyurl.com/wz773bx
Amazon Link: https://amzn.to/37yq0di

Chapter 22
The Source Field Investigations by David Wilcock
Book Depository Link: https://tinyurl.com/rlmw79o
Amazon Link: https://amzn.to/2tJf4Lx

BOOK I MEMBERS RESOURCES

All of the resources for this book can be found at:
http://www.PaoloTiberi.com

Chapter 2
VIDEO: Karate Kid – Wax on, Wax off

Chapter 6
To test for heavy metals, like lead, mercury, aluminum, fluoride, etc.: https://amzn.to/2RnTZzk, https://amzn.to/2RdcBlP, https://amzn.to/2ra0vz2

VIDEO: The Matrix - The Pill scene

Chapter 8
VIDEO: Infant crying until Heart Transfer recipient holds the baby

PDF: 1998, Hameroff; "Quantum Computation in Brain Microtubules: The Penrose Hameroff Orch OR Model of Consciousness."

Chapter 9
Two great videos showcasing this experiment can be found by typing on YouTube: "Dr. Quantum - Double Slit Experiment" (https://www.youtube.com/watch?v=DfPeprQ7oGc) or you can see this video in the member's area.

As well as The Original Double Slit Experiment review, which can be seen in the member's area or on YouTube: https://www.youtube.com/watch?v=Iuv6hY6zsd0

Chapter 12
Manifestation Guide PDF

Chapter 13
For a visual of Quantum Entanglement please see: https://www.livescience.com/28550-how-quantum-entanglement-works-infographic.html

Chapter 14
Book of Enoch PDF

Hebraic Roots Version of the Torah PDF

Gospel of Thomas PDF

CHAPTER 17
Gravity-Superconductors Interactions: Theory and Experiment by Giovanni Modanese:
 https://www.youtube.com/watch?v=sH1p6Cn7ft4

Chapter 19
32 Metronomes,
https://www.youtube.com/watch?v=5v5eBf2KwF8)

Video: The Laughing Man in the Train

Video "Pay It Forward"

Chapter 21
VIDEO: What is A Fractal (and what are they good for)?

Chapter 22
VIDEO: "Look Me in the Eye"

ACKNOWLEDGMENTS

I would like to express my deep and sincere gratitude to all the individuals involved directly and indirectly in the creation of these manuscripts.

To Joshua Crook, for being the pivotal push for me to start teaching again.

To all of the authors, teachers, and mentors along the way who have provided invaluable guidance throughout this work.

To all the villains, liars, selfish and self-centered individuals, fake masters, and con artists who have shown me the ways not to take.

I am incredibly blessed and thankful to my wife for her unwavering love, suggestions, edits, illustrations, understanding, and continuing support as I completed this work. Her kind love and everlasting willingness to help me through the lows and highs of life's roller coaster rides, always patient, always caring, always loving, make me the luckiest man alive. Knowing that this beautiful soul has my back and will always be there for me makes this journey much easier to take.

To my closest students and life friends Mitch Gordon and Susan Crook, for reviewing multiple times the different drafts of the manuscripts, offering suggestions and ideas, and helping me clarifying topics that at the time might have been too hard to understand. I am grateful for their sincerity and motivation, which have deeply inspired me. On top of that, their resolute determination and desire to see this message spread to a wider audience motivated them also to financially assist with the cost of editing the books in the series. Your gift to me and others will never be forgotten.

I am extremely grateful to my mother for her love, prayers, caring, and sacrifices for educating and preparing me for my life as a messenger, and my destiny.

The Science of Consciousness

To all the other people that have read the manuscript before the editing stage and offered suggestions and feedback, thank you! But perhaps the most important acknowledgment goes to you, the reader. It is your open mind and heart and the willingness to hear and share this message that makes all this work worthwhile.

A light or a message is useless if no one can see it. It is your open heart and mind that have made the creation of these books possible. But the adventure is far from over. In fact, it has just started.

If you have felt inspired, please look for the next FREE PDF; or if you would like to make a contribution to this work, buy the Kindle, Audible (if available), or physical version of the next book.

I am truly thankful for being on this spiritual journey of awakening with you.

Love and Light,

Paolo F. Tiberi

A Short Summary of Book I

GOALS AND IDEALS OF THIS WORK

All of the books in I have created, including the *Legends of Altai* books (developed to teach values and morals to children in a non-dogmatic way) have been written with the same goals and ideals in mind.

These are:

- To help people of all walks of life, races, creeds, and religions to awaken from the slumber of the illusory reality they call life.

- To help reconcile scientific evidence with ancient and modern mysticism, and in doing so, help individuals have a direct knowledge, awareness, and experience of God and its Source Field.

- Bringing the understanding of our unlimited creative power and light into the heart of every man and woman.

- Bridging religious diversity by understanding our kinship in God and the commonalities that unite us.

- To liberate humans from the delusion of separation and duality, and therefore end the suffering created by the unruly mind and ego and attachment to illusory and impermanent objects and realities.

- To free humans from the grasp of spiritual and religious narrow mindedness, dogma, and ignorance.

- To make individuals from messianic traditions realize that we are all the son and daughters of God, of the Source, as there is nothing that is not God, nothing that is not consciousness expressing, creating, and exploring.

- Furthermore, it is our responsibility to become unified, enlightened, and no one else's.

The Science of Consciousness

- To encourage a life based on light, kindness, compassion, and love for all other sentient beings.

- To enliven life by becoming the alchemist of self, bringing joy where there is sadness, light where there is darkness, kindness and compassion where there is cruelty and selfishness, and love where there is fear.

- To inspire a life based on great spiritual principles like the golden rule: "Do not do to others what you don't want others to do to you" and the eightfold path practices, which include: proper view, proper resolve, proper speech, proper conduct, proper livelihood, proper effort, proper mindfulness, and proper meditative absorption or union.

- To help people awaken from the social hypnosis that has made many feel isolated, lonely, forsaken, unworthy, and ostracized.

- To help regain our self-sovereignty.

This is my journey, which you too can join and be part of if you wish. Most of my books will be made available for free as PDFs. By you sharing this body of work, you too are spreading this message of light to all the far reaches of the world. The spiritually healthier we become, the more society and the world will be transformed by a new wave of light, understanding, love, and compassion.

A Short Summary of Book I

THANK YOU

www.ingramcontent.com/pod-product-compliance
Lightning Source LLC
LaVergne TN
LVHW041330080426
835512LV00006B/389